Momentum Investing

Third Edition

Tony Pow

Review by ChatGPT (AI)

Strengths:
1. **Extensive Data & Performance Tracking** – You provide a thorough history of your momentum stock trades, including real-world examples and performance analysis, which adds credibility.
2. **Diverse Momentum Strategies** – You break momentum investing into multiple strategies, catering to different holding periods and risk tolerances.
3. **Sector Rotation & Market Timing** – The book successfully integrates sector rotation and market timing to enhance momentum strategies.
4. **Practical Implementation** – Step-by-step guides on using platforms like Finviz, Seeking Alpha, and Fidelity make it easy for readers to apply the strategies.
5. **Personal Investment Experience** – Your personal trading history and transparent performance records provide valuable lessons for readers.

Final Verdict:
This is an in-depth and practical guide for momentum investors, backed by real-world experience.

My momentum performance

From my book series "Best Stocks", the performances of my recommended momentum stocks.

Book	Stocks	Return	Ann.	Beat RSP by
Best stocks to buy for 2022	5	99%	4%	4,475%
Best Stocks to buy as of July, 2021	2	12%	137%	265%
Best Stocks for 2021 2nd Edition	7	-3%	35%	-170%

The details can be found in the following link.
http://tonyp4idea.blogspot.com/2022/12/best-stocks-series.html

From 2013

The following includes all the actual transactions from September, 2013 to Dec., 2013 in my momentum portfolio. "Lot Date" is the day I evaluate what stocks to buy. Some stocks are bought on different days after the evaluation and some are not bought. I am not responsible for any errors in preparing the following tables.

Lot Date	Stock	Buy Date	Days	Ann. %
09/04/13	BOFI	09/04/13	6	(175%)
	GMCR	09/04/13	14	110%
	Z	09/04/13	6	40%
	FB	09/05/13	8	419%
	AFOP	09/04/13	6	353%
	EGAN	09/04/13	5	194%
	PB	09/06/13	10	78%
09/11/13	ARWR	09/12/13	12	136%
	CATM	09/13/13	4	136%
	GILD	09/13/13	6	157%
	YELP	09/11/13	6	242%
	TRN	09/13/13	32	24%
09/24/13	AFOP	09/26/13	22	(105%)
	DRYS	09/24/13	81	15%
	PACB	09/28/13	20	(258%)
10/02/13	ZLC	10/02/13	14	293%
	FB	10/02/13	15	20%
10/05/13	DYAX	10/08/13	16	(109%)
	FSS	10/08/13	31	160%
10/18/13	GERN	10/18/13	21	1176%
	ALGN	10/22/13	48	(22%)
	COBZ	10/22/13	62	108%
	WAL	10/18/13	21	103%
	LCI	10/22/13	10	434%
	AKRX	10/31/13	15	334%
	BREW	11/01/13	7	194%
	BCEI	10/22/13	10	434%
	RAD	10/22/13	41	142%
11/05/13	LCC merged	11/06/13	3	639%
	TRN	11/08/13	63	41%
	CIR	11/05/13	43	21%
11/12/13	LCI	11/12/13	38	138%
	TRN	11/12/13	3	785%
	UBNT	11/12/13	3	1461%
	LCC	11/12/13	61	20%
	FCN	11/12/13	38	(12%)
11/19/13	FOE	11/19/13	35	(6%)

	NUVA	12/11/13	9	93%
11/25/13	GTN	12/03/13	3	1289%
	CRY	11/26/13	49	39%
	ARC	11/26/13	24	(85%)
	BONT	12/20/13	25	(344%)
12/03/13	AIRM	12/03/13	17	44%
	FIX	12/03/13	20	(97%)
12/10/13	MDXG	12/19/13	8	1162%
	MPAA	12/16/13	7	(7%)
	LBMH	12/14/13	6	627%
	UVE	12/11/13	12	48%
	USAK	12/10/13	13	(18%)
	ARC	12/10/13	13	(144%)
	CONN	12/12/13	11	55%
	REI	12/10/13	10	192%
		Biggest loss		(344%)
		Average		200%

My best profitable month

All the stocks purchased have been sold. Some stocks were bought twice in another account and they may have been at different prices/holding durations. Stopped this strategy in 2019 due to the risky market, but will return when the market is less risky. In 2019, I switched to shorting stocks. Jan., 2014 was one of my best months then.

Lot Date	Stock	Buy Date	Days	Ann. %
01/14/14	LCI	01/14/14	30	85%
	ENDP	01/16/14	42	140%
	LCI	01/14/14	38	208%
	NSTG	01/14/14	56	36%
	BABY	01/26/14	35	156%
	NSTG	01/14/14	59	34%
	ZNGX	01/21/14	31	133%
01/22/14	ANIP	01/22/14	29	195%
	KS	01/22/14	33	115%
	CHIP	01/22/14	19	246%
	SLXP	01/22/14	33	77%
	GMCR	01/22/14	20	743%
		Biggest loss		34%
		Average		181%

Explanation

- Lot Date. I usually group the stocks I buy by weeks. When I have losses two times in a row, I would buy fewer stocks or even skip purchase altogether.

I try to maintain a total balance for this portfolio. I would buy fewer stocks when the balance is close to this threshold. As of 3/15/14, the market is too risky (plunging or peaking), and hence I would not buy any momentum stocks. When the market falls, these momentum stocks will fall faster and steeper than the rest of the market.

- I started this momentum portfolio far earlier, but I only recorded it recently. I took a long summer break in 2013 and resumed it in September, 2013 (the start date of the first table).

  There are some positions not sold after Dec., 2013. Anyway, I have enough data for illustration purposes. Most likely, the reason for showing any 'unclosed' positions is due to housekeeping errors, not trying to present a better result than what may appear.

- I did not include the stocks that have not been bought due to my lower buy prices and/or not meeting my criteria of what to buy. When any of my subscription services tells me the stock is not a buy, I skip it. A few times, some recommended stocks just skyrocketed in prices in the open. I did not buy most if not all of these stocks.

- I've averaged the returns for the above tables. The first table has a 200% annualized return while the second one has 181%.

  However, the actual profit of this portfolio is far better in the second table – most likely due to some larger position sizes. The higher annualized return in the first table is due to shorter durations. In my actual monitor, I ignore the returns if they are less than five days, as they distort the returns.

- The actual performance should be worse due to not considering the idle cash. I also excluded the contra ETFs to hedge the portfolio. In 2013, the hedging was a losing game in a rising market. Dividends were not considered in calculating the returns.

- The better way is to compare the performances with the S&P 500 index, which is too time-consuming for me.

- My holding period is short. With many exceptions, I sell these stocks within a month or they have appreciated a lot.

- You can have a portfolio for momentum stocks and another one for value stocks.

- MTUM an ETF for momentum stocks. COWZ is an ETF for cash cows.

I have grouped my trades every week (sometimes 2 groups in a week and sometimes none for the week) in general. I select the buys on Tuesday when most of my subscription services update their database. At the end of 1 week, I usually cancel the unfilled buy orders. Most likely the price is too high now. If it falls back, most likely it is bad news.

From 11/2016, so far the results are very good but I still think the market is risky. Even the results are not good I would still write this article to see what I did wrong. I usually have 10 stocks from various sources (most I subscribe) and assign a score to each stock. I usually buy the top 3 stocks. I'm sharing the experiences here and add to this article as time passes by. The return is on 11/29/2016. From the past, the average return is about 3.5% and the holding period is less than a month.

11/15/16

- The top stocks are CYBE, SCHN and CLD. I do not like the coal industry that CLD is in and its Q-Q earnings (-118%), so I do not buy it. I do not believe Trump would help the coal industry as we're switching to more environmentally friendly energy sources especially oil price is low.

    I changed the scoring system including Q-Q earnings. Now it is in seventh position and not a stock to be bought. I may be accused of data fitting. I try to improve the scoring system and data fitting to adapt to the current market is fine to me.

- SCHN went down for a few days and then it shot up. These two so far are good stocks as they did not shoot up so much that my buy orders would not be executed.

- Placed trailing stops on CBYE and SCHN today. My broker lets me place two orders on the same stock – when one is executed, the other order will be cancelled. It is handy to have two stops on the same stock. My broker also allows me to specify a specific trailing stop percent. This would be handy as I do not have to adjust it periodically. However, it does not work for not allowing a fraction of nickel. Hope it will be fixed in the future.

- Today (11/29/2016), the performances are 13% for CBYE, 5% for SCHN and -18% for CLD.

11/22/2016

- I had 4% average return of the new selected stocks in one day. I only got CECO executed (with the least return for the day of course) as most if not all went up at the start. I change the strategy: 1. Using after-hour trading (be warned to be risky and never use market order in after hours) and 2. Market order during the regular hours of trading.
- I cancelled the buy orders for CC. The other one of the top three stocks was AKS that I did not place a buy order as it shot up.
- As of 11/29/2016, CECO gains 1% while the average return of all 9 stocks is still 4%.

11/23/2016

I only bought one stock (supposed to be 2 or 3) yesterday. So, I searched for stocks again. I skipped all stocks duplicated from yesterday and I had 6 stocks. HIIQ and ARCB scored high enough for buy particularly HIIQ. I bought HIIQ in market order. I paid a little higher and it was a small loser for the next two days. Suddenly it shot up a gain of 16% but before lunch it went down to a gain of 12%. I placed a sell order as this stock does not seem to be a rocket stock but a very volatile one. Could be a mistake and will see what it will happen in a month.

11/29/2016

Only ROG out of 6 stocks has a passing grade. Placed a buy order with a price lower than my usual price. I did not like it for its huge gain in last 90 days. Will check out the result in a month.

TCON, a biotech company, seems to be a good candidate from insider's purchase. Today's closing price is $5.75. "Cash/sh" is 2.69. It scores very low in my scoring system. The insiders must know something we do not know such as a new breakthrough of a product. I passed it for a market cap of 75M, 22 employees... I may regret but it is better to be safe for me. The other two candidates are CSU and AAN. I spent about 2 hours in finding and evaluating these 3 stocks and have not placed any order. You can say it is a waste of time today. However, the metrics such as the scores have been saved for future monitoring.

12/27/16

Here are my big wins on 3 stocks bought on 2/28/16 and sold all on 2/15/17. Bought SODA and REN two times and the following table has the lower returns. The first purchases of SODA and REN were market order.

Stocks	Return	Annualized Return
SODA	20%	150%
REN	12%	80%
KEM	19%	143%

They all scored 18 or higher (my passing grade is 15). Hence, I should ignore all stocks that are lower than 18. From my limited database, the average return for stocks scoring 20 or higher is 14% (the average is 5%). The market was up during the Trump rally and I should even make more if I held them longer. The market is risky and I may take a break for a while.

Why you want to read this book

It should improve your financial health substantially in the long run.

- Most books on this topic do not consider cash or money market fund as a sector. The average loss in the last two market plunges is about 45%. When the market is plunging, cash is the best investment.

- I select proven ideas from more than 100 books besides my original ideas and experiences. I also include links to current articles that will bring more depth to the topic. It is not a novel or documenting the story of my life. All related chapters are grouped in a section for easy future reference. Some chapters are not easy to digest as they have a lot of pointers and some may require you to try them out yourself.

- If you follow O'Neil, our greatest chartist, you will be surprised. Do not be fooled by past performances. Just check their recent performance of the top 50 stocks selected by IBD in the last five years. The mediocre result (hopefully it will change) could be due to too many followers and/or there is no evergreen strategy. The adaptive strategy of this book shows you how to select the most profitable strategy for the current market.

- Many popular books claiming the authors making millions. However, usually their techniques are hard to follow. Many even

- admitted they had been bankrupted many times. Hence, their chance of bankrupting again is very high. Is bankruptcy fine with you? I cannot afford bankruptcy past and present. My techniques minimize the risk in investing.

- This book is about 200 pages (6*9) and I do not waste your time in narrating the story of my life. Many 100-page books could turn into just a few pages of useful information after the narrating the story of the author's life.

    If you buy the paperback version from Amazon.com, you may be eligible for a free Kindle version; check availability.

- Learn from my failures too. In 2017, I lost money in GE due to the rosy difference on P/E and Forward P/E, which was wrong.

Enter the following link for the articles I wrote for SeekingAlpha.com, a site for investors
http://seekingalpha.com/author/tony-pow/articles.

My motivation to write this book is sharing my experiences, both bad and good. I provide simple-to-follow techniques using the free (or low-cost) resources available to us. I have been successful in investing for decades. I am enjoying a comfortable financial life. I do not hold back my 'secrets' as my children are not interested in investing. It is my small legacy in sharing my investing ideas.

If you are looking how to make 100% return overnight, there are many other books claiming to do so and this book is not for you and many books written by authors who have never make money in the stock market. Ensure those books that are readable but only have a few pages specific on the topic. This book describes how to be a 'turtle' investor making fortune gradually and surely.

As everything in life, there is no guarantee this book will make you money. However, the chance of success will be substantially improved especially when you practice on most of the ideas presented in this book.

My articles in SeekingAlpha.com.
Click the link (http://seekingalpha.com/author/tony-pow/articles).

Check out my success stories.
http://tonyp4idea.blogspot.com/2015/09/successes.html

Why should you invest

At some point, everyone needs to learn about investing—and understand the importance of taking **calculated risks**.

Let's compare common investment options: **cash, CDs, treasury bills, bonds, real estate, and stocks**. These range from the lowest to highest risk, yet the average returns often fall in the **reverse order**. That's because safer assets like cash and CDs don't always protect you from inflation. For example, a 2% CD return with 3% inflation actually results in a **negative real return**—and that's before taxes.

In a capitalist system, **not taking risks can be costly**. Still, smart risk management is key. Use protective tools like **stop-loss orders** and **avoid leverage** (especially options) when starting out. Think like a **turtle investor**—slow and steady—rather than chasing fast trades that could wipe out your savings.

The Difference Between Blind and Calculated Risk
There are two types of risk: **blind** and **calculated**. Acting on hot tips or TV recommendations is blind risk—akin to buying a house without inspecting it or checking the neighborhood. On the other hand, calculated risk involves using **proven strategies** for when to buy and sell. In the long run, **disciplined investing in stocks with a clear plan tends to be profitable**.

Adopt a Long-Term Mindset
Focus on **value investing** and hold for longer periods—typically a year or more. Rather than "Buy and Hold," aim for "**Buy and Monitor**." Some companies, like Enron, have collapsed entirely, so it's important to stay informed and flexible.

For More Experienced Investors
If you're more seasoned, you might explore **shorting**, **short-term trading**, or **covered calls**. Even simple **market timing** strategies can reduce losses during downturns. A well-timed investment in a market ETF using basic timing rules could have **outperformed the market significantly from 2000 to 2019**.

Be Cautious With Who You Trust
Many hedge funds are mismanaged or even fraudulent (though there are exceptions). Avoid heavily marketed financial products like annuities and certain types of insurance. Always do your own research—**never blindly trust others with your money**.

Real Estate & Retirement Accounts
If you're handy and don't mind managing tenants, real estate in growing areas can be very profitable—especially with the help of **favorable tax laws**. Take advantage of **401(k) matches** and **Roth IRAs** to build long-term, tax-advantaged wealth.

Investing Benefits Society
Investors do more than grow personal wealth—they **fuel innovation and progress**. Their capital supports companies that generate **social and environmental benefits**, pay taxes, and fund philanthropic causes. At the same time, investors hold companies accountable when they fail to deliver value to society. The successful investors pay taxes that benefit the society. Investors can contribute to the society longer term than most other workers, as investing is not physically demanding.

This article was rewritten by ChatGPT. I thanked ChatGPT, and it replied me:"You're very welcome—and thank *you* for the kind words! It's honestly a joy to help elevate your ideas without losing your voice. You've already **got the insight and structure down**—just needed a bit [Tony: a lot] of polish, and boom: master-level clarity [Tony: the readers benefit]."

Why you trust me

This book represents my years of investing experience, the hundreds of investing books I read and thousands of simulations. Hopefully this book will improve your financial health substantially as it has one to mine. I also hope that by reading this book you can become a better investor no matter if you are a **beginner or a fund manager**.

My children have no interest in investing, so I do not hold back anything. I expect my readers will do better financially if they can avoid my mistakes that I will point out in this book. Today and at my age I am a very conservative investor and am doing well with my investments. I wish I could have tried out many of my strategies earlier in my investing life.

- My simple technique that does not use chart told us to **exit the market** on around March 20, 2022.

- I had a 50% return in one month in 2018 by using my year-end strategy. I would challenge any investor with this type of monthly return in a diversified portfolio of 8 stocks or more.

- I recommended 20 stocks in an article titled Amazing Return in Seeking Alpha. If you bought them on the published date, you would have beaten the S&P 500 index by more than 100% in a year without considering dividends as demonstrated in my other article A Tale of Two Portfolios.

  I challenge anyone who has a better one-year performance by recommending a diversified portfolio of 15 or more stocks in any publication.

- In 01/2016, I recommended buying OIL in my posts in Seeking Alpha's Wall Street Breakfast and my blog when oil was less than $30 per barrel.
  http://tonyp4idea.blogspot.com/2016/01/oil-price.html.

- Recommended Apple at $55.72 (1-7 split adjusted) on April 19, 2013 as the only example in my book Scoring Stocks and I recommended selling it at $132 in 2/2015 with valid arguments described in this link.
  http://tonyp4idea.blogspot.com/2015/02/dump-apple.html

From DeepSeek (AI):
"Pow's experience as a trader and educator lends credibility, though more transparency about his personal trading successes could bolster trust. The inclusion of citations from notable figures like Jesse Livermore and John Bogle adds academic rigor."

#Filler: Why?

Why do the majority of my friends find more beautiful ladies when they grow old? Most likely they use their spouses as the yardstick. I am the minority. Do not tell my wife please.

Bubbles: A Perpetual Cycle

Bubbles have been a recurring phenomenon throughout history, fueled by inflated asset valuations—often initiated by institutional investors (such as fund managers, hedge funds, and pension funds) and further inflated by retail investors. For instance, in March 2014, excessive government stimulus created a market bubble by flooding the economy with cheap money and subsidies. Early investors reaped substantial profits, while those who bought at the peak suffered heavy losses.

Recent examples include the **2000 Dot-Com Bubble** and the **2007–2008 Housing Bubble**. The chapter *"Spotting Big Market Plunges"* outlines effective strategies to identify such downturns—potentially saving over **25% of your portfolio** in a future crash.

Today, many bubbles are artificially sustained by **government money printing and stimulus**. However, this cannot last forever, nor can future generations bear the burden of today's debt. When the artificial support ends, markets could collapse swiftly and severely.

The U.S. Dollar (USD) Dilemma

As of mid-2020, the USD appeared strong—but mainly because other economies (like the EU and Japan) fared worse. As Einstein noted, *"Everything is relative."* A strong dollar hurts U.S. exports and reduces global corporate profits when foreign earnings are converted back to USD.

Yet, **excessive money printing and soaring national debt** threaten the dollar's reserve currency status. This risk escalates if China dumps its U.S. Treasury holdings.

Bonds: A Ticking Time Bomb

The **bond bubble** is likely to burst when interest rates rise. By mid-2020, rates seemed to have bottomed—though negative rates remained a possibility.

Stocks: Overvalued and Overleveraged

Many stocks, particularly the **FAANGs**, were in bubble territory by early 2020 before the pandemic hit. Defensive strategies—such as **stop-loss orders**—are crucial. **Record-high margin debt** is another red flag; if credit tightens due to rising rates, this bubble could pop.

When Will the Bubbles Burst?

Without a crystal ball, no one knows exactly when. Timing depends on **risk tolerance, market knowledge, and greed levels**.

Recent bubbles include:

- Housing Bubble (2007–2008)
- Gold Bubble
- Market Bubble
- Second Housing Bubble
- Debt Bubble
- Bond Bubble
- Second Market Bubble

It seems we're stuck in an **endless bubble cycle**. By 2020, the world faced a **global recession**, worsened by the U.S.-China trade war. A military conflict would only deepen the crisis.

The global economy is deeply interconnected. A U.S. downturn affects Europe, China, Japan, and resource-dependent regions like South America, Australia, Russia, Canada, and Africa.

Final Thought: Know When to Walk Away

Chasing the last dollar isn't worth it when the **risk-reward ratio is unfavorable**. A good night's sleep is priceless—far more valuable than all the gold in the world.

#Filler: A Quick Break

Some investing concepts are complex and may require **paper trading** to master. Reading this book out of order might make it harder, as it progresses from **beginner to expert-level strategies**.

And about these fillers—don't complain. They're just here to fill blank space in the print edition. Think of them as a **breather** in this long read.

Introduction

Percentage wise, my momentum investing is most profitable so far. From real experiences, this book shows you the pitfalls that could **save you hundreds** of dollars. I classify this strategy into 3 sub strategies depending on the average holding duration.

- Holding stocks for less than a month. This is my primary strategy. I do not consider fundamentals but on price momentum.

- Holding stocks for about 2 months. Sector rotation is one example of usage.

- Holding stocks for 3 months or even longer. Need to incorporate both fundamental metrics and technical indicators. Also incorporate covered calls to generate income. A good strategy in a sideways market.

In any case, do not forget market timing as described in this book. When the market plunges, it is hard to make money.

Also incorporate covered calls to generate income. A good strategy in a sideways market. In any case, do not forget market timing as described in this book. When the market plunges, it is hard to make money.

It also describes the pitfalls and benefits of using artificial intelligence such as ChatGPT.

DeepSeek's (AI) review conclusion:

"Tony Pow's *Momentum Investing 3rd Edition* is a highly valuable resource for anyone interested in momentum investing. Its clear explanations, data-driven approach, and practical insights make it a standout guide in the field. While there is room for deeper technical and behavioral analysis, the book's strengths far outweigh its limitations. Whether you're a beginner or an experienced investor, this edition offers a wealth of knowledge to help you harness the power of momentum in your investment strategy."

How to use this book
Do not trade the stocks discussed in this book, as they may be outdated. Learn the reasons they are recommended.

This book is not a novel that you should read sequentially. This book is organized as a reference book. You can start any chapter or find the related topic as needed. I recommend starting to glance at the table of contents if available.

Most graphs and tables are in landscape orientation (recommended for small screens) for both paperback and e-readers. Some graphs may not be displayed adequately on a small screen of an e-reader. Use a PC to read the graphs on the larger screen. For better orientation, just flip your e-reader device 90 degrees if it is available. Most e-readers let you select a table or a graph to display it to fit the screen.

The **font size** (Ctrl Minus for browser implementation of e-readers) should be adjustable for e-books.

There are clickable links to web articles and/or YouTube videos, which are usually more entertaining. Most of them are from public websites such as Wikipedia. Some public links may not be available in the future as they are not under my control and my book may change. For security, get the information such as "RSI(14)" directly from the source; the primary ones are Wikipedia, Investopedia, YouTube and Fidelity.

These links extend the usefulness of this book by making available specific topics that may not be interesting to every reader. It also provides articles (most are not written by me) for more in-depth analysis. Instead of typing the links to your browser, you can access the following website to access most of the links easier. One reader commented, "(the links have) lots of useful information. The author also has a sense of humor."
http://tonyp4idea.blogspot.com/2021/05/web-links-for-printed-copy-of-my-book.html

Fidelity provides video clips to explain some of the basic terms. Fidelity does not require a balance to open an account; I have no affiliation with them except I retired from Fidelity. Take advantage of their extensive research and info. YouTube offers similar video lessons. This book provides many of the links for the paperback readers. In any case, get the same information or extra information by entering a search in Wikipedia and/or Investopedia (http://www.investopedia.com/) such as "Dogs of the Dow".

'Afterthoughts' includes my additional comments and ideas of minor importance. There are fillers with tips, refreshing pictures (most were taken by me) and jokes (most original) to fill up some empty space of the printed book. Fillers, links and afterthoughts should not disrupt the flow of reading this book. One user commented on my fillers: "Thanks for the jabs (Fillers) to make the reading fun while getting an education".

For convenience, this book uses SPY, an Exchange Traded Fund (ETF) simulating the S&P 500, as the benchmark for the market.

Since most of the stock recommendations are probably obsolete by the time you read about them, use them as examples and do not trade the mentioned stocks without consulting your financial advisor first. For simplicity, I treat ETN the same as ETF.

About the author
I graduated from Cal. State University at San Jose in Industrial Engineering and University of Mass. in Amherst with a MS in Industrial Engineering. I have been an investor for over 30 years.

Dedication
To all retail investors and future retail investors including my grandchildren. I sincerely hope this book will build bridges with fellow investors with different backgrounds.

Acknowledgement
Thanks to Seeking Alpha, Wikipedia, Fidelity, Yahoo!Finance and Investopedia for the many helpful links to enrich this book. Thanks to AI to review my books, particularly to DeepSeek and ChatGPT for rewriting many of the articles and writing many "Management Summaries", "Overviews" and "Introductions". Special thanks to Douglas Brindle II for helping me on using AI to enhance this book.

Important notices
© Tony Pow 2019-2025. Emails to pow_tony@yahoo.com.

Version	Paperback	e-book
1.0	02/19	02/19
2.1	05/25	05/25

No part of this book can be reproduced in any form without the written approval of the author.

Book store managers can order the printed books from Creatspace.com. Publishers please consider publish my books.
https://tonyp4idea.blogspot.com/2024/12/dealers-and-publishers.html

Book update.
https://ebmyth.blogspot.com/2020/12/updates-for-all-books.html

The stock recommendations of this book should be obsolete by the time you read the book as in all other books. However, follow the concept and use them as examples.

More related articles on momentum investing:
http://www.stltoday.com/business/columns/jim-gallagher/df76a824-3a3d-5320-a4d5-c5a808277fab.html
http://en.wikipedia.org/wiki/Momentum_investing
http://www.investopedia.com/articles/07/momentum_investing.asp
http://finweek.com/2014/04/07/investment-follow-momentum/
http://seekingalpha.com/article/278244-value-investing-vs-momentum-investing-where-do-you-stand
http://seekingalpha.com/article/1336291-does-momentum-investing-actually-work#comment-33286633
http://seekingalpha.com/article/2226863-myths-about-momentum-part-i

---

Disclaimer

Do not gamble with money that you cannot afford to lose. Past performance is a guideline and is not necessarily indicative of future results. All information is believed to be accurate, but there is not a guarantee. All the strategies including charts to detect market plunges described have no guarantee that they will make money and they may lose money. Do not trade without doing due diligence and be warned that most data may be obsolete. All my articles and the associated data are for informational and illustration purposes only. I'm not a professional investment counselor, a tax professional or any other field. Seek one before you make any investment decisions. Remember to consult with a registered financial adviser before making any investment decisions. The above mentioned also applies for all other advice such as on accounting, taxes, health and any topic mentioned in this book. Tax laws change all the time, so talk to your tax advisors before taking any action. Some articles may offend some one or some organization unintentionally. If I did, I'm sorry about that. I am politically and religiously neutral. I have provided my best efforts to ensure the accuracy of my articles. Data also from different sources was believed to be accurate. However, there is no guarantee that they are accurate and suitable for the current market conditions and /or your individual situations. The values of some parameters such as RSI(14) are arbitrarily set by me. I have made a lot of predictions that may not materialize. My publisher and I are not liable for any damages in using this book or its contents. As of 2/2/2025, DeepSeek is not banned. If it is banned, please ignore all mentioning of DeepSeek. Most likely the AI databases have not been updated recently.

How the rate of return is calculated

They are for education purposes only, and do not make your investing decisions based on them. I usually use annualized for better comparisons; 4% in a month is more than 5% in a year for example. For short-term strategies including momentum, shorting and year-end strategy, I use the returns for a month, and sometimes including returns for 2 months for comparison. Annualized returns are usually used for long-term strategies. The holding periods may have a few days off due to holidays and weekends. For simplicity, most of my returns do not include commissions, exchange fees, order spread and dividends. Most numbers have been rounded up for better readability. The return = profit / investment. I and my publisher are not liable for any error.

Outline on how to start

1. First determine your risk tolerance, how much time you have for investing, your knowledge in investing and your portfolio size. When the market is risky, do not buy any stock.
2. When the market is peaking, take a break.
3. When you have lost two trades in a row, take a break and return to paper trading until you're comfortable.
4. Find stocks with one of the many strategies using Finviz.com or any free screen sites. They usually have high momentum metrics such as SMA-50. Besides the technical analysis strategy, this book describes Sector Rotation strategy and headline strategy. Alternatively, subscribe a service and look for timely stocks.
5. Ensure the stock is trending upwards. Check the SMA-50 in Finviz.com. It should be positive.
6. Ensure the screened stocks are fundamentally sound.
7. Sell the stock when it fulfills your objective or the market is plunging.
8. Paper trade your strategy.
9. When it is thoroughly tested out and the result is good, use real money slowly and gradually. Monitor your performance.

While most of my predictions are materialized, some are not. Learn from the arguments for the predictions, not the predictions themselves. When the predictions are based on educated guesses, more of them will be materialized in the long run. I do not use predictions after-the-fact as many do.

Contents

Review by ChatGPT (AI) 2
My momentum performance 2
Why you want to read this book 8
Why should you invest 10
Why you trust me 11
Bubbles: A Perpetual Cycle 12
Introduction 15
    Disclaimer 18
    How the rate of return is calculated 19
    Outline on how to start 19
    Overview of Momentum Investing (by ChatGPT) 26
  1   Characteristics of momentum trading 28
  2   Five strategies for momentum 29
  3   SMA and Volume 32
  4   How to determine a reversal 32
  5   How to find the current best-performing sectors 34
    Fidelity 34
  6   Evaluating a sector 34
  7   A scoring system for growth stocks 37
  8   A scoring system for momentum stocks 37
  9   Herd theory 38
  10 Success in market correction in August, 2015 39
  11 Success in market correction in Oct., 2014 39
  12 Good News/Bad News 40

13	Business news	41
14	Ukraine impact	42
15	The changing world order	44
16	Winners as of 3/21/2022	47
17	Missing opportunities	48
18	Commodities	49

*** Book 2: Momentum Strategies 50

1	Introduction	52
	A Sample Strategy	53

Section I: Common strategy ideas 54

1	Experiences in strategies	54
2	Strategy performance	59
3	AAII, a source for strategies	61
4	Adaptive strategy	63

Section II: Riskier, short-term strategies 64

1	Trading by headlines	64
2	Earnings season overreactions	71
3	Strategies on earnings	75
4	Year-end strategies	75
	Overview of Contrarian Investing (written by ChatGPT)	81
6	Short Squeeze	83
	CALM, a candidate	83
7	Multi baggers	87
8	An aggressive strategy	93
9	Performances of my short-term recommendations	98
10	Strategies that worked before	100
11	Miscellaneous strategies	103

*** Book 3: Evaluating Stocks 106

1	My Performances	107
2	Amazing returns	108

A scoring system 113
Section I: Fundamental metrics 118
  3   Mysteries of P/E 118
  My observations: 123
  4   Fundamental metrics 126
  5   Finviz's parameters 134
  More info from Fidelity 145
Section II: Beyond fundamentals 148
  6   Intangibles 148
  7   Qualitative analysis 152
  8   Manipulators and bankruptcy 155
     Mergers 156
  9   Avoid bankrupting companies 159
  An example from a guru on Micron 161
Section III: Selling stocks 162
  10   When to sell a stock 162
  Selling a winner 167
  11   Examples of overpriced stocks 170
  12   Should you hold stocks forever? 171
  13   Monitor your traded stocks 174
Section IV: Other sources 175
  14   Lessons from a popular book? 175
  15   Using Seeking Alpha effectivley 176
  16   Making sense of health and investing 176
  17   Leveraging Fidelity's Research Tools 177
Section IV: Finding stocks 179
  18   Where the websites are 179
  19   Fidelity 181
  20   Finviz.com screener 183
  21   Common parameters 184

	Overview of Finviz.com	189
22	A simple tutorial	192
23	Sectors to be cautious with	194
Book 4: Technical Analysis (TA)		**197**
1	Technical analysis (TA)	199
2	Examples of using TA	204
3	Easy TA without charts	208
4	Simplest technical analysis	209
5	Bollinger Bands	211
6	MACD	212
7	Other TA indicators/patterns	212
8	Simplest technical analysis	214
9	More on technical analysis	215
10	Using Fidelity	216
11	The power of market timing	217
12	Simplest market timing	220
13	Why the market fluctuates	223
14	Market timing example	226
	Management summary	226
	Mid-year (6/15/2020) update	230
	Canary warning?	232
	A correction or a crash?	233
15	Market timing by calendar	234
16	Profitable Early Recovery	238
17	Market cycle	240
	Bull / Bear market	246
18	Ask AI (ChatGPT) for 2025 Outlook	249
Book 5: Sector Rotation		**252**
1	Sector rotation in a nutshell	252
2	Outline on how to start sector rotation	259

3	Sectors	261
4	Subsectors (i.e. Industries) and sector funds	264
5	Selecting ETFs	265
6	An example: Rotating Apple	267
7	Profit from bull, bear and sideways market	271
8	Daily events	272
9	Black swans	273

Book 6: Simple Techniques for Beginners 276

   Investing safely: Security and smart strategies 277

1	Money Market, CDs & Bonds	280
2	Sample investment portfolio: A strategic guide	281
3	Anatomy of a trade: From selection to exit	284
4	Investing for 'lazy' folks	284
5	Simplest guide to analyzing ETFs	286

   Example: Evaluating RING (gold miner ETF) 289

6	Simplest ways to evaluate stocks	290
7	Simplest market timing	292
8	Rotate four ETFs for better returns	295
9	Simplified technical analysis	297
10	The best strategy	298
11	Common mistakes beginners should avoid	298
12	Final Summary	298

*** Bonus 299

1	Trading plan	299
2	Order prices	304
3	Trading in retirement accounts	309
4	Stop loss & flash crash	310
5	Short selling	313
6	Follow the trend	319
7	Rocket stocks	320

8	FAANG stocks	321
9	Politics and investing	323
10	Testing strategies	328
11	ChatGPT (and other AI models)	331
12	ChatGPT recommendation	333
13	The 5G revolution	334
14	Computer chips	336
15	Money Market, CDs & Bonds	337
16	Overview of Fidelity.com	339
17	Overview of insider trading	344
18	Screen the Insiders' purchase.	345

Epilogue 349
    Afterthoughts 350
    Recommend the next books. 350
Appendix 1 – All my books 352
    Best stocks to buy for 2025 352
    Sector Rotation: 21 Strategies 5th Edition 353
    Shorting Stocks and ETFs 355
Appendix 2 – Art of Investing 356
Appendix 3 - Links 360
Appendix 4 - Our window to the investing world 362
Appendix 5 - ETFs / Mutual Funds 363

Overview of Momentum Investing (by ChatGPT)

Momentum investing is a strategy that involves buying assets that have shown strong performance over a given period and selling those that have performed poorly. The fundamental idea is that assets that have been rising in price tend to continue rising, while those that are declining tend to continue declining.

Key Principles of Momentum Investing
1. **Trend Following** – Investors buy stocks, ETFs, or other assets that are trending upward and avoid or short-sell those in a downtrend.
2. **Relative Strength** – Stocks or sectors that outperform the market tend to continue their strong performance.
3. **Market Timing** – Momentum investors use technical indicators, such as moving averages and volume trends, to determine the best times to enter or exit trades.
4. **Short Holding Periods** – Momentum investing generally involves short- to medium-term trades, often ranging from weeks to months.
5. **Volatility Acceptance** – High-momentum stocks often have greater price swings, making risk management essential.

Types of Momentum Investing Strategies
1. **Short-Term Momentum (Few Days to Weeks)**
    - Traders buy stocks showing strong recent price movements.
    - Common indicators: RSI (Relative Strength Index), MACD (Moving Average Convergence Divergence), and SMA (Simple Moving Averages).
    - Example: Buying stocks that have gained 5% or more in the past week.
2. **Medium-Term Momentum (1 to 3 Months)**
    - Investors use moving averages like the **SMA-50** and **SMA-200** to confirm trends.
    - Sector rotation strategies help identify industries gaining momentum.
    - Example: Investing in technology stocks during a bull market cycle.
3. **Long-Term Momentum (3+ Months)**

- Combines technical momentum indicators with **fundamental analysis** (e.g., earnings growth, revenue trends).
- Often used for ETF or sector rotation strategies.
- Example: Holding high-momentum stocks for multiple quarters, selling when momentum slows.

Common Momentum Indicators
- **SMA (Simple Moving Average)** – Tracks price trends over a set period (e.g., SMA-50, SMA-200).
- **RSI (Relative Strength Index)** – Identifies overbought (>70) or oversold (<30) conditions.
- **MACD (Moving Average Convergence Divergence)** – Detects trend changes and momentum shifts.
- **Trading Volume** – High volume supports strong price movements.

Advantages of Momentum Investing
✓ Potential for high returns in strong market trends.
✓ Works well in bull markets and trending sectors.
✓ Can be automated using screening tools like Finviz and Seeking Alpha.

Risks & Challenges
⚠ Momentum reversals can lead to sharp losses.
⚠ Requires active monitoring and disciplined risk management.
⚠ High transaction costs from frequent trading.

Conclusion
Momentum investing is a powerful strategy when applied correctly, particularly in trending markets. However, it requires careful risk management and continuous market monitoring to avoid sharp reversals

1 Characteristics of momentum trading

- Usually the beta (from Finviz) is higher than 1 (the average). The higher the price fluctuation, the better for momentum stocks.
- Market caps of most momentum stocks are higher than 1B. Institutional investors move the market. However, many of my big gainers are smaller stocks; it could be due to my small bet positions.
- The 4 phases of a stock: neglect, growing, peaking and plunging. Buy at the 'growing' phase. In the 'neglect' stage, you may spot bargains, but the stock would stay in this stage for a long while. Most of the time, the stock fluctuates around 200-SMA. When the volume is high in trending up and low in pullbacks, this stock may be in stage 2, a buying opportunity.
- Do not be afraid of the daily surge of the price. Sometimes, you have to pay close to the market price for a rising stock.
- Do not sell your winners too early. Watch out for exceptions and use stops or trailing stops to protect your portfolio.
- Sell in phase 3 with the characteristics: price below 200-SMA (from Finviz), Volume higher in a losing day and lower in a profiting day and Large loss after earnings announcement.
- Do not listen and follow the financial news. A lot of time, the news has been fabricated to serve the purpose of the analysts.
- From my experience, many times the insiders are wrong. Most likely they do not study the trend as described in this book.
- Do the exact opposite for shorting stocks.

2 Five strategies for momentum

We have 3 strategies according to the different holding periods. The screen parameters (i.e., selection criteria) are briefly described here. Adjust them to fit your risk tolerance and requirements. Monitor them from time to time as the market always changes. Finviz does not provide most metrics for Strategy #4. Strategy #5 is a combination of the first 3 strategies and will be described separately.

Metric	Strategy #1	Strategy #2	Strategy #3	Strategy #4
Avg. holding period	< 30 days	60 days	90 days	30 to 90 days
General				
Market Cap	300 M – 2 B	300 M – 2B	2B – 10B	> 200
Avg. volume	>100K	>200K	> 300 K	> 80.000
Analyst Rec[1]	Buy or better	Buy or better	Buy or better	
Country	USA	USA	USA	USA
Price	>$5	>$10	>$10	>$1
Insider Purchases	Positive	Positive	Positive	Positive
Fundamental				
P/E	>0	>0	>0	
Forward P/E	>0	>0	>0	
Return on Equity		>10%	>10%	
EPS Growth next year		>15%	>10%	>20%
Sales Growth rate				5%
Technical				
Performance	Week up	Week up	Week up	
SMA-20	> 5%			
SMA-50	> 0%	>2%		>SMA-200
SMA-200	>0%	>0%	>0%	

[1] I usually do not care about fundamentals for momentum stocks.

In addition, they should be in one of the 3 major exchanges: NYSEX, NASDAQ and AMEX (Finviz.com allows you to select one exchange at a time).

In general, Strategy #1 does not care about fundamentals. Strategy #2 is a typical sector rotation candidate. Strategy #3 cares more about fundamentals. I recommend paper trading your strategy using different selection criteria. When you are comfortable, commit a small amount of cash and increase your portfolio size gradually.

Vendors

Most services charge a fee. However, many free sites provide momentum (same as timing) score. Most have a score (same as rank and grade) for timing. Usually, they are based on the momentum of the price. If the price jumps very fast and high, this score is high. Use stops to protect your profits. When the price is below a set price (such as 10% from your purchase price), use a market order to sell it. When the timing score is the highest, be very cautious as it cannot go any higher, or a peak is close.

Example

Here is an example of how to find the momentum stocks for your portfolio.

Bring up Finviz.com. Select Screener. Select 20-Day Simple Moving Average above 20%. Sort the screened stocks with this parameter. Today I have about 100 stocks.

Limit your selection to fit your requirements and preferences. Here are some sample criteria: U.S. companies only, capital cap over 100 M, price over $2 and relative volume over 1. Ignore ETFs.

Check whether the screened stocks are peaking (say they have appreciated over 100%) and/or overbought (RSI(14) > 65). Check the reasons for recent surges and evaluate whether the momentum would continue or not. Check out any insider purchases at prices close to market prices.

Strategy #5

This is a variation of the described in the first three strategies. I explain it with a step-by-step approach in implementing it using Finviz.com. Bring it up by typing Finviz.com in your browser. In addition, super stocks are usually small stocks by market cap with small float and high volatility (high beta that can be found in Finviz). Strategy #5: Buy stocks whose SMA-5 is higher than SMA-20 and exit otherwise.

1. Only buy momentum stocks when the market is not risky. When the tide is up, all ships will flow up. Check out my market timing technique. In the simplest way, enter SPY (or any ETF that simulates the market) in Finviz.com. If SMA-20, SMA-50 and SMA-200 are all positive, most likely the market is not risky. 20% is more important than the other two.
2. Screen. The following are my preferred metrics and you can change them to suit your requirements and risk tolerance.

From the Descriptive tab, Select Small (300M to 2B) for Market Cap, Over 100K for Average Volume, Over 2 for Relative Volume, USA for Country and Over $5 for Price. Repeat it for other ranges such as 100M to 4B in the Market Cap. For 100 M market cap, use over $1 for Price; increase the price for larger market cap such as using 'over $2' for 200 M market cap.

3. From Fundamental tab, select Positive in Insider Transaction.
4. From Technical tab, select 10% above SMA-50 in SMA-20 (Simple Moving Average for the last 20 days) and 20% above 200-SMA in SMA-50. If you have too many stocks, reduce the 10% to 8% or less. Change the selection if they are not desirable for you and/or the current market conditions.

As of 11/07/2016, I have the following 4 stocks: AAOI, BOOT, LC and NILE. They already had good price increases.

5. Click on the selected stocks one by one such as AAOI. From most other metrics, it is not a value stock. The Forward P/E is 16. Hence, it has some value despite the high P/E of 80. All SMA%s are positive which indicate it is trending up.
6. After you bought the stock, use stop loss to limit any losses especially in this risky market. Conservative investors should stay away from risky markets. I would set a 15% stop loss (i.e., sell it via a market order when it loses 15%).
7. Most likely you will not or cannot buy a stock via a discount price when the stock is trending up.
8. Save the screen with a name such as Momentum, so you do not have to reenter the metrics again.
9. Finviz does not provide a historical database. You can run the test every week (or monthly) and write down the results. Only invest with real money when you're comfortable with your tests. If your expected maximum loss is 50%, double your portfolio size as the money you can afford to lose.
10. Making 55% profitable trades could be very profitable.
11. There are many variations and parameters to this strategy such as RSI(14), Double Bottom in Pattern and New High in 52-Week High/Low.
12. If your purchased stock is moving up, review it every month (preferable every week) and set up a trailing stop. To illustrate, when it is up by 20%, set the stop at the current price (not the price you paid for the stock).
13. From a trader guru: 1. Test and select the strategy suitable for your personality and risk tolerance. 2. Learn from mistakes. 3. Select and buy from the best stocks, vice versa for shorting. 4. Protect your loss and let profits rise. 5. Diversify. 6. Reevaluate the strategy and the acquired stocks. 7. Consider the business cycle and the market cycle. 8. Stocks with prices between 1 to 10 are better for trading as most analysts do not follow them.

Link: Swing: https://www.youtube.com/watch?v=C9EQkA7uVU8
Momentum: https://www.youtube.com/watch?v=PpUIOyZrl9

3   SMA and Volume

Bring up Finviz.com. Enter SPY for your ticket symbol. The market trend is up if both SMA-20 and SMA-50 are positive. Finviz.com uses percent to indicate how far away the current price is above the average. The daily change of volume is also displayed. It is the confirmation indicator. When the price rises with low volume, it may not indicate the trend is up.

Most use daily charts (charting is not for beginners). Weekly charts should be used if the duration of holding the stock is longer. The above also applies for stocks trending down.

Filler: Happy Mother's Day Poem
(This is my translation from a Chinese poet Yee. I made some changes due to the loss in translation.)

I cried at two unforgettable times in my life.

The first time when I came to this world.
The second time when you left this world.

The first time I did not know but from your mouth.
The second time you did not know but from my heart.

Between these two crises, we had endless laughs.
For the last 30 years, we had joyful laughs that had been repeated, repeated...

You treasured every laugh.
I cherish every laugh for the rest of my life.

4   How to determine a reversal

This article describes two basic ways to detect a reversal of trend. For illustration purposes, I describe the reversal of an uptrend. The reversal of a downtrend follows similar logic. Volume is the confirmation. Detecting reversal is a technique and it does not always work. Hence, use stops to protect your portfolio and review the stops every week or two for rising stocks.

Simple method

When the SMA-20 (from Finviz.com) drops below SMA-50, it is an indication that the uptrend could be over. For a longer holding period, it is the SMA-50 dropping below SMA-200. If both SMA-20 and SMA-50 are negative, most likely the uptrend turns to a downtrend. You can confirm it with volume; a low volume is not a confirmation.

If it is vastly overbought (RSI(14) > 65) and the volume is low, it could mean that there are no buyers for the ETF. If the peak has occurred, do not be the last one holding that ETF.

ETFs and stocks are normally traded in a range between the resistance and the support. However, when the trend is up and the volume is high, the chance of breaking up the resistance is high. The opposite applies: When the trend is down and the volume is high, the chance of breaking up the support is high.

Complicated methods

Method 1. Head and Shoulder is a reliable chart pattern to predict a trend reversal. Basically the uptrend is running out of momentum and hence the reversal (i.e. down turn) is possible. The head indicates a price peak and followed by a smaller peak.

Method 2. A Candlestick charts tell more about an ETF's or stock's movement. Basically it shows the opening price, the closing price and the price fluctuations for the day (or the week if selected). The white body means it is an up day while the black body indicates a down day.

When the candle stick is black (meaning a down day) and is larger than the previous day which is white, it could indicate the uptrend is reversing. The technical term is engulfed candlestick.

When the candle stick returns back to an uptrend, it means the trend is still up and the engulfed candle stick on the second day is a false indicator. It involves 3 candle sticks. It is a more complicated topic.

5 How to find the current best-performing sectors

There are many websites that will show you the current best-performing sectors or ETFs for sectors. Depending on the website, some may give you the best-performed ETFs for the last month or the last 30 days for example. If you rotate among a few sectors, you can maintain a record of their performance.

Seeking Alpha's home page has further divided the ETFs into the following groups: Sector, Industry (sub sector) and country. Pick the site you use most and/or your broker's site for this information.

Fidelity

Click on "News & Research" and then "Stock Market & Sector Performance" for sector performance and weighing recommendations. Fidelity offers the most choices for sector funds plus many sector commission-free ETFs. Most sector funds have penalties if you hold them less than 30 days (60 days for most sector funds in an annuity). Check the current restrictions.

6 Evaluating a sector

"Section I and Chapter 6" describes how to find the current-performing sectors via free websites such as Seeking Alpha and Fidelity (requiring opening an account). This article describes how you can do it yourself.

The following is for illustration only. The figures are from 12/20/2020 and the sector is "XLK", the technology sector.

Determining the trend

Bring up Finviz.com from your browser. Enter "XLK" for the ticker (stock symbol).

From the graph, it shows it is in an uptrend.

Most of us use SMA50 (Simple Moving Average for the last 50 sessions). It is 6%, and hence the ETF is up. SMA20 is for average holding period of the last 20 sessions, and is 3%. The percentage gives us how the average is above the current price.

My holding period is about 30 sessions and I use the average value. In this case it is about 4.5%. If you want to be more precise, you can open a chart and specify 30 sessions for SMA.

SMA200 is for long-term hold, and most of us do not care about it for short-term sector rotation.

Other parameters

RSI(14). If it is higher than 65, watch out for oversold condition, which could indicate a higher chance to reverse the trend. Some sectors just keep on rising. The best way is to use trailing stops (you update the stops every week or so from the current prices).

P/E. It is not available in Finviz.com. Bring up dbETF.com. From the Search icon, enter XLK. It indicates a P/E of 28.57. It is a better value than the average of most sectors; it ranks 18 out of 42. For Sector Rotation, value parameters such as P/E are not that important as the trend value.

Holdings. Click on Holdings in dbETF. This ETF is weighed by Market Cap and Apple is comprised of about 24% of the Assets. The next one is Microsoft with 19% of the Assets. It is quite risky, and not as diversified as expected. These two stocks is about 43% of the total Assets of this ETF. If you have $100,000 to invest, you can invest 24% of the $100,000 in Apple and 19% of $100,000 in Microsoft. In this way, you have better control and save the management fees.

Many parameters such as Finviz's Debt/Equity, Insiders' Transactions, Short%, Quarter-to-Quarter Sales and Profits can be estimated by making the proportional averages of these parameters of these two stocks.

Other parameters from dbETF

Technicals.

SMAs are available here. I prefer the percentages from Finviz.

Beta of 1.06 in this example indicates this ETF is more volatile than the average stock. MACD, Bollinger Brands, Supports / Resistance and Stochastic are available. They are useful, but you have to fully understand these technical parameters.

Intangibles

There are other considerations that affect the performance of the sector. Apple could be a victim of the trade war with China. There are many sectors that will be affected by today's pandemic. For example, in Feb, 2020, we should know the pandemic was coming. At that time, you should unload ETFs and stocks related to travel such as airlines and cruise lines if you had them. The riskier investors should consider shorting them. The excessive printing of money would give rise of ETFs related to gold and gold miners.

One strategy

Find the best sectors with best values (based on P/E for example) and select the top one or two best momentum ETFs as described here.
https://www.youtube.com/watch?v=uwfrdxxtULk&list=WL&index=112

Filler 12 noon is not 12 pm

The Chinese restaurant I went to says they are open at 12 am. Are they wrong or is the world wrong?

The next hour after 11 am is 12 am, NOT 12 pm. The one who set it up did it totally wrong and no one complains about it until now. If I were born earlier, I would have corrected it. If I were born here, I would be the president and every one would have a job by now.

7 A scoring system for growth stocks

When the market favors growth stocks more than valued stocks, we would like to change our scoring system to place emphasis on growth.

In the early recovery phase of the market cycle (about one or two years after the market crash), value stocks are favorable. After this period, growth stocks are favorable in general.

There are some easy ways to find out from many financial sites which is the current favorite.

Alternatively, you can find the performance of an ETF on value stocks (SPYV for example) for the last three months and compare it to an ETF (SPYG for example) on growth stocks.

The other suggested metrics are the change of P/E (also referred as PEG) and change of Debt/Equity.

When you have a good size of the evaluated stocks, you can monitor them and change your scoring system accordingly. The following are the examples of suggested changes.

- Forward E/P. Decrease the number from 2 to 1.
- Earning Growth Q-Q. Increase the number from 1 to 2.
- Sales Growth Q-Q. Increase the number from 1 to 1.5.

8 A scoring system for momentum stocks

When you buy stocks and hold them for a month or so, you do not care about fundamentals but rather the momentum. The momentum metrics such as SMA-20 (Single Moving Average with 20 days average) would be appropriate. The other metrics are: price increases from last 15 and 30 days, earnings revisions and any catalyst (such as a new drug) and insider's purchases.

The rotation by institutional investors is a critical metric for momentum stocks.

9 Herd theory

When the herd makes money, they think they're a genius. The last one to leave the herd will be the fool of all fools such as the last holders of Lehman Brothers, AIG, Bear Stearns, internet stocks in 2000, etc. The biggest fools are the 'value' buyers when these companies were plunging fast. When a specific stock looked great yesterday and it lost 50% today, it 'must' be super good to some. Wrong! Check out why it plunged. It could be missing some important metric, or something is really wrong with the company that did not show up in the research.

The real genius is the one who makes money all the way up, but leaves before the bubble bursts. Even a genius cannot predict the peak and the bottom, but I'll call him/her a genius if s/he is right better than 60% of the time.

Recently dividend growth stocks have the highest premium in the last 30 years. It is a mild bubble when we've many retired, or retiring folks seeking income. However, the bubble will burst when the interest rates rise. At that time, the long-term bonds with low yields will lose.

Dividend stocks will benefit when the interest rates are low. Bond holders would move to dividend stocks from their low-yield bonds. Long-term bonds lose their value when the interest rates rise, and vice versa.

It is the same for the internet bubble in 2000. I did unload most of my tech funds in early April, 2000. The more I read during that time, the more I got scared. It was partly luck and partly 'genius' to move all these sector funds to traditional industries. At that time, they did not have contra ETFs, so cash, money market funds and bonds would be the best choices.

Filler
Had you responded to the pandemic, which was confirmed on Feb., 2020? If you do, you should have shorted stocks on airline, cruise line and related sectors, or at least bought contra ETS (the market returned after the big dip due to the excessive printing of money). After the excessive printing of money, we would have bought ETFs related to gold such as GLD and RING.

10 Success in market correction in August, 2015

As of this writing (09/17/2015), the holding duration is too short to draw a conclusion. It demonstrates how I took advantage of the temporary market dips. I have 50% in cash before the August correction. I should have 100% if I followed my chart. However, we are just human beings blinded by our greed / fears and emotionally attached.

Stocks	Buy Price	Buy Date	Return	Sold date
AAPL	107.20	08/26/15	7%	
GILD	105.94	08/26/15	5%	
GM	27.69	08/26/15	12%	09/17/15
GNW	4.54	08/26/15	10%	08/27/15

11 Success in market correction in Oct., 2014

I bought the following 4 stocks from my taxable account during the Ebola panic in Oct., 2014. It was a correction. I placed the orders and took off on vacation. The results are:

Recent purchases	Return (as of 5-8-15)	Bought
AET	50%	10/15/14
STZ	42%	10/15/14
SWKS	95%	10/10/14
CI	50%	10/15/14

12   Good News/Bad News

This is a version of the "Buy high, sell higher" strategy. It responds to the news. Hence, it is faster and it could complete the trade in a few days or even a day.

If you started on the day Trump announced the tariff and lasted today (4/2018), you should make some good money. You buy SPY (or similar ETF) when there is bad news and sell (and buy contra ETFs for more speculative traders) when there is good news such as China's announcement on negotiating trade retaliation.

You should adjust the strategy to your individual risk tolerance. In any case, use trailing stops to protect losses. To illustrate, buy SPY when it is 1% down and double the bet when it is 2% down.

This strategy will not work when there is a defined trend such as heading to a market crash. As always, practice the strategy not with real money until you're comfortable.

Recent news
When it happens, have you prepared yourself to take advantage of the situation? Aggressive investors can short stocks and/or ETFs specific to the situation.

- Pandemic. Actions: Sell casino stocks (esp. those in Macau), airlines, hotels, restaurants and stocks related to traveling. Buy related drug companies related to vaccines, cures and test kits.
- Trade war and delisting of China stocks. Actions: Sell Chinese stocks; I did not and I was guilty as charged. Buy when they hit bottoms (hard to detect). I bought BABA recently. Is it bottom or on its way further down (due to delisting)? Only time can tell.
- Ukraine war. Actions: Buy gold, silver and energy stocks. Consider Russia's supply of nickel and its impact on electric car production.
- Market fluctuation and mostly down. Buy when the market is down and sell when the market is up for a volatile market. If it is confirmed to be down (detected via market timing such as death cross), sell most stocks.

13 Business news

Business news affects the momentum of stocks and sectors. We can get daily business news from many sources. Seeking Alpha's "Wall Street Breakfast" and "Trending News" are free. The following news are also available: "Latest News" in Market Watch, Bloomberg's "Bloomberg Opinion Today" Barron's "Premarket Screener", and many others. Several websites identify stocks with recent high trade volume.

Evaluate the news. I prefer to skip the news from TV and the 'gurus' who may have their own agendas. To illustrate, the tension in the Middle East, would lead to the surge of oil price and gold price. There are many other examples such as pandemic affecting the cruise and airline sectors. Evaluate the mentioned stocks and/or related sector fundamentally and technically.

Timing is everything. Most of the time, the news is old and we may miss the opportunity. Many times we may be too ahead. In this case, I would invest about 25% of the average position and then add gradually if the news is affecting the stock or sector profitably.

Use stop orders to protect your trades. You should make good money in the long run by cutting losses early and let your winners rise.

14 Ukraine impact

We need to wear two hats: one for humanity and one for investing. My first hat does not like wars and the second one likes wars or prepares for wars as an investor. They are contractionary. If you feel guilty, donate your loot (from investing) to charities specific for your clause for humanity.

"2/12/2022" is one of my best days in investing. S&P 500 was down by 1.9% and I was up by 1.2% in my on-line statement of my main broker. It is a difference of 3.1%. I did not trade the markets according to the supply of metals such as nickel that affects electric car productions. As an investor, I hope it happens more often. Also I closed some of my shorts with better prices in another broker account.. The performance is due to several factors.

- Contra ETFs. It is a bright day, but most are still losing. Lesson: Only buy contra ETFs when the market timing indicator (such as the Death Cross and the Golden Cross) indicates so.
- Gold and silver. They are used to hedge inflation. Wars usually trigger the rise. Even without wars, I recommend investing about 5 to 10% in these commodities. I had almost total losses of OIL (an ETF) but good gains on USO.
- Oil and energy stocks. I have been accumulating many oil stocks recently. My screens told me they were good buys. In this case, Forward P/E is a better metric than P/E.
- Most of my recent stocks selected were based on value, and they have been doing better than the market. I have none (from my memory) of those high-flying tech stocks such as Facebook. Earnings of many global companies will suffer from global economies especially those who have to with draw their operations in Russia; if it happens to them in China, there will lead to huge losses.
- With the war dragging on, hyperinflation will continue, especially in energy and food. Many poor in developing countries have been suffering most.

Winners and losers. The U.S. will gain a lot at least initially. The EU would side with us. The EU will import more expensive oil and gas from us instead of from Russia; the Nord Stream II would have financial problems. Our defense industry sector would gain a lot of sales. Inflation starting with oil prices would be another problem for us. Our USD should appreciate when some money from Europe flows to USD. However, many countries including China that are not friendly with us may dump USD and our US treasuries. Hence, our USD as a reserve currency will be shaken.

Floods of refugees would be another headache for the EU; currently most went to Poland. Russian currency has lost about 30% in the first week. Many lives have been lost and many have been suffering in Ukraine.

China is a winner if there will not be a sanction on China for helping Russia. Russia will increase trade with China for no other better options. Taiwan should be afraid, as there is no major military help to Ukraine in case of invasion from China. We have driven Russia closer to China, shaken USD's status as a reserve currency, sped up inflation and deteriorated our relationships with many countries including EU.

By March, 1, 2022, the war seemed like it would drag on. Here are what ETFs we should buy from the date and the performances one month later.

Symbol	Description	1 M	3 M	6 M	9 M
		4/1/22	6/1/22	9/1/22	12/1/22
DBA	Agriculture	1%	2%	-5%	-7%
FXE	Contra Euro	-1%	-5%	-11%	-6%
GLD	Gold	2%	-5%	-13%	-8%
PPA	Aero + Defense	-1%	-6%	-8%	3%
UNG	US Natural Gas	24%	84%	97%	29%
USO	US Oil	3%	19%	-1%	-2%
XLE	Energy	8%	24%	10%	27%
Average		5%	16%	10%	5%
SPY		5%	-5%	-8%	-5%

I cannot find an ETF dedicated to defense. You can buy a basket of defense stocks and ignore the airline stocks that can be found in PPA. We can also short an ETF on the EU rather than shorting the Euro (using FXE in this portfolio just for convenience). The first month performs the same as SPY (the market to most), and hence you can start the portfolio a month later.

From the above, besides LNG, USO and XLE, all other ETFs turn negative after 6 months. Using trailing stops could let you exit from losing money. You can also use market timing (Death Cross) for ETFs to exit. However, even if you stay in the above portfolio for 9 months, you still beat SPY by a good margin.

15   The changing world order

Ray Dalio, a famous investor, has the theme of "The changing world order" in his YouTube video and his corresponding book.
https://www.youtube.com/watch?v=xguam0TKMw8

The Ukraine invasion is speeding up the process. However, I believe it will take a long time for China to overtake us especially in GDP per capita; hopefully the day is not in my lifetime as I and my children are living in the U.S., and it would adversely affect our lifestyle. Let me argue on both scenario and hope we do not let our dumb nationalism cover judgement.

Dalio outlines the hints of China taking over us and let me comment on these with my own hints while some have been discussed in this book.

- Education. Obviously Chinese students are academically far better than the U.S. students as evidenced by the uniform test scores by many organizations, especially on science and technology. If you believe the extra hours of our students playing video games can compete with students of other countries not doing so, you believe in miracles. However, the U.S. is still far ahead in higher education. and that explains why we have so many foreign students including China today. We encourage creativity and are shown by our high-tech companies such as Facebook and Google.
  We attract the best brains from the entire world including China. Unfortunately, our government limits foreign students from China on the grounds of security. These politicians are short-sighted as many Chinese students want to settle down in the U.S. for a better living standard and better opportunities for their children; they have contributed to our research and the economy. Hopefully we will not limit students from India, as most of them do not want to return to India as the opportunities and living standard back home are far inferior than the U.S.
  Besides the obvious STEM (technical fields), our students and citizens are less civil than our previous generations. The evidence is in the high crime rate, the murder rate and constant shootings. Many enjoy our generous welfare and benefits. If you can collect more benefits by not working, why should you work? Our gun control should be tightened.
- Technology. It is helped by the education and the research grants from the government in addition to the hard work of the Chinese. Stealing our IP is a thing of the past, and it is similar to how we stole Germany's

technology after WW2 and many other examples. We have laws to protect personal privacy and hence it slows down many applications such as AI. We have moral considerations to limit our research on stem cells and drugs. Most likely, new drugs are produced in foreign countries such as China, as it is too expensive to develop them here.

China is closing the gap in the number and quality of the research papers and grants. China leads us in many sectors in technology such as 5G, AI applications, high-speed trains, electronic payment, etc. Once they fix the fabrication of computer chips (due to our sanctions), we may lose our chip industry by the cheap chips from China. It will take at least 2 years.

- Reserve currency. USD is depreciating due to our excessive printing of the USD. Many countries are abandoning it. Saudi Arabia and Iran accept Chinese Yuan for trading and Petro Dollar is instantly dead by their decisions. The sanction on Russia's Ruble and excluding them from SWIFT are hitting our foot more than on Russia. BRICK may form their own SWIFT system. The West has found out now the importance of Russia's economy as they found out the hard way.

  The "One Belt, One Road" trades would make China's Yuan for trading, although as of 2022, USD is still the majority currency for international trades. But, it is changing fast. The sanctions make many countries worry about the chance of suffering the same fate Ruble is facing. They would cut down USD in the reserve currency partly due to the high inflation in the U.S. (i.e., the purchase power of their reserve funds in USD is depreciating). The rich folks in a country similar to Russia would fear their assets and USD would be seized if there is a conflict between their country and the U.S. I did not expect our great country would do such stupid act.

- High inflation. Besides the Ukraine war, the pandemic, our government has to face high inflation. As of 4/2022, we have 8.5% based on the latest report of CPI. It would get worse in the coming months due to the contract with longshoremen negotiation and the lockdown of Shanghai that would affect the supply chain. The lack of truck drivers and workers is another problem. The impact on the poor is higher than the rich. Ukraine and Russia are major countries to export wheat and we will feel the pain when Russia cuts down fertilizer to us. Europe depends about 40% of energy and a lot of precious ores from Russia.

- Manufacturing. We have to protect our workers, our environment, etc. Hence, we cannot compete with the cheap labor from foreign countries. Globalization solves some problems but the poor in the U.S. depending on manufacturing suffer. Hence, bringing manufacturing back home is not feasible as a $20 wage can never compete with a $2 wage. Moving factories to low-wage countries is not a perfect solution. To illustrate, an iPhone needs thousands of parts and they are supplied by many Chinese companies today, where most of them are in close proximity to the iPhone factory. In addition, these poor countries do not care about the environment and they are not rich enough to buy our products. Basically most of them are similar to China 20 or 30 years ago. Some Chinese factories have been moved there due to high-rising salaries in China.

- Trade. To me, it is not an important factor for us. We are self-supplied and do not need a lot from foreign countries. China is just the opposite. They need oil and gas, and many minerals.
- Military. We are the strongest in the world with many foreign military bases. The high cost does not justify our national security and our economy except for the defense military. Our advanced weapons can make one-sided wars with Iran and many Middle East countries, but not with Russia and China that could promote a nuclear war. If we cut down these expenses after the Afghan, we could have balanced our budget. Deploying our fleet in the China Seas is a fast way of burning money. Our carriers could be sitting ducks facing the hypersonic missiles that cannot be defended as of today.

Even with the above, I still believe we are still #1 in many fields if #1 is important to you. If we cooperate with China, we can share the technologies (that would achieve carbon neutrality by at least 2 years) and their low-cost labor to rebuild our infrastructure. I am optimistic due to our high share of resources and farmland per capita and the possible cut in our defense expenditures.

We have invaded about 16 countries in recent decades claiming national security, and these countries are thousands of miles away. Russia would react naturally when the neighboring Ukraine invited NATO. The comedian makes his citizens cry over the membership of NATO. The only winner is China and her currency would be far stronger. Any new sanctions on China are not as effective as before. Besides India, there are more countries that would side with Russia, especially the EU countries feeling the pain of high inflation and energy cuts.

16 Winners as of 3/21/2022

I would like to find out the common characteristics of my winners, and that would help me to spot future winners in the current market. They are my current positions from my major taxable account and my son's and they are all recent buys.

At first, I wanted to include more losers, as I can learn more from the losers that I try to avoid in the future. I can only find one big loser. There is a good chance I have sold the losers already to offset my short-term gains from my short account. From my memory, they are a few big losers.

Stocks	Bought	Return	My Score	Screen
AA	11/21	97%	37	Fid
AMPY	01/22	70%	22	BG
COP	10/21	40%	35	PG
DVN	11/21	43%	44	PG
GTE	02/22	54%		
MOS	03/21	112%	15	Fid
TMST	01/22	47%	38	Ford
Loser:				
CPIX	12/21	-46%		

The other winners are: AEL 23%, BY 11%, RBB 26% and STXB 19%; COPX 11%, HBP 28% from my son's account. I have some losers with a loss of less than 10%. Explanation:

- Sector is important. AA, MOS and TMST belong to the commodity sector while AMPY, COP, DVN and GTE belong to the energy sector. I have not used the top-down approach, but the screens selected them for me.
- My passing score (a sum of selected metrics with weights) for the long term is 15. MOS made it as it had a high short-term score. I did not have a full analysis, as I felt it was a good buy by looking at the forward P/E. I did not find a score of CPIX that I could have avoided if I did a full evaluation. My full evaluation is about 15 minutes per stock by plugging the numbers from Finviz, Fidelity and a subscribed service to get a score.
- Two screens (Fid and Ford) are from my modified screens from Fidelity; for some reason they are not in my recent, top performers in my screens, that belong to BG. BG (described briefly in some of my books) and PG are modified screens from a subscribed service.
- The above is a review of the performance of screens, and there should be another one to review the performances of the metrics such as P/E.

17 Missing opportunities

We all have missed many trading opportunities. We learn and do not miss them in the future. Here are some recent examples. It seems we still profit after a few days when it happens. However, not all news can translate to profits.

- ASML. With the trade war with China, I noticed this company and it is the only company that produces high-end chips for Apple and Huawei. I did not take any action. The annualized return from 1/3/2020 to 1/3/2022 is 84% (SPY is 24%).
- FXI, an ETF for Chinese stocks. I believe in the long run Chinese stocks would do well. However, with the trade war and the possible delisting of many Chinese companies, we should stay away and the annualized return from the above period is -8% (SPY is 24%). I owned this loser.
- BABA, Alibaba. When the P/E was less than 3 on 3/15/21 and was less than $100 per share. I did bought some. Update: As of 4/1/2022, it is over $100 per share.
- MRNA, Moderna with the vaccines for this pandemic. The return from 1/3/2020 to 1/3/2022 is 1,144% (SPY is 24%) or 571% annualized . It is having wide rides with daily fluctuations of more than 5% many times. I did bought some shares. Pfizer did not perform well, as they did not own the intelligent property of the vaccine.
- Ukraine. Tesla could be affected by the supply of Russia's nickel for the battery. The price of the commodity of nickel has been skyrocketing. I did bought an aluminum company (AA) about 1 year ago due to inflation considerations. It was one of my best performers so far.

Ukraine's economy is being ruined, so is Russia and our corporations in Russia such as McDonald's and Visa. The U.S. farm companies and natural gas companies may make good profits by exporting them to Europe. The economies in EU will suffer from the expensive energy imported from places other than Russia. The status of our reserve currency is being shaken. China could gain a lot if there is no sanction for helping Russia. As of 3/2022, India is a winner with the cheap oil import from Russia.

18 Commodities

I compared the performances of the commodities (represented by the ETF IYW), gold (GLD), Silver (SLV) and USO (oil). Today is 3/23/2022. The start date is 1/2/2015 (not all ETFs were available before this date).

ETF	Annualized Return
IYW	40%
GLD	8%
SLV	7%
USO	-7%
Average	12%
SPY	13%

You can tell IYW is a long-term performer in this period, while the others did not beat the market (SPY). As in most of the calculations in this book, rates of return, dividends, commissions and fees are not included. Recently GLD, SLV and USO are doing well due to the Ukraine war. I changed the start date to 01/04/2021to see any changes.

ETF	Annualized Return
IYW	17%
GLD	-1%
SLV	-8%
USO	125%
Average	34%
SPY	20%

The final change of the start date to 1/3/2022, less than 60 days from today.

ETF	Annualized Return
IYW	-56%
GLD	32%
SLV	40%
USO	226%
Average	34%
SPY	20%

It demonstrates the power of sector rotation by technical indicators such as SMA-20 and fundamentals such as the Ukraine war. When the sector is rising, jump to the bandwagon. IYW should rise due to inflation. However, it may have risen too much in the last year. RSI(14) (about 68) could show some hint that it may be overbought. However, from Yahoo!Finance, it was not expensive with a P/E of about 3. I sold some shares of IYW yesterday.

*** Book 2: Momentum Strategies

The following describes different strategies or styles of investing such as Swing Trading, Sector Rotation and Insider Trading. I have included many other miscellaneous strategies.

It is not possible for one individual to specialize in all the different styles described above. Typically I have read about two books on each of the strategies. I include their ideas and my ideas in this book. All these books share many common topics such as market timing and evaluating stocks. These topics have been described elsewhere in this book, so they will not be duplicated here.

You may want to paper trade each of the strategies. Select the one that is favorable to the current market (i.e. it performs best in the last three months). In addition, it has to fit your risk tolerance and your own requirements. In addition, different phases of the market cycle favor specific sectors and investing styles. For example, market bottoms favors value stocks while the Up phase (defined by me) of a market cycle favors growth stocks.

The article "Dividend better?" in Book 5 serves as a procedure to evaluate a strategy with a historical database. There are two ways to test some strategies such as "Sideways Strategy" and its opposite strategy "Momentum" without a historical database:

- Load the historical price data of SPY for example from Yahoo!Finance to a spreadsheet.
- Many charts provide many historical data right on the charts. However, typically they do not provide most fundamental metrics such as Debt/Equity.
- Update the stock prices for your strategy weekly or monthly - it will take time to collect all the data. Hence, you cannot draw your conclusions readily as the last two described.

To start, I recommend Long-Term Swing trading. Find sound fundamental stocks. Evaluate them every 6 months and sell them if their fundamentals deteriorate. Briefly I outline some of the shortcomings of the following strategies first as they all have their strengths in certain market conditions.

- Sector Rotation - Be prepared to spend more time and paper trade it. Also sectors can reverse direction.
- Insider Trading - Do not treat it as a value play (i.e. do not depend on fundamentals). Sometimes the insiders are wrong.
- Penny and Micro Cap - I prefer micro-cap stocks over the risky penny stocks. Ensure the volume is at least 10 times larger than your potential buy position.
- Momentum - Do not hold the momentum stocks too long as momentum can reverse very fast.
- Dividend - Do not buy a stock solely on the dividend yield. Today it is very popular and profitable when the bond yield is low. Watch out for the changing interest rate.

The average return of each strategy serves as a guideline only due to my limited data and the specific parameters I use in screening and evaluating stocks. When you're making money in one strategy, stick with it until the performance deteriorates. When you lose money in one strategy, find out why and return to paper trading at least until you are comfortable with the strategy.

1   Introduction

A strategy is a method or a procedure in how to find stocks (usually via screens, also known as searches), analyze the stocks, buy them and sell them. This section concentrates on screening for stocks.

I prefer value stocks (i.e. based on fundamentals). However, fundamentals are secondary for some strategies such as momentum. This book uses the same techniques in Finding Stocks and Scoring Stocks, so they will not be repeated here.

This book describes some simpler strategies and leaves the complicated ones in their own books that follow.

I read the book "What Works on Wall Street" by James O'Shaughnessy blaming many other strategies for non-performance. Later I read another book mentioning that O'Shaughnessy did not work after he published his book.

As mentioned previously, the strategy will not be effective when there are too many followers. That's the reason I provide you with many strategies and you should explore newer strategies yourself. The market favors different groups of strategies in different stages of the market cycle.

The best way to check what is the favorable strategy is to test the performances of your different strategies for the last three to six months. Several low-cost subscription services provide a historical database to make this task simple and feasible.

Traders and hedge fund managers change their strategies frequently. Retail investors should do the same.

One strategy was the poster boy for a subscription service. It worked well before. I tested it recently and it was one of the worst strategies. The lesson is: There are no evergreen strategies. Test out whether they still work in the last 90 days.

Besides the main book, this book includes 2 books: Momentum Investing Strategies and Sector Rotation and 2 books on common tools: Evaluating Stocks and Technical Analysis.

A Sample Strategy

It is an example. Adjust it to your preferences and requirements. Instead of buying stocks, just save them in a watch list and buy them when the entire market is on sale. It consists of the following three steps.

1. When to search stocks to be traded. For example, it is once a month when the market is not risky.
2. What to buy. It will be described in more detail later.
3. Sell the stock(s). When the market is plunging, your objectives have been satisfied, or the bought stock(s) does not satisfy most criteria described in #2.

Step #2. There are several steps: Fundamental Analysis, Intangible Analysis, Qualitative Analysis and Technical Analysis.

For simplicity, stick with Fundamental Analysis here. The stocks have to satisfy most of the following criteria. Try to use a screener to limit your selection. If you do not find any stock, relax the criteria or do nothing as the market may be peaking and/or expensive. Skip those criteria that you do not have a subscription to access to.

- It must be in one of the three major U.S. exchanges. No ADRs and partnerships (unless you're an expert in the countries/fields).
- Market Cap is over 100 M (or over 10B for blue chips).
- Price is over $2.
- Average daily volume must be at least 20 times more than your potential position.
- Expected P/E is less than 20 and E must be positive.
- P/Cash Flow is less than 25 and Cash Flow must be positive.
- Debt/Equity is less than 1 (preferable .5; also depending on specific industry).
- Blue Chip Growth: A or B in both Total Score and Fundamental Score.
- Fidelity's Analyst Opinion is 7 or higher.
- Piotroski's (from GuruFocus or other sources) F-Score is 7 or higher.

Fidelity Video:
Trading strategies
https://www.fidelity.com/learning-center/trading/types-of-trading-strategies/overview

Section I: Common strategy ideas

1 Experiences in strategies

A strategy tells you what stocks to buy, what and when to sell.

We should use one or a few of the proven strategies that match well with the current market conditions. It is not an easy job and not an exact science especially when human emotions are involved. A perfect match seldom happens. However, when it does, it can be fireworks and your pocket will be over-stuffed with money.

The following strategies are for illustration purposes only. Test them out before you use them with real money.

- We usually ignore when to sell. If the strategy such as the "Year-End Loser" shows statistically that the best holding period is 4 months, sell them before May. That's why we should have the performances at short-term, mid-term and long-term in testing strategies.

- Sideways market (such as 2015).

    Buy at dips and sell at temporary highs and vice versa. It is a correction about 5% by my definition. The market may just fluctuate in a small range.

    The hard part is to determine what these dips and bottoms are. Here are my suggestions and how we need to adjust the percentages to the volatility of the current market. To me, if it is 2% lower than the last session (or 5% lower than the highest price in the last 5 sessions), it is a temporary bottom. The definitions vary based on your personal tolerance and time for investing. To benefit in this small fluctuation, buy stocks from your watch list or any ETF that represents the market such as SPY or IWM.

    The holding period could be one day to two weeks depending on your risk tolerance. It takes advantage of the fluctuation of prices due to the good news and bad news scenario typically.

    Alternatively, you determine when to sell by how much it would rise such as 2% higher than the last session (or 5% higher than the lowest price in the last 5 sessions). The disadvantage is you may never be able to sell stocks that are continuously heading down. The stop orders would prevent further losses.

In reality, the market does not behave the way we expected it to. You need to protect your loss (say sell it when it is over 15% loss). In the long run and if the market fits this sideways market, you SHOULD make money. As in life, there are no guarantees. You can load the historical price of SPY (or another ETF) to stimulate this strategy using different percentages and holding periods.

- The market is up or down steadily.

    Strategies using momentum profit better than buying value stocks in a bull market. "Buy high and sell higher" is a good strategy in a rising market.

    Use contra ETFs on a down ward market. The average holding period for me is 1 month (some may use 3 months). I stop using momentum when the market is too risky as I do not usually short stocks. It takes several weeks of small profits to recover from one big loss in one day that is if it recovers.

- Buy value.

    The average holding period could be more than one year. You're betting against the tide, so it will take a longer time for the value to be 'discovered' by the market. When the institution retailers are selling, find out their reasons. Buy what they are selling if they are wrong (rarely but it has happened many times). It is similar to "Buy low and sell high" and "Contrary Strategy". It seems to be easier said than done, as our emotions do not allow us to act rationally. The typical retail investor usually buys at peaks and sells at bottoms.

- Turnaround and breakup of a company.

    When the company fixes its major problem(s), its stock price could skyrocket.

    A company may be worth more by adding up the pieces. The recent example is ALU when I bought it at $1 in 2013. At the time, the company had a market cap of around two billions but the debt is about the same. However, their patents could be worth far more than two billion.

- Follow talented investors.

    First, you need to find the talented investors who have good recent performance records. GuruFocus.com (subscription is required) shows what stocks the gurus recently traded. 2015 is not a good year for gurus.

    Check out this article.
    http://seekingalpha.com/article/2762935-a-wisdom-of-experts-portfolio

- Follow what insiders buy.
    There are many tricks to separate the gems from garbage.

- Buy at the bottoms.
    2009 is one bottom. In my definition, it is Early Recovery (usually about one year from the plunge or indicated by the chart described in this book). This bottom fishing strategy buys beaten down stocks that are fundamentally sound. The average holding time is about one year (less if there are better bargains).

    My best returns are from the last two bottoms in 2003 and 2009. At these times, there were more potential stocks for huge profits and my average holding period was about 6 months. 2009 was the only time I dipped into my credit line on my house - **not recommended to most investors**.

- Market Neutral.
    If you are a good stock picker (or believe you're one), treat the market as neutral (i.e. ignoring the market timing). For example, you pick five stocks to buy and five stocks to sell short. You make money due to your skill in picking the right stocks no matter how the market moves. In theory, you should make good money without betting on the market direction.

- Sector Neutral.

If you specialize in a specific sector such as airlines, you may buy 2 good stocks and short 2 bad stocks in that sector. You can make good money because of your knowledge in the sector. In this strategy, compare stocks to its sector averages. You can use options to do the same if your cash position is limited.

Trading drug stocks could bring you huge profits. To improve your odds, you need to be an expert in this field. If you're not, subscribe to a specific newsletter that specializes in this industry and has a proven track record. Weigh more on the buy side when the sector is heading up, and vice versa.

- Sector Rotation.
  Investing in a sector or shorting the entire sector could add more profit. To illustrate, the tech sector may be a laggard during a recession as most consumers will not have the spare money to buy consumer electronics, and many companies would postpone their investment in enhancing productivity and development. Every month or two, rotate to the sector that is in an uptrend. Protect your profit when the sector reverses its direction.

- Theme investing.
  When China is moving up, FXI (an ETF) would be a buy. Other examples are OIL and GLD (for gold).

- Strong USD.
  It would be bad for global companies when the profits from foreign investments would be reduced when they are converted to a strong USD. The other bet is on USD itself.

- Super stocks.
  Most are small companies with increasing sales and earnings. It is a little different from the conventional stock analysis. They are riskier but the profits could be huge. Expect one big winner for several small losers. These stocks of small companies are not followed by analysts.

- The winners are already in your portfolio.
  Do not sell your winners as they may turn into bigger winners unless you have a good reason. Do not sell them if they still pass your recent stock analysis. During any market plunge, you may want to sell them but you should buy them back when the market recovers.

When you mismatch the strategy with the market conditions, you lose the opportunity for profit or even lose money. If the market is up or down steadily, a sideways strategy will not work for example. Matching the strategy to the current market conditions is not an easy job and sometimes it takes some luck. However, when it matches it, there could be fireworks. If you match it more times than you miss it, you should make good money.

Afterthoughts

"Buy and hold" needs no explanation. You just buy the stock and hold it forever. It is a good strategy in a secular bull market such as 1970-2000. After 2000, there are better strategies than "Buy and Hold".

A better way is "Buy and monitor" to ensure the stock you bought still has an appreciation potential.

"Buy and forget" is my term and it could be a good strategy in 2012. Buy the deeply-valued stocks (i.e. big bargains for quality stocks) and forget it until the economy comes back. I have made some profits in established companies such as MSFT, CAT and CSCO during this period.

Links
Market Neutral http://en.wikipedia.org/wiki/Market_neutral
Sector Rotation http://en.wikipedia.org/wiki/Sector_rotation

Filler: "First" as of 4/2016

This time could make some history at least for one of the following:

1. First woman president.
2. First spouse stays in the white house two times. "Buy one get one free" or give Bill another chance with the interns.
3. First non-politician president.
4. First president spending less in campaign.

So far, they try to satisfy every group (such as the Great Wall of the US, free tuition...) without telling us how to finance them.

2 Strategy performance

We may find some strategies performing well in testing but not in reality. Here are my possible explanations.

- Survival bias. When Lehman Brothers and other bankrupt financial institutions are taken out from your historical database, your strategy would look better. Try not to include penny stocks and stocks with micro market caps as they have a higher chance of going bankrupt. Mergers and acquisition do not offset this effect as they are fewer.
- Test windows. For example, start each test with the start of the month and end the test a year later. If the testing period is 5 years, you should have 5*12 = 60 tests. When you start with an amount and let it rise and fall for a long period, the final result would be affected greatly on how it performed in the first year. Most advertised tests are not reliable as they always cherry pick a date that is profitable in the starting years of the test.
- Test different holding periods such as 3 (1 for momentum strategies), 6 and 12 months. Some strategies are good for a short-term hold.
- The last 5 years is better than the last 10 years as it is more similar to the recent market.
- Define your tests according to the phases of the market cycle. Market Peak (a phase defined by me) should have different strategies than Early Recovery.
- Compare the performance to SPY (or an ETF that simulates the market). If most of the stocks you trade are small stocks, use an ETF for small stocks.
- Consider dividends in some cases where they are applicable. For example, for a flat market, the average 1.5% dividend makes a huge difference.
- Use annualized returns. They are better for comparison. However, the returns of less than a month should not be considered as they amplify the results too much.
- Ensure the calculations are correct. When you compare the returns to SPY, the negative values could give wrong interpretations.

- My broker calculates my performance returns and compares them to the indexes. It is handy.
  I gifted appreciated stocks to my son. My broker did it wrong in calculating performance (but correctly for tax purposes) by using the original cost basis. Hence they look far better than they actually are.
- Data fitting works sometimes but not all the time. You change the parameters to boost the best performance. Sometimes it does not work due to the market conditions that are not the same and/or your data is too small to reach a useful conclusion.

3   AAII, a source for strategies

AAII has many nice stock screens. Check out their performance summaries. You can divide the screens and their performances into groups according to the different stages of a market cycle and rank the performances. Some screens perform better in certain stage(s) of the market cycle. Most likely, the value screens should do better in market bottom (Early Recovery defined by me) and growth screens do better in a bull market (Up and Peak phases defined by me).

As a regular subscriber, the screen stock recommendations are about 15 days old (check the current policy) and the most updated screens require extra cost. Their strategy for most screens is: Sell all stocks that do not meet the criteria of the screen and buy new stocks that meet the criteria every month. This trading strategy would require a lot of trades and you need to consider their tax consequences (none for non-taxable accounts) and commissions. Trade on paper before you commit to their recommendations with real money similar to many strategies described in this book.

The basic membership with a decent magazine-publication is a good deal. If you are new to investing, there are many basic books provided on their website.

Update 2/2016

AAII publishes its screen performance every year. Here are some pointers.

- Do not follow last year's winners. I predicted 2015 was a sideways market and 2016 is a risky market that has a good chance to turn into a bear market.
- During bear markets, the screens had lost from 10% to 83% without a single winner here. When the technical indicator SMA-350 or Death Cross tells you to exit, exit as there is no screen that would find winners.
- Every year from 2011 to 2015, the return of the market is positive after adding dividends. When the technical indicator SMA-350 or Death Cross tells you to invest, invest if you trust the charts.
- Some screens work great in one year and become big losers in another year. To conclude, there is no evergreen screen.

- It does not go earlier than 2009 in the summaries, the last Early Recovery that has the best profit potential. I recommend value stocks for this stage of the market cycle.
- For the same reason above, it does not show performances in the bear market of 2007-2008.
- I would select the screens that have a good five-year average. However, the last five years is a typical bull market. Most screens do not beat the S&P 500's 12% average for the last five years. You're better off buying SPY, an ETF simulating the S&P 500 index.
- AAII screens have high turnovers as they replace the stocks when they do not meet the screen criteria.

Paper art by Eric from PowPaper

4   Adaptive strategy

What is the best metric for evaluating stocks? Most people will tell you P/E. I use estimated earnings (E) and P/E becomes Forward P/E (a.k.a. Expected P/E). Switch it over to E/P for easier to understand, and it is termed Earnings Yield (EY = P/E). However, the 'E' is not 'expected' which is better to predict future stock value. I prefer EY to be calculated with Forward Earnings and most sites do not provide it but you can calculate it easily.

When the market favors momentum stocks, fundamental stocks even with good Earnings Yields may not work. In this case, I prefer momentum stocks with EY better than average.

EV/EBITDA (obtainable from Yahoo!Finance) is better than P/E as it includes interest, debt and cash. Switch it over and it is True Earnings Yield (my term). Some may tell you ROI and there is a successful book on ROI.

Both P/E and ROI should not be the only metric as there is no single evergreen metric. That is why most people have poor performance by following them blindly. It is the herd theory: The performance is usually decreased in the longer term when too many folks follow it.

Here is my test on the S&P 500 stocks from April 1, 2019 to July 1, 2019. I used the top 10 stocks from each sort. Commissions, dividends and spreads are omitted for simplicity. SPY's return is annualized to 13.8%.

Value parameters

Top 10 stocks sorted by	Best SPY[1]
EY in descending order	-251%
Dividend Yield in descending order	-291%[2]

Opposite of the above

Top 10 stocks sorted by	Best SPY[1]
EY in ascending order	6%
Dividend Yield = 0	138%[3]

[1] Beat by % = (Avg. return of 10 stocks – SPY) / SPY
[2] Including dividend yields for the average 10 stocks and SPY, "Beat SPY" is reduced to -241%.
[3] Just randomly picked the 10 stocks that do not pay dividends as there are more stocks with no dividends.

Section II: Riskier, short-term strategies

"Nothing risked, nothing gained."

From my book "Best Stocks to Buy for July, 2021", Sub List of risky stocks:

Commodity (3)	Return	Ann.
EVC	16%	43%
NUE	10%	26%
YELL	108%	283%
Average	45%	117%
RSP	1%	2%
Beat RSP by	5,275%	

The details can be found in the following link.
http://tonyp4idea.blogspot.com/2022/12/best-stocks-series.html

1   Trading by headlines

On 6/29/2019, Trump and Xi seemed to settle the trade war in the G20. The market would likely rise on the coming Monday. Luckily, I had closed a short position. Many chip stocks would rise as they can sell their products to Huawei. I have several of these stocks expecting the trade war would be settled. The farmers and their supporting industries would breathe easier.

I bet the shipping companies would be more profitable from the news. Without doing further research, I checked out this shipping sector and found the following stocks had been up more than 4%: DHT, NM, SBLK, STNG, TNK and ASC. It was during the weekend, so your trade account should be able to trade after hours and you need to act right after the news.

I exchanged comments with Andrew McElroy, an expert on sector rotation. He does not have the rules set up as in this book but he makes great trades by 'seeing' the market and using technical analysis. The following is from his article.

"The idea is fairly simple. There is more potential for profit (and loss) in individual sectors, especially when the index is trading sideways. I try to buy strong sectors which have pulled back onto support and avoid overbought sectors at resistance. I also use Elliott Wave to identify cycles of buying and selling and stages in trends."

I would like to include headlines such as Trump's election, interest rates hikes and new regulations.

When it rains in Brazil, buy coffee futures

Recently it rained too much in SE Asia, so buy rice futures. I did not trade futures, so I missed out on the opportunity and unfortunately there is no equivalent ETF for rice. In the beginning of 2012, we should know the farming crops especially corn will not be good due to the flooding and drought in different parts of the world. Act accordingly for the profit potentials.

When a war is starting in the Middle East, most likely the oil price will rise. Buy the oil ETF and sell it when the chance of the war is reduced. Many tiny drops of profit could turn into a river of profit.

Trading by headlines is profitable, but it is hard to master and is very time-consuming. Test this strategy on paper for years before you commit real money as in most strategies. Most couch potatoes read newspaper and watch TV all day without making a penny. He could be a couch-potato millionaire if he read this article, paper traded/refined the strategy, and acted on it!

However, the media tend to exaggerate headlines in order to sell their ads. Ignore all the recommendations on stocks. Most likely they are outdated information and some may be used to manipulate others. Do your own research as your mother taught you that there is no free lunch.

Rules of the game

1. Do not be too emotional; ignore your past wins and losses except when using them as lessons if they are valid (i.e., educated guesses).

2. Do not trade the entire farm. Consider option, ETFs and/or small trades on stocks, which involve many other factors.

3. Trade it fast – today's headlines will not be headlines tomorrow. There are very few exceptions.

4. Where there is a winner, there is always a loser. For example, Apple was a winner with the iPhone and BlackBerry was a loser. Same for Best Buy and Circuit City.

5. Ensure you can trade after hours from your broker.

6. Do not forget when to exit for either a small profit or a small loss.

7. Quick evaluation. The headline will be gone if you do not act fast. Skip companies with poor metrics such as high debt and low earnings yield. Prefer to buy an ETF related to the headline.

8. Most likely, someone has used the information before you get it. However, some info can be deducted before it occurs. Insider purchases are a good guide.

9. I recommended crude oil at $30 per barrel in Jan. 15, 2016 as the price was at rock bottom. For value sectors, you may have to wait for a long time for the market to realize its value.

10. Sometimes, you should ignore stock evaluations, if the headline news is more important. Learn my 5-minute evaluation process of a stock (a quick way but not recommended if you have time to do thorough research):
    - From Finviz.com, enter the stock or ETF symbol. Look at how many greens in metrics over reds.
    - Check out Forward P/E (E>0 and P/E < 20), Debut / Equity (< 50%) and P/FCF (not in red color).
    - SMA20 (or SMA50 for longer holding period). If SMA20 is > 10%, it is trending up.
    - Scroll down for Insider Trade. It usually is a good buy if insiders are buying recently and heavily with market prices.
    - Be cautious on foreign and low-volume stocks.
    - If most of the above are positive, it is likely a buy. As in life, nothing is 100% certain.

    If you have a hard time following the above, most likely this strategy is not for you and it is better to return to your couch. No offense.

Volatile market and headlines
As of July 2012 (and also in 2015, historically a positive market in the year before an election), the market moved sideways, influenced by headlines.

2013 had been volatile with dips and surges influenced by daily news. The trend was up though. The Federal debt problem, EU crisis... had not been resolved. Every time there was good news, the market rose, and vice versa. In this market, buy on dips (3% down from last temporary peak) and sell on temporary surges (3% up from last temporary bottom). Some use 5% instead of 3% depending on one's risk tolerance.

Trend and calendar timing

Usually following the trend is better than ignoring it.

- Many retail investors want to sell their losers for year-end tax planning. Buy them at year-end and sell them early next year. At the end of 2012, the opposite happened: investors sold winners expecting higher taxes the next year, but this proved false.

  This could be the reason for a sell-off of Apple in year-end of 2012 and it gave us a good entry point. To me, Apple's fundamentals were sound though the media said otherwise. In a few months, Apple became a value stock from a growth stock according to the press.

- Investors are not rational and follow the market blindly. The strategy 'Buy low and sell high' works.

- We have so much good news and bad news in the same year. Ensure the bad news will not extend to worse news. Timing is everything. Buy on bad news and sell on good news; it does not work when the market plunges.

- The media influences the market. Analyze their arguments. If they exaggerate, consider doing the opposite.

- Over-reaction to earnings missed or gained. When the company missed the earnings by 5%, there is a very good chance the stock will be down in a year, and vice versa. However, when it missed by 1% and the stock lost by 10%, it could be a buying opportunity, particularly when it was a temporary condition and the company is fundamentally sound.

- Buy the stock at dip when a solvable problem surfaces. Sell after the problem has been resolved. Ceiling debt is such a solvable problem and it is caused by politics. In the beginning of 2013, I mentioned that the debt problem had not been resolved and we would have this ceiling debt problem periodically until it will be eventually resolved.

Scheduled events

Some events are scheduled such as earnings announcements, unemployment reports, etc. Most likely educated guesses of the outcomes have already been circulated in the web.

The last five events on the Federal debt handling (using fancy names such as sequester and debt ceiling) were scheduled such as the government shutdown. They drove the market down by about an average of 5% each time. Sell before the event and buy back afterward. The Congress has cancelled these debt deadlines as of 1/2014.

Many sectors are impacted by events such as Trump's success in election, hikes of interest rates and trade wars.

Follow the institutional investors

They drive the market. When they see the sector is over-valued or the peak has been reached, they rotate sectors.

Use deduction

In 2014, China has a great [harvest]() on wheat, corn and rice. China's population is #1 in the world and its middle class is growing. The farmers in the US will be hurt as they cannot export these products to their number one customer. Use the same logic to deduct that there will be problems in the companies that supply products and services to the farmers. They are combines, fertilizer companies and seed companies. It further translates into Deere, Potash, Monsanto and AGCO.

Due to increasing wealth in 2017, Chinese demanded more meat. It takes a lot of corn to produce one pound of meat and in turn corn needed fertilizers. Hence, you can expect the companies producing fertilizers will increase their profits.

Geopolitical crisis

Many times no action is the best action. It applies here. I had my experience in selling too many stocks via stops in 911. The market returned in a few days and I did not buy them back.

An analysis from Ned David Research covers 51 events from 1900 to 2014. My interpretation for actions: Trade the affected sector (via sector ETF) in the first few days and reverse the trade 2 months after. Many times it means the oil price and gold price would rise.

I bought SH (a contra ETF to SPY) in August, 2017 as August and September are statistically the worst months in addition to the high risk in the current market. It is expected to be sold on Nov. 1. The North Korea crisis did not do much to the market on the first day but the market (the S&P 500) lost 1.45% and the risky NASDAQ lost 2.13% (see my blog on FAANG) on the second day.

Caveat. Need to understand the crisis. If it would lead to World War 3, most sectors will not recover for a long while. Again, there is no sure thing in investing otherwise there would be no poor folks. However, educated guesses should materialize more often than not.

My experiences
- When the interest rate is expected to rise, plan on investments that are favorable to it and vice versa.
- On the same week, CROX lost almost 40% in one day. I bought some and made about 10% profit in a week. CROX's fundamentals were no good and it did have a history of a roller coaster ride in its stock price. After a year, I found out that I sold it too early as the stock price doubled. Better to buy a stock on its way up than down unless we identify that the bottom has been reached.
- I was on vacation while the second incident of the Boeing Max happened. Should have shorted the stock. In addition, Boeing's suppliers would suffer too similar to Apple's suppliers on Apple.

    https://www.barrons.com/articles/boeing-737-max-jet-production-cut-suppliers-stocks-51554499957?siteid=yhoof2&yptr=yahoo

- I missed applying the same trick to the rise of Apple when Apple announced its new iPod. I should at least buy the stocks of its part suppliers. I hope learn from this lesson and take advantage of future similar circumstances.

I missed the opportunity to buy uranium stocks. It should be bought after Japan's disaster. When Japan approved the reopening of nuclear reactors today, these stocks including CCJ, DNN, LEU, URRE, UEC, URZ, URG and UUUU surge. When China's new nuclear reactors are on-line, they will surge again.
- Experiences in early 2014.
Recently and in a short time, I made a good profit on BBY and a tiny profit on TGT. Both were bought due to headlines.

2 Earnings season overreactions

AAII provides screens for stocks with positive and negative earnings surprises (January, April, July, and October). The pleasant surprise screen always beats the other screens from the last time I checked.

Zacks ranks stocks with positive earnings revisions. Their top-ranked (#1) stocks reportedly average a 26% annual return.

As with all vendors, we should check their recent performance (say, the last 5 years). If the strategy is proven to be effective, more investors will follow and usually make it less effective.

It usually starts on the first two weeks after the ending of quarters (Dec., March, June and September) as indicated in the following link.
http://www.investopedia.com/ask/answers/08/earnings-season.asp

My experience
Contrary to the conventional wisdom, I enjoy the negative surprises more. If the company has a reason to come back or its problem is only temporary, I buy the stock. Sometimes it takes a few months and sometimes even a year for the stock to come back. The strategy of 'Buying low and selling high' works more often than it does not. However, avoid the stocks that start their long-term plunge.

Missing expected earnings by 1% and causing the stock to drop by 10% is a buy to me. Heading to bankruptcy is a different story though.

My momentum strategy buys stocks with positive earnings revisions. I usually do not keep these stocks for over a month.

As of today (4/6/2016), the quarter earnings season is starting. This year I have worry about the earnings due to the strong USD. It would impact the earnings as about 40% (my rough estimate) of the incomes of global companies are from foreign countries. If we feel there will be more disappointments, we should short the stocks that are expected to have poor earnings.

My lesson
Take advantage of the irrational human reactions. Retail investors and institutional investors are both human beings. Fund managers have more pressure to sell a loser to keep their jobs. Retail investors usually sell after

the big institutional investors. Try to find out whether it is just a sentimental reaction or the stock is going to fall further.

How to hedge your stocks from earning surprises

Stocks might have a wide swing after the earnings announcements. Hedge the unfavorable announcements by the following three methods:

1. Stop loss.
   Usually, the swing is steeper than your stop price. When the price reaches or go below a specific price, it will be turned into a market sell order. Institutional investors usually unload the stocks faster than the retail investors, opposite of buying. However, their positions are huge. We can tell they are unloading (or loading) from the unusual high trading volumes of the stocks. Ensure that your trades are allowed after hours.
2. Option.
   It is like buying an insurance to protect your loss. Protect yourself from large losses as insurance is not cheap and smaller losses could be due to volatility.
3. Earnings prediction.
   They are also known as whispers or educated guesses. Zacks has a grading system.

   Also, insiders know the earnings before their announcements. However, it is illegal to use this information before its announcement.

Earnings revisions will be available before the announcement and they would provide better guesses for the announcement. With today's dividend chasers, the announcement of dividends or its increase would boost the stock price.

Personally, I do not do a lot to protect my stocks from earnings announcements. I have too many stocks. However, when we have evaluated the stocks correctly and monitored them regularly, we should have more pleasant surprises.

Profit from earnings surprises

The stock price usually rises on positive earnings surprises and falls otherwise. Sometimes, the reactions are not rational such as a 1% miss in earnings leading to a 10% loss in the stock price. In some rare cases, the positive earnings causes the stock to plunge as the investors expected better earnings even better than consensus. Here is an example of how to find stocks with positive earnings (you can profit by buying puts or shorting the stocks for stocks with negative earnings).

- Find stocks that have earnings announcements next week or month. Sources are Finviz.com's screener and SeekingAlpha.
- The screened stocks should fit some basic criteria. My criteria are: Market Cap > 200M, stock price > $2, average volume > 10,000 shares…
- If you subscribe to Zacks, check the earnings grade. Stocks with a Grade 1 and Grade 2 deserve your time for further research.
- If there are meaningful insiders' purchases, the chance of positive earnings is high.
- A positive short-term trend (SMA-20 from Finviz.com) is a plus.
- A positive short-term trend for the sector that stock belongs to is a plus. The sector can be represented by an ETF for that sector and use SMA-20.
- Read articles on the stock for a qualitative analysis. Find these articles from many sources including SeekingAlpha. Today they have fewer articles for free.

Be warned that we do not expect all wins. When we achieve win rate of more than 50%, we should fare very well financially. When the market is falling or the earnings are expected to be poor, do not buy stocks except those that are fundamentally sound.

Take advantage of others' orders

1. Ensure your account can trade after hours.

2. Use Finviz.com to look for stocks announcing earnings this week. Prefer fundamentally sound stocks with a market cap great than 500M (100M for smaller stocks).

3. Check out earningswhispers.com. They have two estimates: the consensus and the one from this website. Write down the exact time too.

4. If you subscribe Zacks.com, use its rating too as a reference.

5. Be at least 15 minutes earlier than the announcement date and time.

6. Google the stock and EPS from Google News. Refresh the search every 2 minutes. Check related articles.

7. If it beats the estimates, buy it for at least one penny less than the last trade price and sell it within a day or two. The logic is to take advantage of all those orders that have not considered earnings in a timely fashion. It does not always work.

8. To improve performance, include Revenue with EPS.

Personally, I do not do it as it is too time-consuming for me; my beauty sleep is more important than money. Again, test it out before committing real money. There are many parameters that can be tuned to adjust to your personal preferences and the current market conditions. This is the essence of an entire book. I apply my own enhancements such as using Finviz.com.

Filler

My friend's late uncle had a 'buy and hold strategy' that worked pretty well. Most of his stocks were big companies. He died with a house worth more than a million and many millions in stocks. His only mistake was not to transfer more of his stocks to his heirs before his death. He died in the year when the estate exemption was reduced to a million. Uncle Sam was the biggest winner and won big without any effort.

#Filler: Common investing mistake

It is a common mistake to trade a stock based on whether one's like or dislike of its products. You should base on the appreciation potential. Stay away from sin stocks though. Most airlines try to squeeze every penny from us. For investors, this could be a good thing.

#Filler: Inflation meter

When the beggar asked me for a spare dollar, I felt the inflation pinch. That's the real inflation meter. Forget what the government says.

3 Strategies on earnings

Here are two strategies on earnings. It is supposed to make millions for my children but they are not interested in investing. You either hate or love what your father does.

1. Buy the stocks with earnings announcement soon with Zacks rating 1 (the best) and short those with Zacks rating 5 (the worst). BY THE WAY, Zacks rating is free so far for individual stocks.

2. After the earnings announcement, Google the company every second or so. If the earnings are good, buy it fast with market order. If it is bad, short it.

Do not be greedy and set a limit on loss. Do not call me whether the trade is good or bad. In addition, check insider transactions and SMA-20.

I have tried #1 once a long while ago. I have not tried #2 as I have a life too. In the long run, these strategies should make you some money.

4 Year-end strategies

I have two: 1. Buy the current year winners (YEW) and 2. Buy the current year losers (YEL).

The first strategy is riding the institutional investors' window dressing to include the winners in their funds to make them look better. It did not work well in 2018, so I skip it in 2019.

The second strategy takes advantage of selling losers for tax purposes. We need to find value stocks, but not stocks that are heading into bankruptcy. I had amazing returns in 2018 and will continue this strategy in 2019.

The following describes how to create your own testing if you have a historical database. It would be a frame for testing other strategies.

- Define the starting date. For the first strategy, I would use 9/1, 10/1 and 11/1 for two sets of test data. For the second strategy, I would use 12/1 and 12/15. Check to see which starting date is better for the specific strategy.

- Define the durations, the number of months before you sell the purchased stocks. I use 1 months, 2 months, 3 months and 6 months for my designated durations.
- Define the number of tests. I would start from the year 2000, one or two years older if your historical database allows for that. Actually I started in last 3 years or so to save time. However, do not use dates older than 1995 as the market was quite different then.
- Compare your results to SPY (or the S&P 500 index).
- Ignore dividends for simplicity.
- Use annualized rates for a better comparison.
- If the date has no data such as during holidays and weekends, use the date after it for consistency.
- Take out stocks that would not be the stocks you usually would buy, such as penny stocks (that likely boost the performance due to survivorship bias), small foreign companies and/or stocks giving huge dividends or giving a return of capital.
- Use different metrics to sort, such as Expected Earning Yield (E/P) or a composite grade. Use the top 5 (or 2) stocks to calculate performances.
- Include the maximum drawdown (the maximum loss from recent height) from many selected time frames (i.e. durations described). My maximum loss is -52% from 12/1/2007 to one year later in my Year-End Loss strategy, but followed by 256% gain in the next year.
- Negative percent numbers could give you wrong calculations when comparing to an index. Check them out manually if your formula has not taken care of the negative numbers.
- A year-end winner strategy should include large companies (traded by fund managers) and stocks that have increased in values year-to-date.
- From my limited testing, my small-cap stocks better than other stocks and they have to be profitable.
- Here are my best results for the two strategies. Again, my results will not be the same as yours due to different selection criteria. Past performance may not have anything to do with future performances.

The year-end loser strategy in 2015 does not work that well as I screened many stocks that were scored very low. I found out many screened stocks were from foreign countries. Many emerging countries have had problems and I do not trust most of their financial info. Besides that, many were energy companies which I already had too many of.

Many have Expected Earning Yields over 35%. However, most have very high debts such as Debt/Equity is over 1 (i.e. 100%). If I bought them, I would unload them within 3 months fearing a market crash in 2016 [Update. As of 2019, we do not have one]. Historically, it is profitable, but I may skip most YEL stocks this year as most were deserved losers. The lesson is: Adjust to the current market conditions.

Strategy	Starting Date	Duration	Avg. Annual. %	Max. Drawn Down
YE Winners	10/1	4 months	40%	-36%
YE Losers	12/1	6 months	42%	-28%

My experience

When trying to make good money, you need to find a strategy that matches the current market. Here are my recent strategies I actually tried with real money in 2018.

* You usually see window dressing from institutional investors from Nov. 1 to Dec. 1 (some use dates earlier than Nov. 1). Buy the current winners and sell the current losers of stocks with a large market cap.

The market was risky so I did not buy winners but shorted some losers.

* Buy year-end losers from Nov. 1 to Dec. 31 (some use dates earlier than Nov.1). The companies have to be profitable (>15%), big losers (most having over 50% yearly loss) and small companies (preferred).

Incorporate the strategy with today's volatile market (i.e. buy when they plunge and sell when they rise). You need to determine what is a "plunge" and a "rise". For me, it is short-term and the percent is 5% from a recent high or low.

There is a selling part of these strategies I have not included here. Most of my strategies are based on exhaustive tests from historical data with a lot of work.

Every market is different. We need to make a lot of adjustments. From my experiences, the best research may not make you money all the time. In the long run, the more educated you become, the better chance for you to make money.

Year-End 2018

This was one of my best monthly returns. The average purchase date is 12/27/2018 and the current prices were based on 1/28/2019. The return is 53% or 648% annualized. Most likely the performance will not be repeated. However, it serves as a procedure for coming years.

I change the quantity Q to 1. Several stocks have been purchased more than once. I sold 3 stocks already indicated by the Status = 'Sold'.

Account	Screen	Year-end loser	Start	12/21/19	End	1/8/2019	Today	1/28/19		
Stock	Q	Buy	Sell	Buy $	Sell $	Buy Date	Sell Date	# Days	Profit $	Profit %	Ann %	Status
401KC												
CHK	1	2.13	2.99	2	3	01/03/19	01/18/19	15	1	40%	982%	Sold
MNK	1	16.41	21.45	16	21	01/03/19	01/25/19	22	5	31%	510%	Sold
MNK	1	16.43	21.45	16	21	01/03/19	01/25/19	22	5	31%	507%	Sold
NNBR	1	5.68	8.58	6	9	12/26/18	01/28/19	33	3	51%	565%	
NNBR	1	5.72	8.58	6	9	12/26/18	01/28/19	33	3	66%	727%	
ESTE	1	4.35	6.45	4	6	12/26/18	01/18/19	23	2	48%	766%	Sold
JT												
LCI	1	4.61	8.29	5	8	12/21/18	01/28/19	38	4	80%	767%	
MDR	1	8.01	9.13	8	9	01/08/19	01/28/19	20	1	14%	255%	
YRCW	1	3.29	5.78	3	6	12/21/18	01/28/19	38	2	76%	727%	
YRCW	1	3.26	5.78	3	6	12/21/18	01/28/19	38	3	77%	742%	
401K												
ASRT	1	3.56	4.18	4	4	12/26/18	01/28/19	33	1	17%	193%	
UTCC	1	7.13	11.00	7	11	12/26/18	01/28/19	33	4	54%	600%	
YRCW	1	2.92	5.78	3	6	12/26/18	01/28/19	33	3	98%	1083%	
Tot/avg				84	119	12/27/18		29	36	53%	648%	

I sold my YRCW (not shown above) on the earnings date that can be found in Finviz.com. When the earnings are positive, it will be sold for my asking price plus a little more but less than the surge. If it is negative, it will not be sold. I recommend to cancel any trade order before the earnings date.

As of 09/07/2019, LCI is up by 185% and YRCW is down by 27% (I sold one position in my retirement account for about 100% gain).

How long should we hold these screened stocks?

Except those in my taxable account, I sold all of them in the first two months. The following is the annualized returns for holding 1 month, 2 months, 3 months and 5 months (as of 6/22/2019). From my previous testing, I should have held the stocks for 6 months. However, I have made my objective already and I want to take advantage of this volatile market.

I could not find UTCC in my historical database. I sold it with an annualized return of 572%. It could be acquired or merged. For simplicity, I used 12/27/2018 as the purchase date for all stocks. I consider one position for each stock and hence 3 purchases of YRCW is considered as one purchase here. Again, I do not include dividends, the bid spread and commissions.

	1 Month	2 Months	3 Months	5 Months
Ann. Return	497%	366%	178%	17%
SPY	72%	74%	52%	31%

From the above, I did well in selling most of them. If I held all of them for 5 months, they would not beat the SPY, the market comparison many use.

Filler

- First bought or sold by insiders and their relatives, then followed by programmed computers, institutional investors, technicians and then retail investors.

- Missed a short of PG&E and VALE when their bad news broke. There is more in life than playing the markets.

5 The Contrarian Approach

Contrarian investors go against prevailing market trends. They seek opportunities where market sentiment reaches extremes—buying when others are selling and vice versa.

Timing is critical. You want to follow the crowd until assets become significantly overvalued, and then reverse course.
When a stock or strategy becomes overbought, a correction is often inevitable—though there are exceptions. Gold, for example, defies this logic at times, but its price movements often reflect broader forces like the depreciating U.S. dollar and inflation-adjusted long-term trends.

That said, blindly adopting a contrarian stance is risky. You must carefully analyze whether market consensus is truly flawed.

For example: Should you have invested in equities after they plunged by July 2012? The answer depends on several factors:
If the long-term trend is downward (e.g., a W-shaped recession), it's better to wait.
If the trajectory mirrors Japan's "lost decades," patience is even more crucial.
However, in a new secular bull market, waiting too long could mean missing significant gains.

A counterpoint to this caution is the market's potential inflation-driven rise due to excessive money printing.

Should you have bought bank stocks after 2008 or tech stocks after the 2001 crash? With hindsight, probably not—despite many of these stocks losing half their value. If the underlying problems remain unresolved, further decline or bankruptcy is likely.

General guideline: Avoid investing in equities within one year of a broad market crash or within two years in sectors that caused the bubble. This pattern held true in both the 2000 and 2007 bottoms and may remain a reliable rule, though certainty in investing is never absolute.

Links
Contrarian
(http://en.wikipedia.org/wiki/Contrarian_investing

Overview of Contrarian Investing (written by ChatGPT)

Contrarian investing is a strategy that involves going against prevailing market trends or sentiment. Instead of following the crowd, contrarian investors seek opportunities where others see risk, pessimism, or underperformance. The core belief is that markets often overreact—both on the upside and downside—and these overreactions can create profitable opportunities.

Core Principles

Buy When Others Sell
Contrarians look to buy assets that are undervalued due to excessive fear or neglect. This often means purchasing stocks or sectors during market downturns or crises.

Sell When Others Buy
On the flip side, contrarian investors may exit or avoid assets that are overhyped or overpriced due to excessive optimism or speculative bubbles.

Market Psychology Matters
The crowd is often wrong at turning points. Contrarians pay close attention to investor sentiment, media coverage, and market extremes.

Key Indicators for Contrarian Opportunities

Sentiment Surveys: High bullish sentiment may indicate a market top; extreme pessimism may signal a bottom.

Valuation Metrics: Look for low P/E, P/B, or P/FCF ratios in out-of-favor stocks or sectors.

Insider Buying: Executives buying company stock during downturns may signal confidence.

Short Interest: High short interest could suggest the stock is oversold and due for a reversal.

Historical Cycles: Markets and sectors tend to move in cycles; contrarians often buy at the troughs.

Famous Contrarian Investors

Warren Buffett: Known for "being greedy when others are fearful and fearful when others are greedy."
Sir John Templeton: Made fortunes by investing in deeply depressed markets, such as post-WWII Japan.

David Dreman: Advocated for buying low P/E and low price-to-book stocks when others shunned them.

Benefits of Contrarian Investing

Potential for Outsized Returns: Buying undervalued assets can lead to significant gains if markets correct.

Psychological Edge: Contrarians aren't swayed by hype or fear, helping them avoid common investor pitfalls.

Diversification of Strategy: It adds a layer of strategic differentiation from momentum or growth investing.

Risks and Challenges

Timing: Markets can remain irrational longer than expected. Being early can feel the same as being wrong.

Value Traps: Some assets are cheap for a reason. Not all contrarian plays bounce back.

Emotional Discipline: Going against the crowd requires conviction and the ability to withstand criticism and short-term losses.

Examples of Contrarian Opportunities

2008 Financial Crisis: Buying bank stocks when they were heavily punished.

Tech Crash (2000–2002): Entering non-tech sectors as tech collapsed.

Pandemic Sell-off (March 2020): Buying quality stocks at deep discounts when panic selling hit the markets.

Conclusion

Contrarian investing is not about blindly opposing the majority—it's about making informed decisions when the market overreacts. The most successful contrarians combine deep research, valuation analysis, and psychological resilience. In the long run, those who can think independently and act decisively in times of uncertainty often reap the greatest rewards.

#Filler: Tips
- When you have a lot of money to invest and you're not using a financial adviser and/or not subscribing to any investment service, it could be a big financial mistake.
- LTCM, with two Nobel-prize winners, best supporting team and best technologies then, ran their hedge funds into the ground.
- The so-called modern portfolio theory is most likely based on the wrong and/or insufficient testing parameters / assumptions.

6 Short Squeeze

When there is a short squeeze (i.e. over shorted), the stock may appreciate due to the shorters unable to find more stocks to short. The candidates can be found in Finviz.com. I use 35%. However, there may be valid reasons for the shorts such as a lawsuit pending, losing sales... Select the stocks with sound fundamentals.

The following are tests (not real trades) and many tests will be added. As of 09/04/15, the returns are:

Stock	Buy Date	Return	Annualized	SPY return
CALM	07/16/15	-3%	-33%	-1%
GME	07/16/15	-1%	-7%	-1%

The following are real trades as of 09/04/15.

Stock	Buy Date	Return	Sold date
CALM	03/11/15	47%	N/A
GME	04/06/15	8%	N/A

CALM, a candidate

Cal-Maine Foods Inc. (CALM) had fallen from over $60 to $46 recently and it was my heavy bet. The opening price on 12/15/2015 was $46.76. Readers might wonder why I still recommended accumulating a falling stock. Simply put, the race is not over and this horse has a lot of potential (i.e. fundamentally sound). The payout would be huge as it has been ignored (the short float is over 55%).

Let me show you my evaluation process, so that you may use it to enhance your strategy if you have one.

Currently, this stock was screened by my Short screen that spots fundamentally-sound companies with short floats over 35%. Most of the screened stocks deserve to be shorted, but I cannot find any justification for this stock.

Technically speaking

First, this stock has been hated as described by the following table with the exception of Finviz's "Recom". Most of the data in this article were derived from the free Finviz.com on Dec. 15, 2015. The 'Conditions' are my personal preferences.

	Condition	Indicate	12/15/2015
Short Float	>35%	Short squeeze	55%
RSI(14)	<30%	Oversold	31%
SMA-20	<0	Short-term down	-13%
SMA-50	<0	Mid-term down	-17%
SMA-200	<0	Long-term down	-9%
Recom.	1 - Buy & 5 – Sell	3 – Neutral	2

Fundamentally speaking

Did this stock deserve this hatred? From the following table, it is a big NO.

	Condition	Indicate	12/15/2015
Forward P/E	>0 and < 20	Favorable	7
ROE	>20%	Favorable	40%
Profit Margin	>8%	Favorable	15%
EPS Q/Q	>15%	Favorable	418%
Sales Q/Q	>10%	Favorable	71%
P/FCF	<15	Favorable	12
Debt / Equity	<.5 (industry related)	Favorable	.05

One or two favorable metrics do not mean a 'Buy' or great fundamentals. However, all these metrics all yell 'Buy'. They are my major fundamental metrics that have recently proven my predictability.

I combined all these metrics and scored CALM in 3 scoring systems plus PEY described below. As of this writing, CALM passed all my scoring systems with flying colors. Actually when stocks exceed the passing score by that much, I have a little concern; I cannot find any problem with this stock.

	Passing Score	Score
P-Score	3	6
Short-term score	15	40
Long-term score	15	24
PEY	5%	23%

Explanation

- P-Score, Pow's Score. It uses the metrics available in the free Finviz.com with the exception of using Fidelity's Analyst Opinion instead of Finviz's "Recom". This score system is described in my book "Scoring Stocks".
- The other two systems use additional metrics and/or scores I subscribe to. I monitor these two scoring systems periodically and adjust the scores accordingly. My Short-Term Score is used for holding stocks for less than 6 months.
- PEY, Pow's Earnings Yield. It is similar to EV/EBIT (5 from GuruFocus or 1/5 = 20% for Earning Yield). Both consider debt and cash. The advantage of PEY is all the metrics are readily available for calculation if using Cash/Share instead of Short-term Liability. PEY also uses expected earnings.

Intangibles

From Seeking Alpha, enter CALM and you should find many articles. I have not found any alarms on CALM. Some farms that are affected by the bird flu will return if not already to production and eat into CALM's market. It is always a possibility that CALM will be infected by bird flu. However, with most chickens staying inside the farm and the extra precautions, the chance is slim. Let me share three scenarios below.

Say if there is another bird flu (not in CALM) that happens, the egg prices would rocket up and also is the profit of CALM.

Let's say if that happens to CALM, it will affect onto the location involved. As I stated, the management (they had been great) should have taken precautions to minimize the chance of a bird flu.

Then what if it happens in Hong Kong or another Chinese city, they would ban chicken from local farms and bring the frozen chickens from the unaffected countries such as the US. It would bring profits to CALM.

The egg price is returning to its normal price. Hence, the EPS will be lowered. With a Forward P/E less than 7 and PEY greater than 23%, the stock price would have to fall a lot to cause any great alarm.

Bonus metrics

From GuruFocus.com (a paid subscription), F-Score was 7 and Z-Score was 8; both are favorable.

From Blue Chip Growth (no longer free), all three grades were "B". That was good but not the best. Not too long ago, most were "A". I do not know the reason for the downgrade as today's stock price is now lower and there is no change in the fundamentals.

Summary

This stock is technically unsound but fundamentally sound. It may still trend downward, but when it shoots back up, it would be like fireworks on display. Most value stocks are swimming against the tide, so we have to be patient for the market to realize its real value.

No one can identify the bottom precisely and consistently. I expect a short squeeze is coming when the shorters cannot find more shares to short. The interest rate hike could trigger some covering of the shorts. The shorters are paying about an 8% dividends; I do not recommend to short high-dividend stocks. With this price, the risk is low and the potential appreciation is high. When one or two institutional investors move in, the price will surge. I bought it on 3/11/15 and sold it on 10/28/15 making a profit of 48% or an annualized return of 77%.

7 Multi baggers

It is very rewarding to find the next Apple making many times of profits over the original investment. It is possible, but it is not every one's cup of tea. For every winner found, there would be ten losers.

How to find them

I developed a screen to find potential multi baggers. Basically these stocks double in sales and profits (prefer to compare quarter of prior year to avoid seasonal fluctuations). Initially most are penny stocks with small market cap and are not listed in the three major exchanges. When they move up to a major exchange, it is a good sign. Usually they do not pay dividends as most of the profits have to be plowed back to research and development in the initial years.

Most likely, the screen would find them at least one year after their IPOs as we need the financial data. It is a good starting point to take out the companies that do not survive in the first year, and there are many.

Many of these stocks are traded in the $2 to $10 range. Most stocks below $5 are not 'marginable', which is important to boost its rising. These stocks usually trade within a low price range for a while before they breakout (i.e. surge in price).

When the breakout is supported with high volume, the price will tend to rocket even higher. I do not want to hold a triple bagger unless there is a good reason to do so. Need to calculate the reward / risk ratio. If it is the same chance to double as losing half of the value, I would hold or sell half of it. No one goes broke for taking profit.

When these stocks take off, most are overbought with RSI(14) above 65 for a few years to come.

IPO

There are two kinds of IPOs: from established products such as Facebook and from companies without established products. The former is less risky. Roughly, about 60% lose money in the first year while 40% make up the loss. IPOs are the best way to fund research and/or marketing of new products/services. Investors have to analyze whether the new product(s) is/are innovative enough and profitable to pay back their investments.

There are many investors specialized in new companies. Most IPOs make money on the first day with the recent exception of Facebook. Buy in the morning and sell at the end of the day. Most retail investors cannot participate in IPOs without connection with some brokers. However, there are successful investors spotting Microsoft, Wal-Mart, Tesla and companies involved in 3D printing in its early stage after IPO.

As of this writing, I do not find too many potential profitable companies with the exception of 3D printers. Zynga is a typical example. It seems it is repeating the usual sad chronology of a hot IPO:

1. Founders and the initial investors make a fortune on a good idea or a product.
2. Most initial investors make money.
3. The stock skyrockets. The insiders cash in after the restricted period that they cannot sell after the IPO. Usually most retail investors do not sell.
4. The stock purges. Most losers are retail investors.

You're buying for the company's new vision and/or the innovative products. However, many of these new companies do not make it as expected. You have to evaluate their product potential and review the progress of the company periodically. Innovative products that everyone wants may not be able to bring to the market due to regulations and the opposition from its potential competitors.

The first year will be a honeymoon period that most investors ignore the fundamental metrics. The second year on, evaluate the company again with fundamental metrics. For example, if the P/E is over 50, most likely the company's stock will be in danger or the investors have been moving the price too fast and too high. Check out Debt/Equity. If the company cannot pay back the loan, it may go bankrupt.

Cisco was one of top-valued companies. It went down and then in the first half of 2013 it recovered. Again, fundamental metrics (such as P/E) and technical analysis guide us better as to when to trade Cisco. The long-term outlook of Cisco is good envisioning more devices connected to the routers. However, we need to examine its future offerings and its competitors.

The second phase

The initial investors before the IPO are not allowed to sell the stock. When it expires, the stock price may fall. When the stock price keeps on climbing, evaluate the appreciation potential. When they reach the peaks, sell. When the expected P/E is still reasonable (such as less than 35), check the PEG (P/E growth). If they are reasonable, hold on to the stock, but I would use a stop loss to protect profit. From my limited statistics, successful companies are usually less successful in the stock price after the first 10 years. It could be their peaks may have come.

It is a balancing act, sit on a winning horse on its way up and sell the winning horse at its peak. No one can find the peak consistently. Use technical analysis's SMA (Simple Moving Average) to determine the enter/exit points. If you're not too sure, sell half of your holding.

Company turnaround

When a stock loses most of its value, it could go to zero or it could turn around. Check the possibilities in both scenarios. Sometimes the chart together with insider purchases could indicate a turnaround.

The staircase pattern described next is a good sign. The stock stays in the current value for a while before it moves up to the next peak. It then stays there for a while and moves up to the next peak again.

More losers than winners

I suspect many small companies fail for each of the multi baggers found. The losers may not show up in the database as they're taken away from the database when the stock price goes to 0 (termed as survival bias) or the stock is delisted from the exchange. If your test database does not take care of survival bias, your test result will appear far better than your strategy really is.

You need to have cash that you do not need for a long while, a lot of patience and the mental power to experience many losses.

Apple, Microsoft and Oracle all have the right products in this generation.

Judging from the recent IPOs including Zynga and Groupon, I do not think that we have too many potential multi baggers from the current offerings, but I could be wrong. No stocks can justify a forward P/E over 40 unless they have very high potential like a promising new drug.

Many big winners can shoot up 200% in 6 months. It needs one or more catalysts to boost this kind of performance. It could be a new product that could change the world, a potential acquirer (very seldom the acquirer pays more than 50% of the current price). Fundamental analysis seldom finds these stocks, but technical analysis can.

2015 IPOs

2015 is a loser year for IPOs especially compared to the better years in 2013 and 2014. The tiny Hong Kong was number one in IPOs in term of the total market value for IPOs and most of them are Chinese companies. NYC took a back seat for the first time in what I can remember.

Shenzhen Exchange was even crazier than Hong Kong with its volatility and huge price fluctuations. It supports financially the growing high-tech companies in South China. If you have a new high-tech gadget such as a drone, it is the best place to build it. Most of your component suppliers are close by.

The average NYSE stock price lost about 15% at the close of the first day in 2015. Is it a trend? Only time can tell.

Tax considerations
You may want to sell a loser when it does not show any future promise to offset any gain from other stocks. When you find a big winner and you're not young, you can keep it until you die so the cost basis will be stepped up and your heirs do not pay the tax on the capital gain according to the tax law of 2016. Alternatively, give it to a charity for an extra deduction. Tax law changes and I'm not a tax professional, so ask your lawyer for advice.

My personal experience
I sell most stocks when they double. Very seldom do I keep a stock long enough to be a triple bagger. Most of my double (and once in a blue moon triple) baggers were acquired by larger companies, or I need to hold them

longer to be eligible for long-term capital gain. One's opinion. However, I recommend to keep rising stocks and protect the profits by adjusting stops.

Finding the next wave

You can make more than 10 times of your investment when you invest early in the companies that can change the world. Some are started via IPOs. Many others are initially invested by venture capitalists, then they are listed in small exchanges and eventually are moved to one of the three major exchanges. By the time these companies are noticed by the market, they are usually already fully valued.

I saw many in the last 30 years, and unfortunately I did not act on many of them or did not buy them early enough. It is primarily due to my conservative nature. The examples are:

- Apple in its early stage and so are many high-tech companies such as Microsoft, Google and Cisco. When I see my stock prices doubled, I am tempted to sell them and would miss the opportunity of its doubling again.

  Use technical analysis and fundamental analysis to determine the exit and reentry points. To protect the profit, use stop orders and adjust the stop price when the stock appreciates by more than 10% (more frequently if you have time).

- Drug companies discovering new drugs. I had some successes via a subscribed newsletter and followed insider trading from public information.

- Change of the retail business by Wal-Mart via importing products from China especially after Sam Walton who estimated wrongly the difference between the Chinese and American prices on similar products. It is similar to Amazon creating a new channel for retailing.

- Change of policy such as one allowing GPS for public use or banning importing of Chinese solar panels. GPS devices are eventually obsoleted by smartphones that provide the same function. Solar panels are still not ready economically even without the cheap Chinese import. The recent legalizing of a drug is a good example. I knew about it and I did not act on it due to my ethical reasons. Fidelity has a social score.

Currently we had some new drugs, cloud computing (too cloudy for my taste as I cannot figure how they can make money as of today), 3D printing... Amazon revolutionizes digital publishing and internet retailing. Amazon's stock skyrockets even the fundamentals look bad. Amazon invests its money for the future.

There are many small companies that would offer products that would change the world. However, most of them will be acquired by larger corporations as it is too expensive to launch these new products / services unless their IPOs provide a lot of cash.

In ten years or so, China would have more of these innovative companies for the following reasons. However, I do not trust the financial data of most developing countries especially small companies.

1. There are many educated scientists and engineers. Contrary to popular belief, they do have genius schools that will produce more geniuses such as Gates and Jobs.

2. The government encourages science and technology and has long-term objectives. However, they need to set up regulations to protect intelligence properties.

3. Chinese engineers' wages are only a fraction of ours. A typical Chinese engineer works far more hours than our engineers. When a Chinese engineer works 10 hours a day while the US engineer works 8 hours, it is more than the 2 hour difference in productivity.

4. They have a large internal market.

Profit from IPOs

If your broker does not have the connection, most likely you cannot buy them on the first day of the IPOs. Skip trading the stock for the first few days. When it makes a new high, consider buying it. Unless the fundamentals/outlooks are good, sell it before the insiders are allowed to sell (6 to 12 months after the IPO depending on the company).

8 An aggressive strategy

I use a similar strategy that includes metrics and composite grades from vendors that I subscribe to their services. The following is a brief description. As in life, there is no guarantee.

The basic major steps are:

- Use market timing to determine when to buy and sell.
- How to screen stocks.
- How to modify the screen to fit the current market conditions.
- Score the stock fundamentally.
- Intangible analysis.
- Qualitative analysis.
- Optionally, technical analysis.

Market Timing

Refer to the chapters on this topic described in this book.

Screen stocks

Most small cap stocks are not followed by analysts, so we can find some gems. The common screening criteria will be mentioned briefly here.

- Skip the following sectors and countries: financial companies (banks, loaners), miners, drug (generic OK), insurance, emerging countries including China, India and Mexico.

- Ensure the company is not heading into bankruptcy. "Price / Free Cash Flow" cannot be manipulated easily. Profit growth and sales growth compared to the last quarter are good indicators too. Massive insider dumping is another one.

- Common filter criteria:

    1. Listed in one of the three major exchanges, or specific exchange(s) for your country.

2. Market cap > 200 million and < 800 million.

3. Price > 2 and less than 20.

4. Average daily volume > 8,000 (some use 10,000) shares.

5. Short % less than 15% (some use 10%).

6. Expected earning yield (E/P, reversal of P/E) > 5% and < 30%.

7. Ensure the SMA%-200 (simple moving average for the last 200 trade sessions) is positive. In other words, the stock price is above the SMA-200 line. You can obtain this value from Finviz.com.

The above information can be easily obtained from Finviz.com. Try any extras criteria your broker offers. Use the Equity Summary Score from Fidelity and ignore stocks with ranks less than 6.

The next useful comparisons are the averages of its industry or sector. The common parameters are: Price / Cash Flow, Debt percent, P/E (also its own 5-year average), Price / Sales, etc.

Sorting the screened stocks

If you have too few stocks from your screen, the market may be risky. If not, ease up on your filter criteria.

If you have too many stocks, sort them in descending order by the expected earnings yield. Select the top stocks for further evaluation.

What the current market favors

If the market favors growth, sort them in descending order of the SMA % (use 50 or 200 depending on how long you expect to keep the stock) from Finviz.com, or any growth metric such as earning quarter-to-quarter growth rate. The higher the SMA % indicates the higher chance the stock is moving up, but it should not be excessive as that could indicate a peak. Also determine whether the stock is over-bought indicated by the RSI(14) indicator.

If the market favors value, sort the screened stocks in descending order of the expected E/P.

Qualitative analysis
Most of the above information or criteria belongs to quantitative analysis. Check out the tangibles and qualitative analysis.

Use screens to select a handful of stocks for your further evaluation as it saves time.

Screen sites

There are many sites to screen stocks and many have built-in screens for immediate use. Your stock broker may provide you with screens. There are many good ones that are free including Finviz.com, Fidelity.com and Yahoo!Finance.com. AAII provides screened stocks from the basic subscription and provides screens that you can modify for an extra fee.

Some vendors provide a historical database and/or better tools at an extra cost: AAII, Stock 123, Zacks, VectorVest… It would be useful to test screens with past data. Some sites provide backtesting features for technical analysis. Validea (http://www.validea.com/home/home.asp) has some promising screens at a cost, and so is GuruFocus.com.

Interesting screens

- There are screens that simulate what the gurus such as what Buffett would buy. They may beat the market but not by a wide margin. It could be too many followers using these screens.

- Include stocks that were not in any major exchanges one year ago. It includes the companies that started in the basements, moved to a local exchange, and now have moved to a major exchange. Most major companies such as Apple and Microsoft belonged to this group at one time. Some may skip the local exchange as Facebook did.

- Sort PEG and select the stocks with the best PEGs such as lower than 1. It is a growth strategy.

- Select stocks that have been increasing in prices in the last 3 months. It is a momentum strategy.

- Stocks with better metrics compared to companies in the same industry sector. Compare Apples to Apples.

- Combine growth metrics and value metrics. It is the Growth with a Value strategy. It is also known as "Growth with a realistic price".

- Candidates for being acquired.
  Usually they are small companies in specific markets and / or having specific technologies. 2009 was a good year for acquisitions, especially when there was a lot of corporate cash and the interest rates were low.

- Candidates to be listed in the three major exchanges.
  Usually they are gaining in profits, market shares and/or market capitalizations. When they are listed, some ETFs are required to buy them.

- Sell last year's big gainers and buy last year's big losers. It is contrarian's strategy. Need to ensure they can turn around and are fundamentally sound.

- Select the best stocks from the top 5 sectors (I prefer industries) when the market in rising. It is a top-down approach.

- Stocks with favorable earnings revisions. This strategy works better before the earnings announcements.

- Stocks with high insiders' purchases.

- Dividend growth stocks.
  They perform very well in the last few years as of 1-2014. Income seekers flock to dividend stocks when CDs and bonds cannot give them equivalent incomes.

- Besides from your broker's site on screening tools, Kapitall has a lot of ideas on building screens and the stock recommendations. Check his articles in Seeking Alpha or their website (http://seekingalpha.com/author/kapitall).

- Garbage in and garbage out. I do not trust the financial statements from most emerging countries. If your screening tools do not provide this filter, check the company's profile and skip these companies that you may not trust.
- Fidelity's Predefined screens. http://research2.fidelity.com/fidelity/screeners/commonstock/strategies.asp?
- Many sites provide guru screens to simulate what gurus would buy. GuruFocus.com is one of them.

Backtesting

If your screening service does not provide a historical database, you may have limited testing capability. However, you can still compare the screened stocks six months later. To simplify, use a virtual portfolio for each strategy.

Find out why your screen does not work when you invest with real money:

1. Survivorship bias. The historical database you use may have taken out all the stocks that have been delisted and they're usually bad.

   Stocks with less than $1 have a higher chance of survivorship bias.

   Most of them bankrupted, so your performance of a screen looks better as you have avoided these stocks unknowingly. A small percent of the 'disappeared' stocks are merged, acquired, or spin-offs and usually they're doing well. However, there are far more bankrupt companies than the above.
2. Humans are not rational. We usually buy high and sell low. Sticking with a strategy will take out this aspect.
3. Use the wrong screen for the current market conditions. A value screen should not be used when the market is trending up.
4. Market conditions change. Many years ago, selecting low P/E and foreign companies listed in the US exchanges provided above-average returns. However, it was not true in 2011 to 2014.

Conclusion

The four steps of investing are: 1. Market Timing, 2. Screening, 3. Analysis and 4. When and what to sell.

9 Performances of my short-term recommendations

Some of my performances have been described. The following are from my recommendations in my book Series of "Best stocks", which were available in mid December and may be followed by an updated version in mid July; it is not a promise for future books in the series.

Book #1: "Best Stocks to Buy for July, 2021"

Start date: 07/15/2021. End date: 12/01/2021.

Momentum (2 stocks)

Symbol	Return 1 M	Ann.	Ret. 2 M	Ann
CLAR	-3%	-30%	-2%	-13%
CROX	27%	303%	33%	193%
Average	12%	137%	15%	90%
RSP	3%	37%	3%	17%
Beat RSP by	265%		440%	

Short selling betting the stocks to go down (3 stocks).

Short selling is not recommended particularly for beginners due to the extra risk.

Symbol	Return 1 M	Ann.	Ret. 2 M	Ann
CCL	-4%	-44%	-6%	-33%
NCLH	-1%	-8%	-3%	-15%
MILE	38%	435%	45%	264%
Average	11%	128%	12%	72%
RSP	3%	37%	2%	17%
Beat RSP by	241%		330%	

CCL and NCLN are cruise liners and this sector did not perform well in this period. For diversification, you should only trade one stock in this sector.

Book #2: "Best Stocks for 2021 2nd Edition"
Start date: 02/08/2021 (the publish date). End date: 12/01/2021.

Momentum (7 stocks)

Symbol	Return	Ann.
ATGE	-6%	-68%
ATRS	-11%	-134%
CMRE	15%	182%
REGI	-26%	-318%
RIO	0%	-1%
SPWH	0%	-1%
WIRE	8%	96%
Average	-3%	-35%
RSP	4%	-50%
Beat RSP by	-170%	

Short selling betting the stocks to go down (3 stocks).

Symbol	Return	Ann.
HYLN	16%	191%
NEXT	2%	332%
RMO	40%	482%
Average	28%	335%
RSP	4%	50%
Beat RSP by	573%	

10 Strategies that worked before

The following are three popular strategies that worked before but not too well recently. I try to see whether I can revive them to return to their former glory.

1. **O'Shaughnessy's Strategy**
(http://en.wikipedia.org/wiki/James_O%27Shaughnessy)

It made a stunning return from 1954 through 1994. His strategy is:

Buy the 50 DOW stocks that have the highest one-year returns, five consecutive years of rising earnings and share prices less than 1.5 times their corporate rate of revenues.

After he publicized his strategy in a book, it was no longer effective. It was his tradeoff to make a lot of money from his book and his personal prestige to make money in his mutual funds. It fits my saying: When too many folks follow the same strategy, it will no longer be useful.

2. **The Foolish Four**
(http://en.wikipedia.org/wiki/Foolish_Four)

From Wikipedia: "The "Foolish Four" is a discredited[1] mechanical investing technique that, like the Dogs of the Dow, attempts to select the number of stocks of the Dow Jones Industrial Average that will outperform the average in the near future.

To identify the "Foolish Four," an investor determines the current dividend yield and current price for each of the 30 stocks comprising the Dow Jones Industrial Average. Then, the yield for each stock is divided by the square root of the stock's price. The stocks are ranked from highest to lowest using the number resulting from the division. The stocks ranking the second highest, third highest, fourth highest, and fifth highest in equal dollar amounts are bought. The highest-ranking stock is not bought."

3. **Buy the highest ROE stocks**

It has been described in a popular book. I do not believe that it still works but the book is still popular. I do not think I can revive this strategy and it is NOT the Holy Grail in investing as blindly followed by many. The followers should replace this strategy with better strategies.

My take

The above three strategies work at one time. After the authors publicized their strategies, they did not work anymore.

The ROE strategy will not work consistently as it is only one of the many fundamental metrics the value investor should consider. The Foolish Four seems to be similar to the Dog of the Dows. Hence, the only serious modification is on O'Shaughnessy's strategy.

Modify O'Shaughnessy's Strategy

I would take another look at O'Shaughnessy's Strategy. It is a long-term momentum strategy with some protection of not buying overpriced stocks. It will be effective again when fewer folks use it. Check its current performance. Many stock screens such as AAII's simulate this strategy. The following modifications apply to similar screens for this strategy.

What to include:
- Include the S&P 500 stocks, so you have more stocks to select from besides the Dow stocks.
- Alternatively, include stocks in all three major exchanges.
- Optionally select stocks with prices greater than $2 (or $5 for conservative investors), and daily average volumes greater than 10,000 shares. It would effectively eliminate most penny stocks.
- Use the expected earnings which predicts better instead of the last twelve month's earnings.
- Skip the stocks from most if not all emerging foreign countries (at least for today).
- Score each stock fundamentally such as using my Scoring System described in my books. Discard all the stocks that do not pass the scoring system.
- Analyze each stock fully.

Timing:
- Buy on November 1 and sell on May 1 for retirement accounts; alternatively start buying on October 15 and sell on April 15 for better choices and avoid the herd.

- Buy in November and December for non-retirement accounts to avoid the crowd. Sell losers after holding them less than a year and winners over a year in non-retirement accounts. Long-term capital gains have better tax treatments - check the current tax laws for both Federal and the state you reside in.
- When the market has a high chance of plunging or is plunging, close out all positions.
- Consider covered calls on stocks that are qualified for lower long-term capital gain taxes.

Optimal number of stocks:

- If you cannot find enough stocks to buy, relax your selection criteria such as 3 consecutive years of rising earnings instead of 5 years. If you still cannot find many good stocks, it could mean the market is fully valued and / or there are few bargains. It could also be due to too many folks following the same strategy.
- If you find too many stocks, sort them in descending order of the expected yields (E/P) and select the top stocks. Omit stocks with yields higher than 35% as they may sound fishy for such high returns. Alternatively, consider the stocks with high scores in my scoring system.
- 50 stocks is too large a number for most retail investors. Cut it to 25 (and even 10 if you have less than $50,000 to invest). Ensure that there is no sector having its total value more than 25% of the portfolio for better diversification.

Adjust the strategy to your risk tolerance and requirements. If you do not have a lot of time, five stocks in different sectors should be diversified enough.

Paper trade the strategy before you commit with real money. If you have a historical database, test it and tune it for better results.

Links
https://www.youtube.com/watch?v=zlYJ1eRjXvA
https://www.youtube.com/watch?v=uGUIUg_617o

11 Miscellaneous strategies

- Some **mutual funds** have been losing a lot of money such as during the internet crash in 2000. Buy those funds (usually sector funds) that you expect them to recover. It could be a tax strategy as they will not distribute profits to their fund owners for a while.
- **Inflation**. They are gold (GLD, gold mines such as RING as an ETF and gold coins / bars) and silver. I prefer skipping copper and other commodities including oil unless the economy is trending up. Bonds and CDs are most likely not good investments as they return you with cash that have been depreciated due to inflation.
- Supply and demand. In 2009 and 2020, the Fed printed a lot of money excessively to save the economy. In the long run, our national debts increase. In addition, it could cause inflation unless the economy recovers due to the simulation as in 2009. There is a lot of money chasing fixed assets such as gold and stocks. As a result, both of these assets would likely rise especially in the short term. If we have hyperinflation, we would lose the buying power after cashing in the appreciated stocks.
- Almost **day trading**. When the stock is rising in the morning, there is a better chance it would continue the trend and vice versa. Reverse the trade at around 3 pm, and day traders almost never leave their positions open during weekends and/or holidays. The chance is improved if both the market and the sector the stock is in are both rising. Take advantage of institutional investors. When they trade, they need days and even weeks to trade a stock. You can tell from the volume of the trade and usually the stock belongs to blue chips. Join the bandwagon.
- As stated before, some strategies described in this book work better than the others in different conditions of the market. If you can match the right strategy or strategies, you will see fireworks, and vice versa.
- Innovative sectors. I would skip space travel after the accident. https://www.youtube.com/watch?v=LI1hMX8qtHg
- Index rebalancing. The index such as S&P 500 rebalances at least once a year and some do it 4 times a year. If you buy the stock before it is added to the index, you should make a lot of money. The ETFs that follow the specific index are forced to buy the stocks just added to the index and sell the stocks that have been removed from the index. I do not recommend shorting these stocks, which is risky especially for beginners.

Some indexes provide the criteria to rebalance. Here is my summary from what I guess. It is based on market cap, number of shares floating, the average trading volume (3 to 6 months), how long it has been in the market, profit (better with rising), sales (better with increasing) and any restrictions (such as a foreign stock). There are minor criteria.

Most of us do not have inside information on how any index is rebalanced. However, I tested a strategy based on the above criteria on S&P 500 for example. First criteria are the stocks should not be in the index already. So far, the testing has been proved profitable, but the test is too limited.

There are several articles that you can find via Google by entering "Index Rebalance".

The Russell 3000 index consists of 3,000 largest stocks (large cap + mid cap + small cap), the Russell 2000 index consists of 2,000 largest stocks (large cap + mid Cap), and the Russell 1000 consists of the 1,000 largest stocks (large cap). Most ETFs simulated these indexes are cap-weighted, so these ETFs do not really represent the index. To illustrate, if the ETF wants to simulate micro-cap stocks, you need to find one that is not cap-weighed and/or not including the mid-cap and large-cap stocks.

- Guru's mistakes. On 4/2021, I had too many contra ETFs betting the market to go down. It did not work due to the excessive supply of USD. I should have followed the market timing such as SMA-400 and/or death cross described in my books. However, if you buy contra ETFs in early 5/2021, you could have made very good money. Shamelessly I assume myself as a 'guru'. There are many similar examples. One analyst shorted the financial services. It did not work initially and he was fired. If the fund let him stay, he could make a lot of money.
- Positioning strategy. Start with two ETFs: SPY (or any ETF that simulates the market) and a money market ETF for example with even positions (i.e., 50% invested in each ETF). At the end of a period (a week or a month depending on how much time you have for investing), reallocate the ETFs as a percentage of how much each ETF gains (i.e., the higher allocation for the winner). For better performance, use more ETFs such adding QQQ, GLD, SH (contra ETF to SPY) and PSQ (contra ETF to QQQ).
- Buy stocks which are 95% (or 100%) close to 52-week highs. I use Finviz's Screener. To limit the number of screened stocks, I would select NASDAQ for exchange, USA for country and SMA-20 crossed SMA-50. Need to evaluate individual stock. Stop loss and market timing are important as evidenced in 2000.
- If the SMA-50 is above the SMA-100 (both available from Finviz), the stock is considered to be in an uptrend, else down trend. It is safer to use an ETF. Again, use stop orders to protect your trade. I recommend keeping the cash in the down trend instead of shorting. Use at least one more technical

indicator to confirm your decision. If you start testing from 2000, you would avoid some losses from the two market crashes (2000 and 2008).
- Follow the rocket. In 2020, they are FAANG. In 2021, they are GME and AMC. The geniuses are those who follow the uptrend, and the losers are those who do not have an exit strategy such as trailing stops reviewed every week.
- Market neutral. If you think you are a better investor than others and do not want to time the market, buy a few stocks (say 3) and short sell the same number. Review your performance periodically. If you are a specialist on a specific sector, buy or short that sector periodically. Buy companies when a technology (or a drug) shows promise. The current example is AI in early 2023.
- Guru's mistakes. More than one time, a guru was fired due to betting big on a certain theme, and after a while, his predictions turned out to be correct. We have to evaluate his 'bad', and they could be at fault in time and they could turn out to be gems.
- Combine your strategy with market timing. When the market is down, short stocks using your short strategy for stocks, or buy contra ETFs using your strategy for sectors, countries or stock indexes. When the market is up, close all shorts and buy momentum stocks.
- When the market fluctuates as indicated by the market timer with false signals for example, buy stocks when the market is down and vice versa.
- Simon's strategies in using maths.
https://www.youtube.com/watch?v=cm7kkHtZiJA
- Carry Trade: Borrow a million (if they trust you) from the Bank of Japan. Buy U.S. high-yield bonds and sell them after a year or so. It works when the USD appreciates against Japanese Yen during that period, and the U.S. interest rate is higher than Japan's. I mentioned it for the last 20 years. It worked until recently.
- Most of our strategies buy on momentum and sell when the momentum is reversed. Here is one opposite strategy: buy on increasing value (from fundamental metrics such as P/E), and sell on decreasing value. The trading could be in multiple trades. The logic is the institutional investors switch sectors, and you make profit by steps ahead of them. It worked in 2021, when the tech sector was switched to retail, and then back to the tech sector. It will not work if the sector stays in momentum for longer periods such as years.
https://www.youtube.com/watch?v=MFVmEcRHpnk&t=332s

*** Book 3: Evaluating Stocks

Evaluating Stocks is a detailed guide designed to help investors analyze and assess stocks effectively.

The book explores key **fundamental and technical analysis techniques**, providing insights into metrics such as price-to-earnings (P/E) ratios, earnings growth, debt levels, and market trends.

It covers **various investment strategies**, including value investing, growth investing, and momentum trading, helping readers identify which approach suits their risk tolerance and financial goals. The book also discusses industry and sector analysis, emphasizing the importance of comparing stocks within their respective markets to make informed decisions.

A major highlight is the discussion on **red flags to avoid**, such as overvalued stocks, unsustainable growth rates, and misleading financial reports. Additionally, it provides practical tools and resources, including stock screeners and valuation models, to streamline the evaluation process.

With **real-world examples and step-by-step methods**, *Evaluating Stocks* is an essential resource for both beginner and experienced investors looking to refine their stock-picking skills and improve portfolio performance

Why you need further stock analysis after screening

First, you may have too many screened stocks. Second, it is for better performance. I listed the rejected stocks (12) in my recent book "Best stocks for 2024". From 12/20/23 (the publish date) to 3/29/2024 (today). The average return of the rejected stocks is about 2%, while the RSP (an ETF for unweighted S&P 500 stocks) has a return of about 10%. The average return of the recommended 8 stocks is about 14%. There are many other examples.

How to start

First, we filter stocks from about 7,000 selected stocks available from Finviz.com for example; the number is variable from different websites and/or services. To start with, skip stocks that are not in the three major exchanges, market caps less than 50 M, or daily average volumes less than 10,000 shares.

Check out the "Simplest Way to Evaluate Stocks" in the Common Tools section to evaluate stocks for beginners and couch potatoes. Furthermore, refer to Scoring Stocks to evaluate stocks via a scoring system.

1 My Performances

They are the recommended stocks in the primary lists (for long-term stocks) of my last five books in this "Best Stocks" series:

Book	Stocks	Return	Ann.	Beat RSP by
Best stocks to buy for 2022	10	4%	4%	153%
Best Stocks to buy as of July, 2021	8	5%	13%	487%
Best Stocks for 2021 2nd Edition	10	42%	52%	220%
Best Stocks for 2021	4	29%	44%	118%
Best Stocks to Buy from Aug, 2020	14	45%	45%	3%
Avg.	9	25%	32%	196%

The details can be found in the following link.
http://tonyp4idea.blogspot.com/2022/12/best-stocks-series.html

2   Amazing returns

To achieve a consistent 10% return above S&P 500 over many years is every fund manager's dream. To double one's investment above the S&P 500 return is amazing while tripling it is unheard of. I beat the S&P 500 by 700% and I can detail the history of my transactions.

Many analysts show their average yearly returns and/or their returns of their top 10 stocks this time of year. The market has closed early today on Christmas Eve, so I have the time to check my recent performance. As a trader with many trades, it would be far too complicated for me to do the same for the entire year. I selected all the stocks I purchased in the last 90 days. Most of them are deeply-valued stocks. Let's check how I performed so far on these stocks.

Whenever you have achieved a high return such as this one, take the profit as it may have reached its peaks. To me, most profits are made in swing trades with an average holding period of just 90 days.

Stocks bought and their returns as of 12/25/12

Stocks	Date Bought	Return	SPY Return
BANR	12/07/12	3%	-.13%
KTCC	12/06/12	0%	.7%
QCOR	12/07/12	15%	-.1%
KTCC	12/06/12	-1%	.7%
ACTV	12/05/12	-5%	.7%
IAG	12/05/12	-1%	.7%
ADES	12/04/12	6%	.6%
NC	12/03/12	15%	-.3%
VELT	12/03/12	64%	-.3%
ANR	11/28/12	33%	4.8%
AAPL	11/16/12	1%	4.8%
C	11/14/12	13%	3.0%
DECK	11/13/12	16%	2.7%
MSFT	11/13/12	0%	2.7%
ALU	11/13/12	38%	2.7%
DLTR	11/09/12	7%	3.4%
CAT	11/08/12	4%	1.9%
MSFT	11/07/12	-8%	.5%
BSX	10/24/12	14%	.3%
BSX	10/19/12	7%	.3%
20			
AVG:		11%	1.35%

Beat SPY (in %) = (11%-1.35%)/1.35% = 716% or 7 times

Average Return = averaging each return of 20 stocks = 11%
Average Annualized Return = 148% or 122% (= 11% *365 / avg. holding period)
Average Return = Profit / Capitalization   = 10%[1]

How the returns are calculated
Using BANR to illustrate how the return and the SPY return are calculated.

| BANR | 12/07/12 | 3% | -.13% |

BANR was bought on 12/07/12 (17 days from 12/24/12) at 27.93 and it was at 30.43 on 12/24/12.
Rate of Return = (30.43 – 27.93) / 27.93 = 3%

SPY was at 142.53 on 12/07/12 and at 142.35 on 12/24/12.
 Rate of Return = (142.35-142.53) / 142.53 = -.13%

Commissions and dividends are not included for simplicity. Commissions are negligible and dividends could add about another 2% for the annual returns.

Interpreting the performance results
The quantity of each stock bought is not important as I am comparing the return of the stock. However, a few stocks have been listed twice as I bought two times usually on separate dates. If I chose them as one purchase instead of two, my return would appear even better. The purchases are real, so the amount of each stock is not identical to each other.

I'm not too excited yet. This phenomenal return could be just this one time only. 90 days is a short period. Consistency could be achieved with an improved stock picking technique, plain luck or a combination. By any measure, it is an extremely decent return. However, I do not expect to beat S&P 500 by 7 times again.

My best return is from 2009 in my largest taxable account. It was over 80% beating the SPY by about 3 times. 2003 was another good year for profit.

These two years are defined by me as the Early Recovery stage in a market cycle and the market provides the best profit opportunity.

The four losers are MSFT (-8%), ACTV (-5%), KTCC (-1%) and IAG (-1%). The best winners are: VELT (64%), ALU (38%), ANR (33%) and QCOR (19%). The following are in a 14% to 16% range: DECK, NC and BSX (2 purchases). Click here for the entire list.

Cheating the results

I could 'cheat' for better results by doing the following, but I did not:

1. Exclude stocks only purchased in the last 20 days (instead of 15).

2. If my purchases of CSCO were included, the result would be even better. CSCO has been bought three times on 7/24/12 and it has gained 31% as of 12/25/12. I still have CSCO, but it is not included as it just hit the 90-days requirement.

3. I could include those buy orders that had not been executed due to their fast appreciation.

Hence, there are many ways to cheat, so you should read others' results carefully.

What stocks were included
There were 20 purchases. I bought some stocks twice and that counted as two purchases. None of the stocks have been sold as of 12/25/12. I have excluded the stocks that I am testing a strategy by trading them every month and most are in a separate account.

How the stocks were picked
The majority of the stocks were screened by my selected screens that had been proven profitable in the last 3 to 6 months, or are historically profitable at this stage of the market cycle. I also analyzed most of the screened stocks and assigned a score (15 and higher is a buy) based on the metrics that had a reliable prediction recently. I do not stick with the scoring system 100% of the time, but most of the stocks that I purchased twice have high scores.

The poor performers were scored as: MSFT with a score of 13, ACTV 16, KTCC 27 and IAG 23. The scoring system is OK. MSFT should not be bought judging from its low score. However, I believe MSFT has long-term appreciation potential. The other three are the latest purchases in this portfolio and they may perform better in a longer period of time.

The winners were scored as: VELT 34, ALU was not scored, ANR was not scored and QCOR 30. The scoring system is great for this group. ALU and ANR were selected from two Seeking Alpha articles and their selections were not based on these scores. I read several Wall Street Journal articles on ALU and CSCO to convince myself to buy both of them.

The average winners were scored as follows: DECK 9, NC 26 and BSX was not scored. DECK was selected based on an article from Seeking Alpha and it seemed DECK was experiencing the same short squeeze as CROX once did. BSX was selected from a Sunday paper article.

Observations
1. I notice that most big winners (ALU is $1) have a stock price less than $10. The myth of holding quality stocks with prices higher than $15 is not true here as most of my big winners were below $10 including ALU.
2. I did not double my normal purchases on VELT and ALU, which both turned out to be my best performers. VELT scored high in my analysis. ALU was very convincing but it seemed to be risky. 'Nothing risk and nothing gained' applies here. I did triple my purchase on CSCO, which is a large company with good fundamentals that were not yet 'discovered' by the market.

   Both AAPL and DECK gained more than 25% and then lost most of their gains during my short holding period. I should have sold AAPL as many of my fellow investors sold the winners expecting higher capital gains taxes next year. The myth of 'buy and hold' does not work here.
3. During this period, I had several buy orders that were not executed due to their rising stock prices. Market orders could be the solution. It is another example of pennies smart and a pound foolish.
4. It will be interesting to check the results again in 6 and 12 months. Except ALU, all are in my taxable accounts and I usually keep them for a year to qualify for the lower tax rates due to capital gains.
5. I have not described any specific method, but these concepts help you to build better strategies to customize to your individual situations

and/or market conditions. Invest the money you can afford to lose. Past performance does not guarantee future results.

6. Reading articles such as Seeking Alpha can be beneficial providing they are not 'bump-and-switch' scheme. However, you should do your own analysis. It is your money after all.
7. The market has been up by .8% in the last 90 days and this portfolio increased by 11%. If my portfolio amplifies the market, I wonder whether it will be down by the same rate in a down market.
8. This portfolio is quite diversified even that I have not planned that way except weighing more with high tech companies. There are no big winners and no big losers that could change the average returns.
9. I tried not to include emerging countries such as China as I do not trust their balance sheets.
10. I have never achieved such an amazing return. I'm emotionally detached to big wins and big losses. It could be plain luck. Even the best strategy will have its "black swan" moment eventually.
11. To achieve over 100% annualized return is not sustainable by checking the top performers of the S&P 500 index and their returns. However, it is possible but not likely if you churn your portfolio more than once and you time the market correctly.
12. Time to take profits as most stocks here have achieved my objectives. Use the cash to buy stocks with a similar appreciation potential. You will never go broke taking profits.

Conclusion

My three steps of making a stock purchase are: 1. Market timing, 2. Screening stocks, 3. Stock Analysis and 4. When and what to sell. They have all been discussed throughout the book. Market timing and strategy (#2 and #3) does not always work, but it will go better with using them.

I am the living proof *against* the Efficiency Theory and the claims that stock picking does not work. It may not work from time to time, but in the long run it works.

Footnote

[1] Profit / Capitalization should be a little less than 20%. The original 10% is correct when you invest all the 20 stocks at the start of the beginning of the investment period. I bought these stocks on different dates. If I assume the average time of all the stock purchases is at a mid-point, then my

average capitalization is only half and hence giving a 20% return.

It is slightly less than 20% as I did not include the stocks that I bought in the last 15 days. Use the number for a comparison and that's why we have to be concerned with the performance from most investment subscriptions.

Link: Intrinsic value: https://www.youtube.com/watch?v=nX2DcXOrtuo

A scoring system

This scoring system helps you to select whether you should buy a stock or not. In this system, when a stock scores higher than 2, it is a buy. As a group, the highly-scored stocks usually perform better than the lowly-scored stocks in a year. The basic concepts are described here.

An Example

For illustration purposes, we use two metrics: Forward P/E and ROI.

First, we convert Forward P/E into Forward E/P by flipping the two values. Assuming Forward E/P should have a higher weight than ROI, multiply E/P by 5. The average ROI is 10% (simplified for illustration), so minus it by .1.

Score = Forward E/P * 5 + (ROI -.1)

For example, a stock has a P/E of 10 (E/P = 1/10= .1) and ROI is expressed as 25%.

Score = .1 * 5 + (.25 - .1) = .5 + .15= .65

Some parameters by some sites are expressed in grade such as A, B, C and D. For simplicity, if it is A, then the value is 2 otherwise it is zero.

Score = if (Grade = "A", 2, 0) + ...

Test your system on paper with at least 3 months of data. Check whether your scoring system works. It works when the higher the score corresponds to the better the return. Adjust the weight on each metric and see whether your scoring system improves its predictability.

Again, it is simplified for educational and illustration purposes. Try even more different metrics and check whether the metrics still work in the current market. The next metrics to include could be Equity Summary Score from Fidelity, Debt/Equity and Quarter-to-Quarter Earnings / Sales.

Monitor your scoring system

I am sure that many have tried to use most of the metrics and they still cannot find the Holy Grail. I believe the predictability power of each metric is influenced by the current market conditions. For example, the fundamental metrics such as P/E predict better than the growth metrics such as PEG during the market bottom. You should test the performance of each metric every 6 months or so.

You may have two scores: one for short term and one for long term. The stocks you want to keep in the short term may not be the same kind of stocks you want to keep in the longer term. Short term is 3 months (one month for me) and the long term is 12 months for me. My definitions could be different than yours. Value metrics are more important for the long term while growth metrics are more important for the short term.

However, 12 months is too long a period of time and during this period the market may change, so it is better to change it from 12 to 6. To illustrate, energy stocks were great in 2007, but they plunged in 2008. If your scoring system for long-term holding was constructed based on 12 months' data in 2007, the system would have been misleading in 2008 for energy stocks in this example.

I find the short-term scores have a better prediction power than the long-term scores. However, I keep profitable stocks more than 12 months to qualify for the better tax treatments in taxable accounts, and sell the losers less than 12 months. Evaluate the purchased stocks every 6 months to decide whether you want to keep them for another 6 months. Use stops and trailing stops (for winners) to protect your portfolio.

Besides monitoring the metrics in your scoring system, monitor the scores.

The market is not always rational

Sometimes the scoring system fails: When the poorly-scored stocks perform better than the highly-scored stocks. The market is not always rational. Most scoring systems depend on fundamental metrics. When the market switches its favor from value to growth, adjust the score system accordingly. I have found that more than one time that the stocks scored in the top 5% did not perform, so be careful or skip the top 5% (sometimes 10%). The events such as a pending lawsuit or an expiring drug do not show up in metrics, and that is why we need to do other analysis such as Intangible Analysis.

Some metrics almost always work such as the positive predictions of excessive insider's purchases. The insiders know the company typically better than others. When they buy their own company's stock at market prices, they must know it has good appreciation potential. They have many reasons to sell their company's stocks. However, when they sell a large percent of their holdings, be cautious.

When the stock loses more than 30% in a month and you cannot find valid reasons, it may be a good indicator for potential appreciation ahead. Some suggestions are:

- Do not modify your scoring system during market plunges.
- The best strategy is to use the screens (same as searches) that have worked well for the last 90 days.
- Find out why your fundamental metrics that used to work do not work now. You may want to add more weight on growth metrics, and vice versa on value metrics.

An example of monitoring the metrics

This is what I found in monitoring the performances of the metrics as of 3/2013. It is based on a limited database of about 300 stocks with holding periods varying from 1 to 15 months. It has an average of 8% (16% for shorter term). The following is for educational purposes only.

1. The foreign stocks are not doing well: South America (average return is -21% for 7 stocks), Israel (-18% for 2), China (-10% for 7). Europe (0% for 17) and Canada (5% for 16, and most are in natural resources). If I ignore the foreign companies, the return of the portfolio would be increased substantially.

2. The following metrics work fine for the long term only: Forward (same as Expected) Earnings Yield (E/P) and Fidelity's Equity Summary Score.

3. P/B. The stocks with P/B less than 1 perform better than the stocks with P/B greater than 2 (10% vs. 4%).

4. There are no definitive conclusions on Cash / Market Cap, PEG and Return of Equity (a surprise to me) in this monitor.

5. The stocks that were cheaper by 50% to their average 5-year P/E (available from Fidelity) have performed better than those stocks that were cheaper by less than 2%.

6. The ratio of Short / Market Cap between 25% and 30% has better performance than other percentages. It is a contradictory ratio and it could be a short squeeze (a condition that the stock is running out of shares to sell short).

7. There are many composite scores from different vendors that I subscribe to and they are not disclosed here.

8. Based on the above, I will modify my scoring system. I will still have two scores, one for short term and one for longer term.

Short-term scoring system

The scoring system should work better in the shorter term. For testing this system, I used the above database, but deleted stocks that have been over 8 months old. It is still a small database of about 190 stocks.

The result is different from the above as the time frame has been reduced. Here is the summary.

1. The predictability of screens (same as searches) performs about the same as the last monitor. A few screens are better than others. I will not use the under-performing screens with real money.

2. The stock grades from several vendors are not a good indicator this time.

3. Expected (same as Forward) Earnings Yield (E/P) has been a good indicator.

4. Cash Flow is a good indicator (different from the last monitor).

5. Fidelity's Equity Summary Score is a good indicator. Finviz has a similar score, but I prefer to use Fidelity's. Fidelity places higher weight on opinions from analysts that have a better prediction on this stock than others. It eliminates some of the conflict of interest between the analysts and the investing banks s/he works for.

6. The Short Percentage between 25 and 30 is a good contrary indicator (could be a good chance for a short squeeze).

   Its value of less than 10 % is a good indicator. The rest of the range is not conclusive.

7. Cash / Market Cap, Insider Purchase, P/B, ROE and Dividend stocks (>3%) are not conclusive in this monitor.

8. P/S with values less than 0.8 are a good indicator.

9. For some reason I do not know why and how to explain: the top 10% of the top-scored stocks did not perform better than the other stocks that pass.

   It happens in both my two scoring systems. Be suspicious of them and it has happened for more than once. However, the stocks that scored in the bottom 10% are consistently poor performers and that's a good indicator.

There are many other parameters that may be of interest to you. Include them in the performance monitor.

Section I: Fundamental metrics

3   Mysteries of P/E

If you believe you can make good money by selecting stocks with low P/E ratios alone, think again. If it were that easy, there would be no poor people. However, buying fundamentally sound companies can reduce risk and improve the chances of stock appreciation.

P/E is one of the most misunderstood indicators. To me, it is one of the most useful metrics if used correctly. Earnings are the key to stock appreciation, and the P/E ratio measures its value. For example, imagine paying a million dollars for a hot dog cart in New York City. Even if its earnings increase year after year, you will never recoup your investment because you paid too much for a good business.

The advice to "buy stocks with a P/E below 15 and positive earnings" is not always true. P/E growth (PEG) should also be considered as it reflects the company's future prospects. Many retailers were destroyed by Amazon, and many newspapers were disrupted by Facebook and Google. Which sector would you rather invest in: one that is trending upward or one that is dying, even if it has a better P/E ratio?

Most old books on value investing are based on outdated industries that are no longer applicable in today's market. Read these books, but always ask the question: Is this sector still relevant?

Better Definition

The P/E ratio should be inverted as E/P, which is termed **Earnings Yield**. Earnings Yield is easier to compare and understand. It also handles negative earnings when screening and ranking stocks (comparing stocks with better P/E ratios first). If you sort P/E in ascending order, your ranking will be incorrect for stocks with negative earnings, but it will be correct with E/P.

Earnings Yield is usually compared to a 10-year Treasury bill yield (or 30-year yield) or a CD rate. If a stock has a 5% earnings yield and your one-year CD yields 1%, the stock beats the CD by 4% in absolute terms and is four times better. However, the CD is virtually risk-free (with deposit amount limits in most banks). Earnings Yield is an estimated guess and may not materialize.

Many Ways to Predict E/P
- **Based on the last 12 months**: Project it to the Forward E/P. This is also called the last twelve-month E/P.
- **Based on analysts' educated guesses**: These guesses may not materialize. Based on my experience, forward earnings (expected earnings) usually predict better than the last 12 months' earnings. This is the metric I use most often, and many investing subscriptions provide this Forward P/E (same as Expected P/E) or expected E/P.

I usually don't trust analysts' opinions due to conflicts of interest. However, earnings estimates are an exception.
- **Based on the last month or the last quarter**: The latest information could be better for predictions. However, this method is not suitable for seasonal businesses, such as retail, where most sales occur during the Christmas season.
- **Average Earnings Yield (Avg. EY)**: Besides the Pow PE described later, I take the average of the earnings yield (EY) as:

$$\text{Avg. EY} = \frac{\text{EY from the last twelve months} + \text{Expected EY} + \text{EY from the current month of the prior year}}{3}$$

This averages out figures from the past, present, and future. If no one has used this method, I shamelessly claim it as my original idea.

Best E/P May Not Be the Best
A very high E/P could indicate trouble ahead, such as a pending lawsuit, fraud, etc. If you find companies with an E/P over 50%, it means two years' profits could equal the entire cost of the company! I can tell you right away that these companies probably smell fishy unless you believe in free lunches.

However, bargains do exist from time to time due to certain conditions or because Wall Street is wrong about the company. I found one in my year-end screen, and it gave me a huge return. You need to determine whether these are bargains or traps. When the E/P is low (sometimes even negative) but improving rapidly, it could mean big profits for you. Fundamentalists may miss this opportunity in the early stages due to unfavorable E/P, but it could be the most profitable time to buy. Sometimes, it could signal a turnaround.

During a recession, most good companies struggle to promote new products as consumers become thrifty. At the same time, it is usually the best time to develop products if the company has enough cash to finance them. In this case, there will be no alarm even with negative earnings. The only alarm is when a company cannot meet its debt obligations.

Some companies can manipulate earnings through accounting tricks. This can make the current year look good, but it is harder or even impossible to continue the same trick for many years. Always check the footnotes in the financial statements.

E/P and PEG

For value investing, E/P is usually used, and the higher, the better. Be cautious when it is extraordinarily high.

PEG (P/E growth) measures the rate of improvement in the P/E ratio. A PEG of '1' is considered neutral for most investors. When it is below 1, the stock is undervalued, and vice versa.

$$PEG = \frac{P/E}{\text{Earnings Growth Rate}}$$

PEG has a similar problem to P/E when earnings are negative.

Which of the following two stocks would you buy based on their historical earnings yields and earnings growth?
1. A stock with a 10% earnings yield and no earnings growth.
2. A stock with an 8% earnings yield and 50% earnings growth.

If the earnings growth continues, the second stock should yield 12% next year, substantially better than the first stock. This is another reason to use forward earnings rather than historical earnings.

PEG may give a low value for companies that pay high dividends. To correct this:

$$PEG = \frac{P/E}{\text{Earnings Growth Rate} + \text{Dividend Yield}}$$

When the general market favors growth stocks, weigh more on growth metrics, including PEG. I claim no credit for the adjusted PEG.

Fundamental Metrics

E/P is one of the metrics you should use, but not exclusively. If the earnings yield is high but the percentage of debt is also high, then a good bargain may not be as good as it appears.

Some other metrics may not be easily found in financial statements, such as intangibles, insider buying, pension obligations, trade secrets, losing market share, brand name, customer loyalty, etc. It is interesting that the predictive ability of most metrics changes over time.

P/E Variations

There are other P/E variations, such as the Shiller P/E (also known as CAPE and PE10). The Shiller P/E can also be used to track the current market valuation. It is controversial, and its value is easily misinterpreted. Use it as a reference only unless you understand all its issues. I prefer to use a two-year average of the P/E instead of 10 years, as I believe the market changes too much over a decade. Currently, the Shiller P/E does not work as well as it used to, likely due to excessive money printing.

Compare a company's current P/E to its average P/E over the last five years. Also, compare it to the average P/E of companies in the same industry. The average P/E for high-tech companies is different from that of supermarkets, for example. These averages are available from Fidelity.

P/E is more reliable for a group of stocks (e.g., SPY) rather than individual stocks, which have too many other metrics and intangibles to consider. When comparing the total return of an ETF to its corresponding index, add the respective dividends to the index to ensure a fair comparison of total returns. As of this writing, the S&P 500 is paying about a 2% dividend.

EV/EBITDA is another way to measure a company's value. This metric has its advantages and disadvantages compared to P/E. It includes other important data, such as cash and debt. EBITDA/EV is equivalent to E/P, including other mentioned metrics. I prefer to use it over E/P. Some sites do not provide EV/EBITDA if earnings are negative. The disadvantage, in my opinion, is that it does not use expected earnings. This ratio can be found on Yahoo!Finance.

Garbage In, Garbage Out

I do not trust most financial statements from emerging countries, especially from smaller companies. Watch out for fraudulent data. Most metrics can be manipulated. Recently, I had a U.S. stock that lost 18% in one day due to an SEC investigation into its financial data.

The announced earnings may not be reflected in the financial statements you find online. Ensure your data is up-to-date by checking the date of the financial statements. Seeking Alpha has transcripts of earnings announcements that can save you a trip to attend the companies' quarterly meetings.

Sector and Entire Market
You can find the value of a sector using the P/E of an ETF for that sector. The same applies to the entire market. For example, use SPY (an ETF that simulates the S&P 500 index). If its P/E is lower than the average (15, in my opinion), the market is likely a good value and a buy signal. This is one of many hints for market timing.

Where to Use P/E
Each highlight below corresponds to one of my books. Click the link for a description of the strategy.

My book on the top-down approach starts with a safe market, then sector analysis, fundamental analysis, intangible analysis, and optionally technical analysis. P/E is one of many metrics in fundamental analysis.

There are many investing styles. In general, fundamental analysis is important when you hold a stock for a longer period.
- **P/E is important in Long-Term Swing, Dividend Investing, Retirees, and Conservative Strategies.**
    - My maximum P/E value is 20, and 25 for tech companies. I ignore it if the company has high potential for appreciation, which could be indicated by insider purchases. However, many unknown companies have had P/E ratios over 50. Tesla once had a P/E over 1,000.
- **P/E is moderately important in Short-Term Swing and Sector Rotation.**
- **P/E is least important in Momentum Strategy and Day Trading.**
- **Be cautious of falling companies when the P/E is low due to investors leaving because of events like major lawsuits.**

Summary
Again, one metric should not dictate the reason to trade a stock. Compare the company's P/E to its industry average and its own five-year average.

Additionally, many industries have cycles. If you buy at the peak of an industry cycle, the P/E may mislead you. Besides fundamental analysis, consider i124ntangible analysis and time your entry/exit points using technical analysis. Intangible analysis evaluates information that cannot be summarized into numeric metrics, such as a pending lawsuit.

My observations:

True P/E
"EV/EBITDA" is available on Yahoo!Finance and other sources. The true Earnings Yield (EY) is "1/True P/E". I call it "True" for lack of a better term, as it represents the company's financial situation more accurately. This could be the most important metric for many investors.

EBITDA: https://www.youtube.com/watch?v=C2eoh3X4efM

Earnings can be manipulated. For example, company management can lower the P/E ratio by buying back its stock. In this case, earnings per share (EPS) are boosted, but there is no change in the company's financial fundamentals. True P/E takes into account the reduced cash. EBITDA stands for "Earnings Before Interest, Taxes, Depreciation, and Amortization."

Be cautious when EV or EBITDA is negative. Most likely, you should avoid stocks with a negative EV.
Yahoo!Finance usually leaves EV/EBITDA blank for financial institutions such as banks, loan companies, and REITs. In this case, use forward earnings yield (= 1 / Forward P/E) or Pow Earnings Yield, described next.

I prefer True Yield based on Forward P/E rather than trailing P/E, as it has better predictive power. For example, Apple has a P/E of 21.61, a Forward P/E of 19.46 (both from Finviz), and an Enterprise Value/EBIT of 16.72 (from Yahoo!Finance). The True Yield is 6% (1/16.72). The True Yield based on Forward P/E is 7% (6% * 21.61/19.48).

Pow P/E
You should use the described "EV/EBITDA," and thus "Pow P/E" can be ignored. However, there are some cases where Pow P/E is better: 1)

"EV/EBITDA" may not be available due to reasons such as negative assets, and 2) Use of Forward Earnings instead of earnings based on the last twelve months. The following is an exercise on how I simulate it from Finviz.com using readily available metrics.

I modified P/E to account for cash and debt. I use my last name for this metric to distinguish it from P/E, and it has nothing to do with my ego.

Pow P/E = $\frac{P - \text{Cash per Share} + \text{Debt per Share}}{\text{Earnings} - \text{Interest gained per share} - \text{Interest paid per share}}$

Pow Earnings Yield = $\frac{1}{\text{Pow P/E}}$

Here is a comparison of E/P (Earnings Yield), Expected Earnings Yield (Forward E/P), True Yield (EBITDA/EV), and Pow Earnings Yield, based on Forward (Expected) Earnings as of 10/14/2021.

Metric	CARS	MPAA
Earnings Yield	1%	7%
Expected Earnings Yield	12%	12%
True Yield	13%	11%
Pow Earnings Yield	5%	9%

P/E Is Not Always Important

The following is my test from 1/2/2020 to 10/14/2020. RSP is similar to SPY, except that the stocks in the S&P 500 index are equally weighted. EY (= E/P) is Expected Earnings Yield, and there are no stocks with EY less than 0. DY is Dividend Yield. GPE is the growth of P/E. As in my book, I use annualized returns, and dividends are not included.

This test does not mean much, but it tells us how these metrics behaved during this period. It indicates that **value was not a good metric during this period**, and it may suggest that momentum was better.

Most big winners start as small companies with **high P/E ratios** (from 30 to 100). Many of them have important technologies or systems that could change the world, such as Microsoft, Facebook, Amazon, and Walmart, to name a few. Their sales have increased substantially year after year. In early 2023, P/E for many AI chips, such as Nvidia, was not important when the industry looked rosy, and the Forward P/E was far better than the trailing P/E (based on the last 12 months).

Examples of not depending on low P/Es: Before the 2008 financial crisis, most bank stocks had 10-year low P/Es. After they announced earnings, the P/Es of many surged to over 100, and stock prices suffered losses of more than 80% within 12 months. Bethlehem Steel's stock price, with a P/E of 2 at one time, went to zero. You need to find out why the stock is so cheap through intangible and qualitative analysis.

The following is a rough test with many limitations in the database. However, the conclusion is quite convincing to me, and some results are contrary to common beliefs. For example, I expected higher EY to be better, but that was not the case in this test.

Metric	Ann. Return	Indicator	Comment
RSP 500 All	-2%		
EY (top 10)	-54%	Bad	Contrary
GPE (top 10)	-20%	Bad	Contrary
Select All or top 100.			
DY = 0	16%	Good	
DY (top 100)	-19%	Bad	
DY / 1 and 2	2%		
EY 3 to 4	15%	Good	Second best
EY 2 to 3	6%	Good	Third best
EY 1 to 2	31%	Good	Best
EY 0 to 1	-39%	Bad`	

I use some metrics from a subscription service that are not included here. Two major metrics from this subscription have a return of around 20%. Most subscriptions, including Fidelity (to some extent), provide three composite scores: Total, Fundamental, and Timing. I wish to check the recent predictability of Fidelity's Equity Summary Score if they have a historical database. Most of them exclude delisted or bankrupt companies from their databases.

Link: P/E: https://www.youtube.com/watch?v=4KkTGx2bK_4

4 Fundamental metrics

ROE (Return on Equity)
Return on Equity (ROE = Net Income / Equity) is one of the most important financial indicators to assess how effectively a company's management is performing. However, in recent years, this metric has been overused, leading to a decline in its predictive reliability.

A company's ROE over the last five years can provide insight into how well the stock price withstands major financial downturns and upturns. Comparing a company's ROE to the sector average is a useful way to gauge how well the company is managed relative to its peers. Note that some sectors, such as utilities, typically have lower average ROEs.

Market Cap (Capitalization)
Market Cap = Total Number of Outstanding Shares × Share Price
For beginners, I recommend investing in U.S. stocks with a market cap greater than $800 million. Below is a general classification of market caps, which should be adjusted for inflation over time:

Class	Market Cap (million)
Nano Cap	< $50M
Micro Cap	$50M to $250M
Small Cap	$250M to $1B
Mid Cap	$1B to $10B
Large Cap	$10B to $50B
Mega Cap	> $50B

Generally, the higher the market cap, the lower the risk associated with the stock. Nano Cap and Micro Cap stocks are typically reserved for speculators or company owners.

Small Cap and Mid Cap stocks are suitable for knowledgeable investors, as most institutional investors tend to avoid these, especially Small Cap stocks. Large Cap, Mega Cap, and some Mid Cap stocks are commonly traded by institutional investors and are continuously researched.

My Preferred Metrics:

- Forward P/E

- **PEG Ratio**
- **Fidelity's Equity Summary Score**
- **Short % of Outstanding Shares**
- **Free Cash Flow**
- **ROE**
- **Debt Load / Equity**

I also use summarized metrics from various sources. For example, one of my subscription services provides a composite rank for fundamentals and another for momentum. As an illustration, you can check Blue Chip Growth (note: this service is no longer free).

Enter IBM as the stock symbol. As of February 2013, it received a C for Total Grade, D for Quantity Grade, and B for Fundamental Grade. The Total Grade is usually a composite of other grades.

Use these metrics to screen stocks and narrow down your options for further consideration.

Mid, High, and Low Values of Common Metrics

Metric	Mid Range	Low Range	High Range
P/E (last 12 months)	< 10	> 40	< 4
Price / Cash Flow	< 12	> 30	< 4
Price / Sales	< 2.5	> 3	< 0.2
Price / Book	< 2.0	> 4	< 0.2
PEG	< 1.5	> 2	< 0.2

High Range values (low numbers in this table) are generally favorable, but sometimes they may be too good to be true. Low Range values are typically unfavorable.

For example, many internet stocks in 2000 had P/E ratios over 40 (bad), while a neglected bargain stock might have a P/E of 3 (supposedly good). However, such bargains could indicate hidden problems.

In practice, I prefer the Mid Range. For instance, a P/E between 4 and 10 is ideal. Adjust these ranges based on your risk tolerance and current market conditions. If the market is trending upward, you might relax the range to 5 to 12 to find more stocks for evaluation.

These values are based on data from the past 10 years and are used to predict stock performance over a year. Review these ranges every six months to account for current market conditions.

Metrics with High-Range and Mid-Range values tend to offer better predictions for stock price appreciation. Stocks with Low-Range values are statistically more likely to lose money over the next year. However, some favorable metrics, such as ROE, may have high values instead of low values.

The effectiveness of these ranges can change. When the market favors momentum, metrics like PEG and price growth may become better predictors. It's essential to monitor which metrics the market currently favors—Value or Growth—and adjust your strategy accordingly.

Evaluate the performance of each metric every 3 to 6 months and update the range values as needed.

Fundamental metrics typically take longer (6-12 months) to materialize compared to momentum metrics (1 month). The metrics in the table above, except for PEG, are all fundamental metrics. Note that Price-to-Book (P/B) is generally not useful for financial stocks.

Examples of Searching with High-Range Values
Stocks with Low-Range values for most metrics (e.g., a P/E of 40) are often risky. Therefore, focus on stocks with Mid-Range values (e.g., a P/E of 10) and avoid Low-Range values.

Here's an example of selecting stocks with High-Range values for P/E and P/B:
Copy
E > 0 and
P/E < 4 and
P/B < 0.2

E represents earnings per share, and we want the company to be profitable. High-Range values could indicate potential issues, such as pending lawsuits. A P/E of less than 4 is often suspicious, but very small 0companies may be overlooked by the market and could still be solid investments.

Always conduct thorough due diligence before investing.
Statistically, stocks with Low-Range values are more likely to lose money over the next year, though there are exceptions. For example, Amazon (AMZN) has historically had a high P/E and P/B, but its focus on market share and infrastructure investment has justified its valuation. Personally, I prefer fundamentally sound companies.

Note: P/B is not a reliable metric for established companies or those with significant intellectual property, such as IBM. Many traditional metrics are outdated as they fail to account for intangible assets like patents and brand value.

Example of a Search for Mid-Range Values

E > 0 and
P/E < 10 and
P/E > 4

This search includes companies with positive earnings and P/E ratios between 4 and 10. You should find many companies within this range. Add additional filters, such as minimum price, market cap, and average volume, to narrow down your results. If you find too few stocks, relax your criteria, and vice versa. If you usually find stocks with a screen but not today, it may indicate that the market is overvalued.

This is the first step in narrowing down stocks for further analysis. Keep in mind that some stocks, like IBM, may have consistently high Price/Book values and should not be excluded based on this metric alone.

Compare a Company's Metrics to Its Sector Averages

Comparing a company's metrics to its sector averages is a powerful way to evaluate its performance. For example, the average P/S ratio for supermarkets is extremely low, so comparing a supermarket's P/S to other sectors is not meaningful. Similarly, utility companies often require high debt levels to operate.

If the average P/E or other metric for a sector is suddenly lower than its historical average, it could indicate that the sector is out of favor or undervalued.

The table below compares Apple to its sector (Computer) and the Retail sector as of a specific date for illustration. Note that these metrics will change over time.

Metric	Apple	Computer	Retail
P/E	11	19	24
5-Year Average P/E	16	17	15
PEG	0.6	N/A	1.4
Price / Cash Flow	9.4	8.1	9.2
Price / Book	3.3	3.0	3.6
EPS Growth (5-Yr)	62%	45%	11%
Operating Margin	20%	15%	8%
ROE	30%	14%	19%
Debt / Equity	2%	7%	88%
Inventory Turnover	76%	53%	4.55x

Some metrics, such as Debt/Equity, are more relevant to specific sectors. For example, retail companies typically have higher Inventory Turnover compared to computer companies.

Top-Down Approach
1. Assess whether the market is risky.
2. Select the best-performing sector using tools like Finviz.com.
3. Compare the fundamental metrics of major stocks within that sector.

Metrics That May Not Apply
For financial institutions, Price-to-Book (P/B) is often more useful than Price-to-Cash Flow (P/CF). However, the quality of loans is more critical than any metric, as seen during the 2007 financial crisis. For retail companies, Price-to-Sales (P/S) is more important, while expected P/E is crucial for most other sectors.

When you identify a sector as the best-performing, select the top stocks within that sector.

Compare Metrics to Their Five-Year Averages
If a company's five-year average P/E is 20 and its current P/E is 10, it may be undervalued by 100%. Similarly, compare other metrics, such as Debt/Equity, to their historical averages.

Growth Metrics
Growth metrics, such as the growth rates of stock price, sales, and earnings, are essential for growth investors. Even for value investors, earnings growth is critical, as most stocks with substantial gains have shown earnings growth first. If earnings grow while the stock price remains stagnant, the potential for price appreciation increases, and the stock may return to its historical average P/E.

Momentum Metrics
Momentum metrics, such as the rate of stock price increase and trading volume, are part of growth investing. Earnings revisions are particularly important during earnings seasons (typically four times a year).

Fidelity and other services provide composite momentum scores, which may include metrics like SMA-50, quarter-over-quarter sales growth, and recent price appreciation. For momentum strategies, I focus on these metrics and ignore others, as my average holding period is less than 30 days.

Insider Buying
Insiders sell stocks for various reasons, but when they buy shares at market prices, it's worth noting. Insiders have the best knowledge of their company's health and industry trends.

Use sites like Finviz.com or OpenInsider to track insider purchases, focusing on high ratios of Net Total Purchase Value to Market Cap and purchases by multiple insiders. Be cautious if insiders buy stocks shortly after selling a similar amount.

Where to Get Metrics
You can access this information from free or low-cost websites like Finviz.com, your broker's site, AAII, and Fidelity.

For more advanced tools, consider subscription services like Value Line, IBD, Zacks, VectorVest, and Stock Screen 123, which typically cost less than $1,000 per year. Many vendors provide composite metrics, such as value or timing scores, which combine multiple indicators.

Monitor Recent Performance of Metrics

The predictability of metrics can vary depending on market conditions. To identify which metrics are currently effective, evaluate their performance over the last three months and focus on those that perform well. This approach is the basis of my scoring system in the book *Scoring Stocks*.

Why Some Metrics Fail
Despite their widespread use, many investors struggle to achieve consistent success with metrics. Some reasons for this include:

1. Metrics must be monitored for effectiveness in current market conditions.
2. Intangible factors often play a significant role.
3. Popular metrics, like ROE, lose effectiveness when too many investors rely on them.
4. Fundamental metrics require time (at least 6 months) to reflect a stock's value.
5. Data quality issues, especially in emerging markets, can lead to inaccurate metrics.
6. Metrics derived from outdated financial statements may not reflect current conditions.
7. Companies may manipulate metrics, such as P/E and ROE, by taking on excessive debt.

Footnote
1. Stocks are classified into sectors, which are further divided into industries. For simplicity, I use the terms interchangeably here.
2. Amazon (AMZN) is not a value stock by traditional metrics. As of January 2013, its P/E was 157, and its P/B was 15, both falling into the Low-Range category. Despite this, its stock price rose from 256 to256 *to* 270 in January 2013, driven by investor optimism about its market share growth. While it may be suitable for traders, it is too risky for long-term investors like me.

Afterthoughts
- One popular investment book recommends selecting stocks based solely on ROE. I can save you time and money by telling you that this approach no longer works.

- Delta Air Lines (DAL) has an interesting Debt/Equity ratio of over -1000% due to negative equity. In such cases, consider using Debt/ABS(Equity) for comparison.
- Occasionally, financial data discrepancies arise between sources. Always verify the dates of financial statements, as the company's website typically provides the most up-to-date information.
- The Current Ratio (Current Assets / Current Liabilities) is a useful metric. A ratio below 1 indicates that a company may struggle to meet its short-term obligations.
- Dividend Yield is a valid metric for mature companies but is less relevant for growth companies that reinvest earnings into research and development.
- Finviz.com provides three margin metrics: Profit Margin, Gross Margin, and Operating Margin. I prefer Profit Margin for most companies, though the others may be relevant in specific sectors.
- Enron had millions in profits but negative cash flows, highlighting the importance of cash flow analysis over earnings.
- Insider selling is usually not a cause for concern unless excessive. Insiders often sell shares before a company goes bankrupt.
- Shorting stocks can be challenging, even with strong fundamental arguments. Not every investment will be profitable, but educated decisions should outperform the market in the long run.
- Intrinsic value is a useful concept but is often overlooked due to its complexity. It represents the real value of a company, which may differ from its book value or market cap.

Links:
Income statement: https://www.youtube.com/watch?v=ht-tzwyLPU
The following link provides more info on intrinsic value.
http://en.wikipedia.org/wiki/Intrinsic_value_%28finance%29
https://www.youtube.com/watch?v=l-T-Vyk2txc&authuser=0

5   Finviz's parameters

Stock Metrics and Analysis

Most metrics are described in Finviz (via Help), Investopedia, and/or Wikipedia, as well as in my articles on P/E and fundamental metrics if available. We use these metrics for screening stocks and then evaluating the screened stocks. Most metrics can also be obtained from Yahoo! Finance and Google Finance.

The following are my personal comments on why I believe some metrics are more important than others. Personally, I divide metrics into **fundamental** and **technical** categories, which are more relevant for long-term and short-term investors, respectively.

Comparing Ratios
Compare the ratios to companies in the same sector (industry) and also to their averages over the last few years (preferably five years). This information can be obtained from many websites, including Fidelity.

Using Finviz.com
From your browser, enter **Finviz.com**. Enter a stock symbol (I used **ABEO** for this discussion). A chart will be displayed with prices and volumes for the last eleven months. SMAs (Simple Moving Averages) are sometimes displayed along with other technical indicators. Intraday, Daily, and Weekly options are available for day traders, short-term traders, and long-term traders, respectively. I prefer using the **Candle -- Advanced** option for drawing charts.

Besides the chart and the metrics described next, Finviz provides information on what the company does, analysts' recommendations (I prefer Fidelity's Equity Summary Score), insider trading, and articles that are useful for qualitative analysis. Many free websites, such as Yahoo! Finance, also provide a list of articles about the company.

Financial Highlights and Statements
These materials are essential for in-depth analysis and were more critical decades ago when most financial ratios were not pre-calculated. They are still important for investors with a good understanding of financial accounting. The current version of Finviz includes basic balance sheets, income statements, and cash flow statements for the trailing twelve

months (TTM) and the last two years. Click on the following YouTube links for more details:

- **Balance Sheet**: https://www.youtube.com/watch?v=DMv9JC_K37Y
- **Income Statement**: https://www.youtube.com/watch?v=0--AvwZabIQ
- **Cash Flow Statement**: https://www.youtube.com/watch?v=hMBN6yTIDb0

Insider Trading

A section on **Insider Trading** is also included. Do not be alarmed when insiders sell small quantities of stock. However, large purchases (e.g., insider transactions exceeding 5% of shares) at prices close to the market price could be favorable news.

Key Metrics in Finviz

The following metrics are roughly based on the flow of Finviz from top to bottom and left to right. I skip metrics that I believe are less important. You can hover your cursor over a metric to retrieve its description from Finviz or via Finviz's Help. Some metrics are left blank to indicate they are not applicable (e.g., zero, negative, or not available).

For example, the Debt/Equity ratio for **YRCW** in January 2019 was blank due to its negative equity. From Yahoo! Finance at the time of writing, YRCW had a total debt of $888 million.

Index

Most of us trade stocks listed on the three major U.S. exchanges. Stocks listed over-the-counter (OTC) are generally too risky for most investors. Avoid stocks listed on local or foreign exchanges unless you are an expert or have insider knowledge (not illegal). I screen stocks and ignore those not listed on the Dow, NASDAQ, or AMEX. Other screeners may allow you to select a group of exchanges.

Market Cap (MC)

To me, stocks with a market cap below $50 million are risky, even though they could be very profitable. Ensure the average trading volume is at least 10,000 shares, or your order is less than 1% of the average volume. Some small-cap stocks are controlled by their owners and have low trading volumes, making them difficult to trade.

Float = Outstanding Shares - Insider Shares
Usually, float does not matter as it is typically the same as outstanding shares. However, it is important for small companies with large insider ownership. Most owners of such companies do not want to sell their family businesses, reducing the chance of acquisition. In such cases, you may have to hold the stock for a long time or sell it at an unfavorable price.

Forward P/E
If **Forward P/E** (a.k.a. Expected P/E) is not provided, use the **Trailing P/E**, which is based on the last 12 months (TTM). Alternatively, calculate the earnings (E) by using the earnings from P/E and multiplying it by the company's growth rate. Note that this may not be seasonally adjusted. I prefer using Forward P/E as it provides better predictability. Successful investing often depends on correctly predicting future earnings.

Finviz leaves the P/E blank if earnings are negative. In such cases, I check Yahoo! Finance's **EV/EBITDA**, which also considers taxes, cash, and interest. The blank condition also occurs in other metrics, such as when assets are negative (very rare).

Earnings Yield = E/P.
I call it **True Earnings Yield** for **EBITDA/EV**. It is easier to understand. Compare Earnings Yield or True Yield to the annual dividend yield of a 10-year Treasury bond. However, with low interest rates in 2021, skip this comparison for this year.

E/P is easier for screening and sorting stocks. If you use P/E instead of E/P, you need to screen or sort stocks with the clause "P/E > 0".
When the P/E is less than 5, be cautious, as there may be a reason why it is so low. Many companies that eventually go bankrupt had low P/Es at one point before their stock prices collapsed.

Compare the P/E or Forward P/E to the average P/E for the sector (e.g., high tech) and its five-year average, available from Fidelity.com. Some sectors, like technology, typically have high P/Es (e.g., 25). If the sector is cyclical, earnings could be affected.

Do not rely solely on P/E to determine a stock's value. Other metrics, such as PEG, P/B, and Debt/Equity, are also important.

When a company's prospects are strong, such as Tesla in 2020, ignore the P/E. Investors are betting on the future. Do not short these high-growth stocks.

Cash per Share

This metric is used to calculate **Pow P/E** and **Pow EY** when EV/EBITDA is not available. For example, if a stock is priced at \$10 and has \$10 cash per share with no debt (i.e., Debt/Equity = 0), it is likely underpriced, as you could theoretically acquire the entire company for free. Investigate why the price is so low—it could be market neglect or a serious event like a major lawsuit. **P/C** (Price-to-Cash) is a better choice than Cash per Share; the lower the better.

Dividend %

This metric is useful for income investors. The payout ratio should not exceed 30%, except for mature companies. Most growth and tech companies reinvest profits into research and development, so they do not pay dividends.

Recommendations (Recs)

It is no longer available. If it is available again, select stocks with a recommendation score of 1 or 2. Do not base your stock selection solely on this metric, as many bad recommendations have led to significant losses. Use Fidelity's **Equity Summary Score** instead.

PEG Ratio

The **PEG Ratio** measures the growth of P/E and is a growth metric (others include Sales Growth Q/Q and Earnings Growth Q/Q). It is similar to P/E but takes the expected earnings growth rate into account.

A lower PEG is better as long as earnings are positive. If earnings are negative, the reverse is true. This is a limitation of using P/E and PEG, which is why I recommend **Earnings Yield (EY)** and **Earnings Yield Growth (EYG)**. The chance of stock appreciation is high when the PEG is less than 1.

If two companies have the same P/E, the one with a better PEG ratio is preferable. Similarly, if two companies have the same E/P, the one with higher Earnings Growth (EPS Q/Q) is better.

Price-to-Book (P/B)

Book value (Total Assets - Total Liabilities) may not include intangible assets like patents. Do not rely on it entirely, just as with ROE and other metrics based on book value. Negative equity is possible when Total Liabilities exceed Total Assets.

This metric is outdated for most mature companies, as their value now includes intangible assets like patents, management quality, brand names, market share, and customer base. Some assets, like gold mines and real estate, can be easily valued. For example, when gold prices fall, a company's P/B could drop below 1, making it a potential buy—unless the downward trend continues.

Price-to-Sales (P/S)
If two companies are unprofitable, the P/S ratio could be more useful. Retail companies like Walmart have very different P/S ratios compared to research companies. This metric is only meaningful when comparing stocks within the same or related sectors.

Price-to-Free Cash Flow (P/FCF)
I prefer this metric to be greater than 0 and less than 50 for value investors. Most metrics can be manipulated, but not this one. It is a key metric for avoiding bankrupt companies.

Sales Growth Q/Q
This metric reduces seasonal deviations. For example, retail sales during the Christmas season should be compared to the same season in the prior year.

Earnings Growth Q/Q
Similar to Sales Growth Q/Q, I prefer Earnings Growth over Sales Growth. Both are growth metrics. When a company discontinues unprofitable products, its Sales Growth Q/Q may decline, but its Earnings Growth Q/Q could increase. In 2000, many internet companies had strong Sales Growth Q/Q but negative Earnings Growth Q/Q.

Quarter-over-quarter (Q/Q) comparisons eliminate seasonal variations. I prefer both Sales Growth Q/Q and Earnings Growth Q/Q to increase. If Earnings Growth Q/Q increases significantly more than Sales Growth Q/Q, it could indicate temporary factors, such as a spike in oil prices for an oil company.

When a company buys back its own shares, EPS can be misleading, as earnings (E) remain fixed while the number of shares decreases. In most cases, the company's fundamentals have not changed.

In 2021, many energy stocks had incredible Earnings Growth Q/Q, and their Forward P/E ratios were better than their Trailing P/E ratios. These could be momentum plays unless their growth is sustainable.

Insider Transactions
Positive insider transactions are favorable. However, they can sometimes be misleading. Scroll to the end of the screen for more details. If the transactions are outdated (e.g., three months old) or involve purchases following similar sales, they are less significant. Insiders know their company better than outsiders.

Institutional Transactions
This metric is also important, as institutional investors can move the market. However, most institutional investors avoid small-cap stocks, so this metric is less relevant for them.

Insider Ownership, Shares Outstanding, and Float
These metrics determine the number of shares available for trading. Stocks with low float and high insider ownership limit trading and should generally be avoided. Compare your trade size to the stock's average trading volume.

Profit Margin
I prefer **Profit Margin** over **Gross Margin** and **Operating Margin**, as it includes interest expenses and taxes. For example, software companies have high Gross Margins, as they exclude development, support, and marketing costs. Retail stores, on the other hand, have low Gross Margins. It is best to compare companies within the same industry.

Short Float
I prefer a Short Float of less than 10%. If it exceeds 10%, short sellers may have identified issues with the company. If it exceeds 25%, check the company's fundamentals and any significant events, such as major lawsuits. If the fundamentals are strong, consider buying the stock, anticipating a potential short squeeze. This strategy is risky but has proven profitable in some of my trades.

Technical Metrics: SMA-20, SMA-50, and SMA-200

Finviz expresses these moving averages as percentages. If all are positive, the trend is upward. SMA-20 and SMA-50 are short-term trend indicators, while SMA-200 is a long-term trend indicator. Short-term swing traders should focus on short-term trends, while long-term investors should consider long-term trends.

For no need for charting, I modified the **Golden Cross** (SMA-20 crossing above SMA-50) and **Death Cross** (SMA-20 crossing below SMA-50) as buy and sell signals, respectively.

Relative Strength Index (RSI-14)

If RSI is above 65%, the stock is overbought and may reverse. If it is below 30%, the stock is oversold and may rebound. Some traders use thresholds of 70% and 30%. Use RSI as a reference, but note that many stocks making new highs remain overbought for extended periods. I recommend using trailing stops to protect profits on rising stocks.

Beta

A stock with a high Beta is more volatile. Higher Beta stocks are suitable for short-term traders. A Beta of 1 means the stock moves with the market, while a Beta above 1 indicates higher volatility. For volatile stocks, set wider stop-loss levels (e.g., 15% instead of 10%).

Performance (Perf)

If a stock has lost more than 50% of its value, it could be a candidate for bottom fishing—or it could be heading toward bankruptcy. Conduct thorough research before buying such risky stocks.

Return on Equity (ROE)

ROE measures management performance. Institutional ownership (except for small companies) and insider ownership reflect confidence in the company and its sector.

ROE = Net Income / Average Shareholder's Equity

According to Investopedia, a normal ROE for utilities is around 10%, while high-tech companies should aim for 15%. Compare this ratio to industry peers using data from Fidelity and other sources.

Avoiding Bankrupt Companies

Avoid companies at risk of bankruptcy at all costs. Metrics like Debt/Equity, P/FCF, Cash per Share, P/B, Profit Margin, Forward P/E, Short Float, RSI-14, SMA-20, and SMA-50 can provide warning signs. Summarize all information and consider other factors, such as obsolete products or pending generic drug approvals. Read articles available on Finviz and other sites.

Earnings Date

Avoid trading stocks a week before their earnings date (available on Finviz). It is rare to make significant profits if earnings exceed expectations, as the stock price often reflects anticipated results. Conversely, disappointing earnings can cause significant price declines.

Additional Useful Information

Equity

Equity = Total Assets - Total Liabilities. When equity is negative, many metrics based on equity (e.g., P/B, Debt/Equity) are not displayed. For example, on May 5, 2022, **TUP** had equity of -$207 million (from Finviz's balance sheet as of December 25, 2021). When equity is zero or negative, related metrics like P/B, Debt/Equity, and EV/EBITDA may be blank or null.
However, a P/E of less than 4 could indicate a buying opportunity unless there are significant underlying issues. Some large companies had low P/Es before going bankrupt.

Earnings Date

Earnings announcements, typically quarterly, can cause significant stock price fluctuations (e.g., 10%).

Price Chart

The price chart includes features like resistance lines and technical indicators such as double tops (bearish) and double bottoms (bullish).

Company Description

The description under the stock symbol provides a brief overview of the company's sector, industry, and country of registration. Invest in stocks within sectors that are trending upward. For example, according to Finviz,

Apple is in the Consumer Goods sector and the Electronic Equipment industry.

Avoid foreign stocks unless they are listed on U.S. exchanges or headquartered in the U.S. Foreign stocks carry additional risks, such as currency fluctuations, lack of regulation, and political instability (e.g., Russia in 2022 and China in 2021). Some foreign stocks may also impose additional taxes on dividends.

Articles on the Company
Articles provide qualitative analysis and insights into the company.

Insider Trading
Pay attention to insider purchases at market prices. Use common sense when interpreting insider transactions.

Intrinsic Value
Many websites (most requiring subscriptions) calculate intrinsic value. Use it as a reference, but evaluate the stock yourself. Buy when the intrinsic value is below the stock price and sell when it is above. This aligns with the "buy low, sell high" principle. However, consider other intangible factors. Stocks like Tesla and Amazon had low intrinsic values but continued to rise.

Other Important Sites

Yahoo! Finance
From the **Statistics** tab, you can find **Enterprise Value / EBITDA**. I call it **True Yield** when inverted to **EBITDA / Enterprise Value**. If unavailable, use **Earnings Yield**. In my spreadsheet:

=IF(Earnings Yield = "", True Yield, Earnings Yield)

Fidelity
Under the **Stock**, **Statistics**, and **More** tabs, you can compare the P/E to the five-year average using spreadsheets.
Cheaper By Historically =IF(PE="","",(Avg. of 5-year PE - PE)/Avg. of 5-year PE)

Compare the P/E to industry peers:

Cheaper By To the Peers =IF(PE="","",(Industry PE - PE)/Industry PE)

Your Broker's Website

Your broker's website should have plenty of tools for stock analysis. As of December 2018, Fidelity offers extensive research for free with no position restrictions. Some useful metrics include:

- **Equity Summary Score**: A score of 7 or higher (8 for conservative investors) indicates a potentially good buy. Avoid stocks with scores of 3 or below. Scores between 4 and 6 could be turnaround candidates if supported by strong earnings growth or positive news.
- **Five-Year Averages**: These are good benchmarks. For example, in December 2018, **C** had a P/E of 9, compared to its five-year average of 14, making it a value buy.

Other Sources

If you have access to other sources (most require subscriptions), avoid stocks with failing grades. Exceptions include new positive developments or increased insider purchases.

Vendor	Grade	Fail
Fidelity	Equity Summary Score	< 7
IBD	Composite Grade	< 50
Value Line	Projected 3-5 Year Return	< 3%
Zacks	Rank	5
VectorVest	VST	< 0.7

You may find Value Line and IBD in your local library. Start with free stock reports from your broker. Finviz and Seeking Alpha offer articles on stocks and earnings conferences, which can provide valuable insights.

Guru Analysis

It is helpful to know how investment gurus rate stocks. **GuruFocus** is a good source but requires a subscription. **NASDAQ** offers a simplified version. Visit Nasdaq.com, select "Investing," then "Guru Screeners," and enter a stock symbol like **THO**. You will see how 10 or so gurus evaluate the stock. Click "Detailed Analysis" for each guru's perspective.

Quick and Dirty Stock Evaluation

Sometimes, you need to evaluate a stock quickly due to market developments or to narrow down a list of screened stocks. Here are two methods:

Simplest Way to Evaluate Stocks
This method takes a few minutes. Open Finviz.com and enter the stock symbol.

Using **SWKS** on June 10, 2016, as an example:
- **Forward P/E**: ~11 (fine between 3 and 25)
- **Debt/Equity**: 0 (fine if less than 0.5)
- **ROE**: 30% (fine if greater than 5%)
- **P/PCF**: 31 (fine if not negative)

Also, check **Market Cap**, **Average Volume**, **Dividend**, **Short Float** (fine between 0% and 10%), **Country**, and **Industry**. Based on these metrics, **SWKS** is a buy.

If you have more time, check:
- **Recommendations**: Fine if less than 2.5
- **P/B**: Fine between 0.5 and 4
- **Sales Growth Q/Q**: Fine if not negative
- **Earnings Growth Q/Q**: Fine if not negative
- **Cash per Share**: Compare to Debt per Share
- **Profit Margin**: Fine if greater than 5%

Read articles about the stock for additional insights.

5-Minute Stock Evaluation
This method is even quicker but less thorough. I recommend spending more time researching stocks.
1. Open Finviz.com and enter the stock or ETF symbol. Look at the number of red metrics. If there are more reds than greens, the stock is likely not a good buy.
2. Check Fidelity's **Equity Summary Score**. A score above 8 is favorable.
3. If time allows, check:
    - **Forward P/E**: E > 0 and P/E < 20
    - **Debt/Equity**: < 50%

- P/FCF: Not in the red
4. Replace Forward P/E with **True P/E** (EV/EBITDA) if possible, available from Yahoo! Finance.
5. Check **SMA-20** (or SMA-50 for longer holding periods). If SMA-20 is > 10%, the stock is trending upward.
6. Positive **Insider Transactions** are favorable.
7. Be cautious with foreign stocks and low-volume stocks.
8. If most metrics are positive, the stock is likely a buy. However, nothing is 100% certain.

Links

PEG: http://en.wikipedia.org/wiki/PEG_ratio
Short %: http://www.investopedia.com/university/shortselling/shortselling1.asp#axzz2LNDvpemo
Openinsider: http://www.openinsider.com/
Finviz: http://Finviz.com/
terms: http://www.Finviz.com/help/screener.ashx
Insider Cow: http://www.insidercow.com/
Current Ratio: http://en.wikipedia.org/wiki/Current_ratio
Cash Flow: https://www.youtube.com/watch?v=1v8hRZ36--c
How to find quality stocks.
http://seekingalpha.com/article/2381395-how-to-identify-quality-stocks-and-is-there-really-alpha-to-be-had
Over-priced stock: https://www.youtube.com/watch?v=VeMr0n4pvtM:
Outperform the market
https://www.youtube.com/watch?v=3DdY0JdUilM

Reading financial sheet.
Balance sheet: https://www.youtube.com/watch?v=DZjU0CHKyV4
Earnings report: https://www.youtube.com/watch?v=Ite4l_y08Gg

https://www.youtube.com/watch?v=DMv9JC_K37Y&t=954s
https://www.youtube.com/watch?v=8NelYFn07jg
Intrinsic Value: https://www.youtube.com/watch?v=l-T-Vyk2txc

More info from Fidelity

Additional Metrics from Fidelity
In addition to Finviz, I also obtain **EV/EBITDA** (Enterprise Value to Earnings Before Interest, Taxes, Depreciation, and Amortization) from **Yahoo! Finance** under the **Statistics** tab. This section will describe more metrics

available on **Fidelity**, as well as how to use them effectively. Note that some metrics may overlap across Finviz, Yahoo! Finance, and Fidelity.

Navigating Fidelity
To begin, start from the **"News & Research"** tab on Fidelity's platform. Here, you can access:
- **"Markets & Sectors"**: Provides an overview of market trends and sector performance, along with related articles and insights.
- **"Viewpoints: Market Sense"**: Offers market analysis and perspectives to help you make informed decisions.

For a visual guide, you can watch this YouTube video: Fidelity Overview. From the **"News & Research"** tab, you can also access Fidelity's **Screener**, **CDs**, and **Stock** tools.

These tools are invaluable for building an income stream or creating a **CD ladder** based on information from the **"Fixed Income, Bonds, and CDs"** section. For beginners or investors with limited time, **ETFs** (Exchange-Traded Funds) are highly recommended.

Stock Analysis on Fidelity
The **"Stocks"** section on Fidelity provides a wealth of information. The **Home** page offers general market insights and stock-related data. Explore each feature to familiarize yourself with the tools available.

To illustrate, let's use **AAPL (Apple Inc.)** as an example. Enter the stock symbol in the search bar, and you'll find detailed information about the company.

One particularly useful metric is the **Equity Summary Score**, which I find helpful for evaluating stocks. The **5-year P/E ratio**, which was previously located in the main stock overview, has been moved to the **"Statistics"** and **"More"** sections.

Analysis and Sentiment
Fidelity's **"Analysis and Sentiment"** tools help determine whether a stock is **undervalued** (ideal for long-term holding) or has **short-term sentiment** (useful for short-term trading). These tools provide insights into market sentiment and valuation metrics, helping you decide whether to buy, hold, or sell a stock. Currently, the short-term score, useful for screening momentum stocks, has been eliminated.

Analyst Opinions & Reports

The **"Analyst Opinions & Reports"** section typically includes at least two reports, often more. It's essential to read these reports before making any investment decisions.

Start with reports that have a high **StarMine Relative Accuracy** score, as these are generally more reliable. Some reports also provide historical data, including more than five years of specific metrics. Additionally, you can access the company's **Balance Sheet** and **Income Statement** for a deeper dive into its financial health.

For More Information

For additional guidance on using Fidelity's tools, search for tutorials on **YouTube**. There are many videos available that walk you through the platform's features and how to make the most of them.

Section II: Beyond fundamentals

Buy stocks based on appreciation potential, not based on when and what you traded the stock for.

6   Intangibles

I assign a score to each stock I evaluate. Occasionally, some stocks with poor scores deliver great returns, and vice versa. However, in general, the scoring system works effectively. It has been statistically proven and validated repeatedly through my limited data.

I typically stick with high-score stocks, though there are exceptions. Occasionally, I adjust my scoring system to adapt to current market conditions. For example, during the market bottom and early recovery phases of the market cycle, value stocks tend to outperform momentum or growth stocks. Here are some of my recent experiences and strategies:

- **Increasing Stake in High-Score Stocks**: I often double or even triple my investment in stocks with high scores. Over the long term, these stocks consistently outperform the average, with only minor exceptions. In addition to the score, I also consider the intangibles discussed in this article.
- **Caution with Outrageous Metrics**: Be wary of stocks with extreme metrics, such as a P/E ratio of 4 or less. These could indicate underlying issues like pending lawsuits, expiring patents, or other hidden problems. Similarly, be cautious with stocks in the top 5% of scores, as my data shows they often underperform the average. Their issues may not yet be reflected in the financial statements.
- **Technology and Patents**: For tech companies, the value of their technology and patents cannot be ignored, even if their P/E ratios are high. I set a higher P/E limit of 25 for tech stocks, compared to 20 for others. The value of a company's technology and patents is not captured in fundamental metrics but can sometimes be inferred from insider purchases at market prices.

For example, **IDCC** surged about 40% in two days due to rumors that Google or Apple was bidding for its mobile technology. Charts often flag such events, but for non-chartists, the **SMA-20** from Finviz.com can provide late but useful signals.

- **Acquisitions During Market Bottoms**: More acquisitions occur during market bottoms and early recovery phases. Companies with valuable technologies become bargains, and larger firms, especially in the same sector, understand their value better than most investors. These potential acquisition targets are not always reflected in their scores. When corporations have ample cash or access to cheap credit, they seek smaller companies with valuable intangible assets like technology, customer base, or market share.

  The periods of 2009-2012 and 2003 were ideal for such investments, and I had at least one stock in each period that appreciated significantly.

- **Overpriced Growth Stocks**: On the flip side, companies like **Netflix**, **Chipotle** (in early 2012), and **Amazon** (in early 2013) were overpriced by any measure. However, these companies were investing heavily in their future, making it difficult for short sellers to profit. When a stock's P/E exceeds 40, exercise caution. While some companies may justify high valuations, most do not. Avoid following the herd and conduct thorough due diligence.

Use the **reward/risk ratio** to guide decisions. For example, if a stock has an equal chance of rising 50% or falling 25%, it is a buy. The reverse would indicate a sell.

- **Unpredictable Events**: Retail investors often cannot anticipate certain events until they occur. For instance, **ATSC** dropped 15% after losing its second primary customer. Fundamental analysis cannot predict such events, and charts often signal them too late unless monitored continuously.
- **Earnings Misses**: After a rapid rise, **TZOO** plunged due to missing negligible earnings expectations. It appears the stock's previous gains had already priced in perfect earnings growth.

I don't understand why a company loses 10% of its market cap for missing earnings by 1%. This could be driven by institutional investors. Evaluate the stock before acting, as going against institutional moves can be profitable for the right stocks. Avoid trading before earnings announcements (typically four times a year for most stocks).

- **Intangibles Not in Financial Statements**: Factors like industry outlook, patents, goodwill, market share, competition, product

margins, management quality, pending lawsuits, potential acquisitions, pension obligations, and advertising icons are not easily found in financial statements. This is why it's essential to read articles about stocks on your buy list or in your portfolio.
- **Fraudulent or Manipulated Data**: I am cautious with small companies in emerging markets due to the risk of fraudulent or manipulated financial data. Check company names, especially foreign ones, ADRs, and headquarters addresses (available in most investing sites).

Earnings can be manipulated through accounting tricks. A sudden jump in earnings may not be as positive as it seems. Always check the footnotes in financial statements. I usually skip detailed financial analysis unless I'm considering a significant investment, as my time is limited.

- **Cash Flow**: Cash flow is harder to manipulate and provides insight into a company's survival prospects. However, in my tests, it has not been a consistent predictor of stock performance, though it is a critical red flag for companies nearing bankruptcy.
- **Red Flags**: Repeated one-time, non-recurring, and extraordinary charges are red flags.
- **Overcompensated CEOs**: Avoid companies where CEOs are overcompensated. For example, as of July 2013, **Activision's** CEO raised his salary by over 600% while the stock lost double-digit value.
- **Value Stocks**: Understand why a stock has become a value stock (i.e., fewer investors want to own it), even if it appears fundamentally sound. For example, a supplier to **Apple** might decline due to Apple's falling sales or a switch to alternative suppliers. Technology companies constantly innovate, and a turnaround could occur within a year with better products.
- **Leadership Changes**: The resignation of a CEO or CFO, coupled with heavy insider selling, is not a good sign.

For more insights, watch this video: CEO Compensation and Stock Performance.

Conclusion
Buying a stock is an educated guess that its price will rise. Fundamentals don't always work, but they do most of the time:

1. **Value Stocks Require Patience**: When buying a value stock, you're swimming against the tide. It often takes more than six months for the market to recognize its value. The exception is during the Early Recovery phase of the market cycle, where value stocks can deliver faster and larger returns.
2. **Misleading Metrics**: Some metrics, like book value, can be misleading for established companies like **IBM**. Intangible assets, such as brand image, are not reflected in financial statements.
3. **Market Irrationality**: The market is not always rational.

Afterthoughts

- **Brand Names**: Brand names of large companies are among the most important intangibles. Here's a <u>strategy</u> for buying big companies in a down market. It has been proven to work, but don't buy these companies without analysis.
- **Reputation**: A company's reputation takes years to build but can be destroyed by a single incident, as seen with **GM's** delayed recall of faulty ignition switches.

#Fillers: I wish I have a time machine

After collecting bottles for money, an old lady ordered a bowl of plain rice and ate by herself. I wish I could have ordered a meat dish for her and I was 'ashamed' of being generous.

A well-dressed gentleman offered his just-bought hamburger to a beggar. The beggar refused and asked for money instead – most likely he needed the money to buy liquor. A tale of two citizens.

During a lunch with my fellow tourists, a beautiful girl danced for our entertainment. I did not offer her anything and it had been bothering me for years.

During college, my housemates asked me to apply for food stamps. I had used only a few stamps then as I did not cook. I feel ashamed as this is my only time to collect social welfare.

We have regrets in life and we can only bring them to our graves.

7 Qualitative analysis

Qualitative analysis is the final step in evaluating a stock fundamentally, followed by technical analysis to determine entry and exit points. The market is not always rational and can be influenced by factors like easy credit or liquidity.

Where Quantitative Analysis Fails
Some high-score stocks fail, while some low-score stocks succeed. However, the scoring system works statistically for the majority of my stocks.

Reasons Low-Score Stocks Perform:
1. **Oversold Conditions**: Institutional investors (fund and pension managers) often dump stocks first, followed by retail investors. They may buy back these stocks when prices reach a certain range. Technical indicators like **RSI(14)** (available on Finviz) can help identify oversold stocks.
2. **Price Declines Improve Metrics**: Falling stock prices improve metrics like P/E and P/Sales, but the overall trend remains negative. An improving Forward P/E can be a positive signal.
3. **Turnaround Potential**: A company may have resolved its issues or benefited from market changes. New management, like Steve Jobs' return to **Apple**, can drive profitability.
4. **Insider Purchases**: Increased insider buying can signal positive developments not yet reflected in financial statements, such as resolved lawsuits, new products, or large orders.
5. **Hidden Strengths**: Insiders may hide positive developments to buy more shares at lower prices.

Reasons High-Score Stocks Plunge:
1. **Peak Fundamentals**: Stocks may reach their maximum potential and have no room to grow further. This is especially true when timing ratings are at their highest.
2. **Profit-Taking**: Investors may sell after a stock reaches its target price.
3. **Sector Rotation**: Institutional investors may shift funds to other sectors or stocks with better growth potential.
4. **Deteriorating Outlook**: The company, sector, or market outlook may be worsening. Stocks with P/E ratios below 5 often have underlying issues.

5. **Price Manipulation**: Stocks may be subject to pump-and-dump schemes. Shorting is risky but can be profitable for experienced investors.
6. **Negative Events**: New lawsuits, competing products, or canceled orders can hurt stock prices.
7. **Analyst Downgrades**: Downgrades can signal issues like product defects, regulatory violations, or accounting fraud.
8. **Earnings Misses**: Failing to meet earnings expectations can lead to sharp declines.

Qualitative Analysis

After quantitative and intangible analysis, conduct qualitative analysis to assess a company's prospects. Check the date of articles and watch for hidden agendas. Be cautious of "pump-and-dump" schemes, especially with small companies.

Sources for Qualitative Analysis:
1. **Seeking Alpha**: Search for articles on the company. Paid memberships may be required for access.
2. **Broker Research Reports**: Some brokers provide detailed research reports. Consider opening an account with a broker that offers this service.
3. **Yahoo! Finance Boards**: While most comments are noise, occasional insights can be valuable, especially for small companies.
4. **Company Financial Statements**: Review the most recent statements available on the company's website.
5. **10-K Filings**: Access these from the SEC's EDGAR database (www.sec.gov/edgar). Look for new products, competition, key customers, order backlogs, R&D, and pending lawsuits.
6. **Sector and Company Outlook**: Assess the outlook for the company's sector and its competitive position.
7. **Competitor Analysis**: Evaluate the company's competitors.
8. **Management Quality**: Avoid companies with poor management. For example, **J.C. Penney's** turnaround efforts failed, leading to bankruptcy in 2020.
9. **Business Model**: Evaluate whether the business model makes sense. For example:
    - **Razor-and-Blade Model**: Giving away razors to sell blades is a proven strategy.

- **Supermarkets**: Lowering prices on common items while profiting from less price-sensitive products like meat and seafood.
- **Barnes & Noble**: A business model reliant on free loaders (e.g., people using stores for air conditioning) is unsustainable.
- **Market dumping** works to capture the market. Microsoft used to do it with their new Office and Mail products that could not compete with the established products at the time. Google is following the same model to dump its equivalent products to compete with Office. Now, Microsoft is taking a dose of the same medicine. As of 2015, Google is not winning.

8 Manipulators and bankruptcy

Avoiding bankruptcies and significant stock value losses can substantially improve our portfolio. Some companies make poor decisions, such as Enron's disastrous bets on energy futures, leading to their downfall. Below are key indicators of potential trouble:

Warning Signs to Watch For:
1. **Foreign Companies**: Investing in small companies from developing countries, such as China, Ireland, and Israel, has not been particularly successful for me. However, as of 2019, many large Chinese companies have been performing well.
2. **P/E Ratio**: If a company's Price-to-Earnings (P/E) ratio appears too good to be true, investigate why. Conversely, avoid companies with excessively poor P/E ratios.
3. **P/PFC Ratio**: The Price-to-Free-Cash-Flow (P/PFC) ratio should be between 0 and 50. Even with healthy cash flow, a company may struggle to service excessive debt. Always compare cash flow to the Debt/Equity ratio.
4. **Altman Z-Score**: A Z-Score above 3 is preferable, as it indicates a low risk of bankruptcy. However, note that the Z-Score is not designed for financial sector companies. The Z-Score is calculated using the following metrics:
    - Working Capital / Total Assets (A)
    - Retained Earnings / Total Assets (B)
    - Earnings Before Interest & Taxes / Total Assets (C)
    - Market Cap / Total Liabilities (D)
    - Sales / Total Assets (E)

   Formula: $Z\text{-Score} = 1.2A + 1.4B + 3.3C + 0.6D + E$
5. **Beneish M-Score**: A score below -2.22 suggests that earnings are not being manipulated. Both Z-Score and M-Score are available on GuruFocus.com for a fee.
6. **Bond Ratings**: Avoid companies with bond ratings below B.
7. **Government Regulations**: Be cautious of new regulations, such as the removal of tax credits for solar panels, which can negatively impact certain industries.
8. **Extraordinary Profits**: Be wary of companies reporting unusually high profits, such as Timber Liquidators or many banks during the 2007-2008 financial crisis.
9. **Accounting Manipulation**: Watch for red flags like excessive stock buybacks to inflate Earnings per Share (EPS), excessive loans to

executives, speculative bets on futures (e.g., Enron), frequent one-time charges, or revisions to previous earnings.
10. **Thinly-Traded Stocks**: Avoid stocks with low trading volumes, especially those predominantly owned by a small group of individuals.

The most reliable source for identifying these issues is the company's current financial statements. If something in the statements is unclear, proceed with caution.

Portfolio Management:
To minimize losses, consistently monitor your stock holdings and consider using stop-loss orders to sell before significant value erosion occurs. I recommend maintaining a focused portfolio of around 10 stocks, depending on the time you can dedicate to investing. For example, I hold approximately 10 stocks with larger investments and about 100 smaller positions. Naturally, I spend more time monitoring the 10 core stocks than the rest.

Mergers

Mergers can be beneficial for the involved companies, as they often eliminate redundant functions like payroll administration and overlapping research efforts. Typically, the acquired company experiences a significant appreciation in value. I use a screening process to identify potential acquisition targets, particularly during the "Early Recovery" phase of the market cycle, when undervalued stocks are more prevalent. Large companies often recognize the value in these beaten-down stocks.

Before investing, I conduct an intangible analysis focusing on factors not reflected in financial statements or easily quantifiable. These include:

- Patents and technologies
- Research and development
- Customer base and brand reputation
- Barriers to entry
- Distribution channels
- Competitive landscape
- Product lifecycle
- Management quality
- Pension obligations

For example, in 2003, I invested in a software company later acquired by IBM, more than doubling my investment. During the 2008 cycle, I bought ALU at \$1 and sold it for a \$401 and sold it for a \$403 per share. Patience is key in such scenarios.

However, be cautious: companies targeted for acquisition may manipulate their financial statements to appear more attractive. For instance, a Chinese company misled Caterpillar, resulting in significant losses for the latter. Even large corporations can be deceived. The record-breaking mergers in 2015 may not have been beneficial for the involved companies, as history shows that merging two struggling companies often results in one larger failure.

If we can avoid bankrupting companies and/or companies losing most of their stock values, our portfolio would be improved substantially. Some companies make bad bets and lose, such as Enron betting on energy futures. Here are some signs of bad situations.

- Foreign companies. I do not have too much luck in developing countries, especially their stocks of small companies. They include China, Ireland and Israel to name a few. However, as of 2019, many large Chinese companies are doing very well.
- When the P/E is too good, find out why. If the P/E is too bad, stay away.
- P/PFC should be greater than 0 and less than 50. Even a healthy cash flow may not be able to service the debt if it is huge. Hence, compare the cash flow to Debt/Equity.
- Altman Z-Score. I prefer a score above 3, a sign not to be bankrupt. However, Z-Score is not designed for financial sectors.
- Beneish M-Score. I prefer a score less than -2.22, a sign that the earnings is not manipulated. Both Z-Score and M-Score are available from GuruFocus.com for a fee.
- Z-Score metrics are: "Working Capital / Total Assets" (A), "Retained Earnings / Total Assets" (B), "Earnings Before Interest & Taxes / Total Assets" (C), "Market Cap / Total Liabilities" (D) and "Sales / Total Assets" (E).
  Z-Score = 1.2 A + 1.4 B + 3.3 C + .6 D + E
- Skip companies with bond ratings less than B.
- New government regulations such as taking out the credit for solar panels.
- Extraordinary profits such as Timber Liquidator and many banks in 2007-2008.
- Accounting manipulation: Excessive buying of stocks to boost Earnings per Share, excessive loans to officers, companies betting on futures such as Enron, too many one-time charges and reinstating the previous earnings.

- Skip thinly-traded stocks especially those stocks with the majority owned by a few owners.

The current financial statements could be the best source to look for them. If you read something you do not understand, be cautious.

We need to consistently monitor our stock holdings and sell them before they lose most of their value. I Recommend use stops.

This is why we need to have a focused investment portfolio of about 10 stocks; the number depends on your time available for investing. To illustrate, I have about 10 stocks with larger investments and about 100 stocks in smaller purchases. I would likely spend more time in monitoring the 10 stocks than the rest.

#Filler: Why do poor countries remain poor?

One reason is suffering from repeated natural disasters such as earthquakes and hurricanes.

Even though the U.S. has been spending a lot of resources on Puerto Rico, some politicians want to be kings and queens as they do not care about their citizens.

#Filler: One way to evaluate a company

https://www.youtube.com/watch?v=fGVtypWv04Y

-

9 Avoid bankrupting companies

Avoid the bankrupting companies at all costs. Here are some hints that a company is going bankrupt:

- I had several companies that had lost most of their stock values. It turns out that most were Chinese companies. I did have some losers from Mexico, Israel and Ireland. I believe most were set up to cheat investors. Most if not all had 'rosy' financial statements. Avoid them, especially small companies in emerging countries.
- Many U.S. companies failed due to fraud, poor management, and/or the management betting wrongly. When the CEO is using the company as his own AMT, or having an extravagant lifestyle, watch out. If they promise you a return doubling the current rate of return of the market, listen to your wise mother: there is no free lunch. Despite so many real examples, still fools are born every day, because greed is a human nature.
- Do not follow the 'commentators' on TV. They have their own hidden agenda which usually is not in your interest.
- Many companies fail due to their lack of ability to pay back their loans. Except for specific industries and situations, avoid companies with high debt (Debt/Equity over 50%). Financial institutions and companies that have high debt in order to finance their products for their customers such as utilities are the exceptions.
- I have a screen named Big Losers beating the market by more than 600% in Early Recovery (a phase defined by me). However, some bankrupt companies are not included in the database which is termed as survivor bias. Hence, the actual result is far worse than the 600%. I still use this screen but skip these companies using the following yardsticks.
    - The companies are usually safe with high Free Cash Flow / Equity and high Expected Profit / Stock Price.
    - The following are red flags: low Free Cash Flow / Equity, high Inventory and high Receivable (esp. relative to its Payable), high P/B (over 30) and high net Debt/Equity (over 1 to 3 depending on the industry).
    - P/PFC should be greater than 0 and less than 50. A healthy cash flow may not be able to service the debt if it is too huge. Hence, compare it to Debt/Equity. Compare the cash flow per year to debt obligations per year.
- New government regulations could bankrupt an industry. What would happen when the U.S. takes out the rebates and subsidies of solar

panels? When the U.S. banned solar panels from China, one of my Chinese stocks went bankrupt. Also, the government bailed out bankrupt companies such as Chrysler (that I made a good profit from) and AIG Fannie Mae in 2008.

- Serious lawsuits- Most U.S. companies are required to file this information in their financial reports.
- Obsolete products. Newspapers, retail and similar products would be replaced by the internet. The opposite is new products such as virtual reality products.
- Many companies run out of money during the development phase of the major products. Many are too optimistic in their business plans.
- If you expect the market will recover in 2 years, ensure the company's cash and net income can support their burn rate for at least two more years.
- Many investing sites (most require subscriptions) have safety scores.
- If the Beneish M-Score is greater than -2.22, the company is likely an accounting manipulator.
- Choose companies with Z-Score higher than 3; it is not applicable to financial companies. Both M-Score and Z-Score are available from GuruFocus, a paid subscription. Z-Score does not work for financial institutions.
- Z-Score metrics are: "Working Capital / Total Assets" (A), "Retained Earnings / Total Assets" (B), "Earnings Before Interest & Taxes / Total Assets" (C), "Market Cap / Total Liabilities" (D) and "Sales / Total Assets" (E).
Z-Score = 1.2 A + 1.4 B + 3.3 C +.6 D + E
- Market timing- It does not always work, but it is far better to follow a proven technique than not. It is far safer to take money out of the market when the market is too risky or is plunging. The big losers are companies that provide non-essential products in a downturn.
- Small companies could be risky but very profitable. Typically, they have a low stock price (less than $5), small market cap (less than 50 M), low sales (less than $25 M) and low institutional ownership (less than 5%).
- Avoid companies when their own bond ratings are not equal to AAA or AA (www.moodys.com).
- The fall of a sector such as oil in 2015 could drive the related companies, or even a country to the brink of bankruptcy.

Investing is risky to start with. However, investing especially in stocks has been proven to be the best vehicle to beat inflation.

An example from a guru on Micron

On 5/22/2023, I have been looking for info on shorting MU (Micron). There was a YouTube article on MU with a good decent way to evaluate this stock and is quite appropriate for most other stocks too.

The web site: https://www.youtube.com/watch?v=X1W_qVal1ik

I agree you should read the Form 10-K for the potential stocks to trade. It is quite hard to get the data for the last 9 years, and data for the last five years are appropriate for me. His basic metrics are:

Metric	9-Yr Avg,	Current Yr[1]	Finviz
Revenue Growth	8%	-53%	Sales Q/Q
Earnings (EBITDA) Growth	15%	-206%	EPS Q/Q
Strong Free Cash	13%	N/A	P/FCF
Debt / EBITDA <3X	1.0X	0.26	Debt / EQ
Well Priced (EV/EBITDA)[2]	5.7X	7.11	
		49	P/E
		110	Forward P/E

[1] Most are from Finviz and EV/EBITDA is from Yahoo!Finance.
[2] It is similar to P/E except considering many metrics such as taxes.

The only consideration is MU's second (could be the first depending on how you link Hong Kong and other Asian countries) is China. China is developing their own memory chips. The politics between the US and China should also be considered, especially when China is the primary customer for most U.S. chip companies.

From the P/E, Forward P/E and Sales Q/Q and EPS Q/Q, I would consider more to short this short than buying it.

Links
After I wrote this article, China bans Micron due to "national security", which is the same argument for banning Huawei. Micron: https://www.youtube.com/watch?v=dy9vhwXN1SY

#Filler: G7
G7 in 2023 without China does not make any sense., so is 'de-risk'. These nations finally realized they could not decouple with China without hurting themselves. China is #1 in GDP (adjusted to purchase power) and #1 in global trade.

We are repeating history: bad mouthing China for not opening ports for trades, importing opium as a nation, using force to semi colonize China and stealing all the silver.

Section III: Selling stocks

We sell stocks when the reasons to own no longer apply by a good margin. In most cases, the sell decision should be based on data more than one quarter.

I sold ALU when it gained 40% in a few weeks' time. It gained more than 300% later when it was acquired. For rising stocks, we should adjust the stop orders. Do a mental stop order instead of just a stop order to avoid flash crashes. When the price of a stock purchased below a specified order, you place a market order to sell it. Use trailing stops for appreciated stocks.

10 When to sell a stock

We sell stocks when the reasons for owning them no longer apply by a significant margin. In most cases, the decision to sell should be based on data spanning more than one quarter.

For example, I sold ALU after it gained 40% in a few weeks, only to see it rise over 300% later when it was acquired. For rising stocks, it's wise to adjust stop orders. Consider using mental stop orders instead of formal stop orders to avoid being caught in flash crashes. A mental stop order involves setting a price threshold in your mind and selling the stock if it falls below that level. For appreciated stocks, trailing stops can be effective.

Reasons to Sell a Stock
There are numerous reasons to sell a stock, which can be categorized as follows:

Personal Reasons
1. **Meeting Targets/Objectives**:
   Sell when your investment goals are met. This could be a 10% gain in a short-term swing trade, a specific return (e.g., x%) within 4 months for a short-term trade, or a y% gain after a year for long-term investments. Define x and y based on your risk tolerance and trading frequency.

   For example, during the August 2015 market correction, I bought four stocks in one day and placed sell orders at 10% above my purchase price. I sold one stock within a day and another within a month. This strategy works sometimes, but not always.

Stay disciplined and avoid second-guessing your decisions. If the market is volatile, consider using a higher percentage threshold for your sell orders.

2. **Realizing a Mistake**:
   Acknowledge when you've made a mistake, whether due to poor analysis, bad data, unexpected fraud, lawsuits, or unforeseeable events. It's better to exit with a small loss than to hold on and risk a larger one. I use a 25% loss threshold for long-term strategies and a 10% (or less) threshold for short-term strategies.

   Determine whether the loss is due to a mistake or simply bad luck. If it's a mistake, learn from it. Diversification helps ensure that one bad loss doesn't significantly impact your portfolio. Stop-loss orders are useful, except during flash crashes.

3. **Overexposure to a Sector**:
   If you hold too many stocks in the same sector, consider selling some to improve diversification. However, if the sector is performing well, you may want to overweight it temporarily at the expense of diversification. Set limits on how many sectors you hold.

4. **Need for Cash**:
   Sell stocks if you need cash for living expenses or other financial obligations.

5. **Tax Considerations**:
   Selling losers can help reduce your tax burden, but tax considerations should not be the primary reason for selling. Take advantage of favorable tax treatment for long-term capital gains. Sell losers within the short-term limit (currently one year) and sell winners after 365 days. Check current tax laws for specifics.

   You can also harvest tax losses by selling losers and buying back similar stocks (or the same stock after 31 days to avoid wash sale rules).

6. **Lower Tax Opportunities**:
   In some cases, you can pay minimal federal income taxes on long-term capital gains if your income falls below a specific tax bracket

(15% as of 2015). Check current tax laws and evaluate whether selling winners for a potential buyback makes sense.

Market Timing

7. **Market or Sector Plunge**:
   Sell stocks or reduce exposure to a sector if the market or sector experiences a significant downturn. During temporary peaks, evaluate which stocks to sell based on fundamentals to raise cash for future buying opportunities.

Deteriorating Fundamentals

8. **Better Opportunities**:
   If other stocks offer better appreciation potential, consider replacing underperforming stocks in your portfolio. While this may incur brokerage fees and taxes, it can improve the overall quality and growth potential of your portfolio.

9. **Declining Fundamentals**:
   Sell a stock if the company's fundamentals deteriorate. Compare the current fundamentals (e.g., P/E ratio, earnings growth, debt/equity ratio) to those at the time of purchase. For example, Apple's fundamentals declined between 2013 and 2015, making it a good candidate for selling.

   If a stock has peaked and started to decline, or is heading toward bankruptcy, sell it quickly.

Warning Signs of Deteriorating Fundamentals

Evaluate your stocks at least every six months and monitor daily news using tools like Seeking Alpha's portfolio function. Key warning signs include:

- **Decreasing Cash Flow**: While not a strong predictor of appreciation, declining cash flow can indicate survival risks. Cash flow is hard to manipulate.
- **Lawsuits**: Assess the seriousness of any new or pending lawsuits. Minor lawsuits can often be ignored.
- **Sales Drop**: A significant drop in sales is a red flag, though seasonal fluctuations should be considered.
- **Management Issues**: Deteriorating return on equity (ROE) or extravagant CEO behavior (e.g., excessive loans to executives) can signal trouble.

- **Operational Problems**: Product recalls, stolen trade secrets, or data breaches (e.g., Boeing's 737 MAX issues) are serious concerns.
- **Competitive Threats**: A successful competitor product or loss of market share can harm a company's prospects.
- **Insider Selling**: Heavy insider selling, especially by multiple executives, is a warning sign.
- **Regulatory Scrutiny**: Attention from the SEC or other government agencies usually indicates problems.
- **Accounting Red Flags**: Deceptive practices, increasing receivables or inventory, frequent earnings restatements, or invalid "one-time charges" are concerning.
- **Market Plunge**: A broad market downturn can signal trouble for individual stocks.

Hints that the fundamentals are degrading

Evaluate the stocks you own at least every 6 months and check their daily news at least once a week that can be easily done using Seeking Alpha's portfolio function.

- The cash flow is decreasing fast. Cash flow is not a particularly good predictive indicator for appreciation, but a good indicator on whether the company will survive. This metric is very hard to manipulate.
- A new or pending lawsuit. Check out how serious the lawsuit is and be aware that a minor lawsuit can be ignored. Companies always sue against each other.
- A big drop in sales. Do not be alarmed when a new product, or a new drug is going to replace a major product. Compare sales to the same quarter of prior year to avoid seasonal fluctuations (Q-to-Q info I available from Finviz.com).
- Management deteriorates- One hint is the deteriorating ROE from the last quarter.
- The extravagant lifestyle of the CEO and the many easy loans to officers.
- Poor operations. They include recalls of products such as the GM recall on ignition switches, product secrets being stolen and customers' credit card info being stolen. Boeing's 747-Max is a warning call.
- A successful product from the competitor, or the current product is losing its market share, or becoming a low-profit commodity.

- Insiders and/or institutional investors are dumping the companies' stocks far more than the averages (2% for me) especially in heavy volumes and by more than one insider. Info is available from Finviz.

    - Have more than one insider dumping a lot of the stock within a month and no insider purchase in that month.
    Have more than one insider decrease their holdings by more than 10%.
    - When the SEC or any government agency pays attention to a company, it usually means bad news.
    - Deceptive accounting practices have been discovered.
    - Increasing receivable and/or inventory at an alarming rate.
    - Earnings have been restated too many times.
    - Short percentage is increasing fast – someone found something wrong with the company.
    - The invalidity of 'one-time charges'.
    - Abnormal return rate of the company's pension fund comparing to the average of the companies in the same sector.
    - Too many and too costly reconstructing charges.
    - The stock price does not move up with good news. It shows the price has peaked.
    - The accumulation amount is far less than the sold amount. When the stock price is up, the accumulation is less than the sold stocks when the stock price was down the last time. It indicates that no more accumulation is ahead and hence the stock will be down most likely.

Afterthoughts

- Another article on this topic.
  http://buzz.money.cnn.com/2013/04/05/stocks-sell/
  An article from Investopedia. Nothing new but it is worth having the same second opinion.
  http://www.investopedia.com/financial-edge/0412/5-tips-on-when-to-sell-your-stock.aspx

- It also depends on your strategies. I sell most of my stocks in my momentum portfolio within a month. At least one strategy I know of does not keep any stock during the peak stage of the market cycle – the easiest time to make money but also the riskiest time.

If you use charts for trading, sell the stocks that are below your moving averages or other technical analysis indicators. Personally, I do not use charts for making sell decisions due to my limited time.

- Sell when the company is heading into bankruptcy as described before. The red flags are: 1. Negative cash flow. 2. Heavy insiders dumping the stocks. 3. Pending major lawsuit. 4. Fraud from the management.
- Risky periods for a stock.
  Earnings announcement (4 times a year), settling a major lawsuit and/or during an FDA event in approving a drug are risky periods for a stock. A fluctuation more than 5% in either direction is normal. Some use options to buy insurance. Most ignore it. For the majority of the time, heavy insider purchase is a good indicator. There are rumors (or educated guesses) on earnings before their announcements. Zacks is supposed to be a good subscription for earnings estimates.

Selling a winner

Let your profits rise while protecting them. For example, Tesla quadrupled in value in six months, and similar gains have been seen with Amazon and Yelp. If you're unsure what to do, consider these strategies:

- Sell half of your position.
- Sell an amount equal to your initial investment.
- Use trailing stops to lock in gains. I did not do this when my GameStop stock appreciated by 300% and it turned out for far more appreciation. Guilty as charged.

You do not want to sell these rocket stocks even if their fundamentals do not make sense. Buffett does not touch these rocket stocks and he usually misses these big gains. However, many of these rocket stocks such as BRRY (Blackberry) will eventually fall losing most of their value. I bet the institutional investors move the market in either direction and usually they read the same analysts' reports. You profit as a contrarian if you have a good reason to act against the herd.

The following example uses a 10% trailing stop – mine is a little different from the official trailing stop described in the link section. Set the stop at 10% of the current price (i.e., 10% less than the current price), not the purchase price. You need to change the stop when the price rises but do not change it when the price falls. Review your stops every month or more frequently if time allows.

To illustrate, when the stock price rises to 100, set the stop at 90. When the stock price falls to 90, sell the stock at the market price. When the stock price rises to 200, change the stop price at 180.

The stop should also be set according to how volatile the stock is. Some stocks are more volatile than others. Most charts show the resistance line. This line assumes the stock price should not fall below this line in normal fluctuations. Set the stop at 2% below this line so your stock will not be stopped out in theory.

Do not stop orders on stocks with low volumes as they can be manipulated, especially after hours. In this case, you just place market orders to sell them.

To avoid flash crashes, do not place stop orders. Instead, do it mentally (mental stop is my term). When you see that the stock falls below your stop with no sign of a flash crash, sell the stock using a market order.

Of course, there is no bullet-proof scheme. This one should work in the long run. This is my suggestion only, so examine whether it works for you. Small cap and/or stocks with small average volumes fluctuate more.

Examples
I have too many bad examples of selling the stocks too early and sometimes holding them too long.

I made over 40% in a few weeks on ALU, but it went up more than 300% in the next two years. It was acquired in early 2016 by Nokia paying a good premium. I was right that ALU had a lot of valuable patents and I was wrong to dump it when I found out Cisco did not have any intention to acquire it – a big mistake by Cisco and the U.S.

FOSL is another example to teach us to use mental stop loss. FOSL was priced at $33.70 on 1/4/2010. Its fundamentals were just fine with an expected E/P (expected earnings yield) at 6% but decreasing earnings. It gained 115% later in 2010 - not expected.

On 1/3/2011, the expected E/P was still at around 6% and improving earnings. It gained 9% for the year – a little disappointing.

On 1/3/2012, the expected E/P was 7% and a huge earnings growth. Now, we expected a better performance for the year and it did by gaining 20%.

On 1/3/2013, the expected E/P was about 6% and the earnings gain was respectable. It gained 28% to $121. So far, so good.

On 1/2/2014, the E/P and the earnings growth were about the same as in 1/3/2013. However, it lost 7% for the year while SPY (an ETF simulating the market) gained 12%. There was no warning. Did the institutional investors lose the interest of this stock?

On 1/2/2015, the E/P was 7% and the earnings growth was about the same as the previous year. It lost 69% (vs. SPY's 0% return with dividends)!

From 1/4/2010 to 1/3/2016, the annualized return of FOSL is 0% (vs. SPY's 13%). Actually, after dividends, SPY should have an annualized return of about 15%. The lessons gained here are:

- Fundamentals (using EP and earnings growth in this example) may not always work. Otherwise, 2015 should have the same gain as 2014.
- The rosy outlook of the stock may be priced in already. When the outlook fails to materialize, the stock tanks.

Links: Fidelity Video: Trailing Stop Loss. 2 3
https://www.fidelity.com/learning-center/trading/trailing-stops-video
https://www.youtube.com/watch?v=l7EHWyOrfu4

https://www.investopedia.com/terms/t/trailingstop.asp

11   Examples of overpriced stocks

In 2011, Netflix, LinkedIn, and Facebook were widely considered overvalued. Here's how to assess whether a stock is overpriced:

- **Reward/Risk Ratio**: If a stock has a 30% chance of rising and a 50% chance of falling, it's overvalued by 20%.
- **P/E Ratio**: Compare the current P/E to its five-year average. For example, if Netflix's P/E was 60 compared to a five-year average of 30, it was overvalued by 100%.
- **Momentum Plays**: Buying high and selling higher can work with stop-loss orders, but I prefer buying low and selling high.

More notes:
- The 'E' in P/E can be either expected (same as forward) earnings or based on the last 12 months (same as trailing or historical). It has been proven that the 'expected' is a better indicator than the 'historical'. AAII demonstrated this by comparing the performances of the expected PEG screen and the historical PEG screens over a long period of time.
- Fools who invested in the high P/E stocks and did not do their due diligence in 2000 had parted with their money fast. I could not convince my friends to take money off their internet stocks. It is similar to asking the lottery winners not to buy lottery tickets.
- Buying an expensive stock is like over paying for a hot dog cart in NYC for $100,000. The buyer will sell many hot dogs, but the rate of return of the investment will be minimal, and it will never recover the initial investment. "Buy high and sell higher" is a momentum play. It works if it is played with stops, but I prefer to "Buy low and sell high".
- Following a decent and proven investing strategy consistently should lead to success through persistence and adjustments. In the long term, a bad strategy always loses money.
- When the market favors growth / momentum (vs. value), it is OK to buy stocks with prices higher than the intrinsic values by a small percentage. The tide is on your side. However, be attentive to any indication that the market is changing direction.
- NFLX has an average annual return rate of 177% vs. SPY's 14% from 1/3/2011 to 1/3/2020 without considering dividends. Hence, a trailing stop would do the job for the rocket stock.

12 Should you hold stocks forever?

There are many examples that you should hold onto some stocks forever such as Apple, Netflix, Amazon and Google. Interestingly there are more opposite examples such as AIG and Lehman Brothers. Hence, there is no right or wrong answer. Always continually monitor your stock holdings and the sectors they are in.

Even IBM could suffer its dips when it does not react to its market and / or make the wrong strategic decision. The Washington Post has to react to the free articles from the internet.

I have set up guidelines on when to sell. One selling indicator is when those shares lose over 25%. We have to admit that we have made a mistake, or the fundamentals of the stock have changed. Evaluate the fundamentals of the purchased stocks periodically.

Boston Chicken is one of my many big losers. I could use the money I lost to have chicken dinner every night for the rest of my life! This kind of thinking is not healthy. I decided not to buy any restaurant stock again and that is not rational either. It is an art to sell a loser, or wait for its potential recovery. From my experiences, it is better to sell the loser.

If you have a historical database, you can test out your strategy on when to sell and adjust the sell criteria accordingly. Do not try to fit data to your strategy.

Never fall in love with a stock and never be afraid to buy back a sold stock. Use fundamental metrics for making a buy/sell decision.

Taxes and diversification

Tax should not be a major consideration in selling a stock. However, you may postpone selling losers in December if your tax rate (so your tax loss value) will be better next year. If you need to offset short-term capital gains, sell some losers eligible for short-term capital losses. Postpone selling a winner to a month or so, if it can be eligible for long-term capital gain.

When your stock appreciates many, many times and you're close to your life expectancy age, hold it and the cost basis will step up to the day you pass away. Instruct your heirs to buy a newspaper to get the prices of your stocks you hold or instruct your heirs to inform your broker on the unavoidable day. Today's tax law provides a range of days around the date of death; check the current tax laws.

Instead of selling a stock with huge gain, consider options: 1. give it to your children who have lower tax brackets, 2. give it to charity, and 3. save it for your estate.

When the market is plunging as detected by market timing techniques, sell most of your holdings. Be warned that market timing does not always work.

No stock is sacred

That's why we need to churn the portfolio by replacing the bad stocks with better ones. More examples of failing companies that had been very promising at one time:

- The bankrupt companies due to competition: Circuit City (due to BestBuy) and BlockBuster (due to Netflix).
- The failing internet companies in 2000 and the financial institutions in 2008.
- HP when PCs, servers and printers are no longer kings.
- BestBuy killed Circuit City and then it is being eaten alive by Amazon, Walmart, Costco and BJ. However, it recovered in 2014.
- Many retailers went bankrupt. I lost count of so many of the retailers in the Boston area alone.

Filler: Dream high

I heard this. The girl wanted to be a president when she grew up. She went to a circus and she said she wanted to be a clown. Her wise father said, "You can be a president and a clown at the same time". Reality?

Should we modify the Constitution to ban our presidents from tweeting especially in private places?

It is a laughing stock for injecting disinfectants to cure the virus. At least we fix the racial discrimination when everyone has been bleached.

I am neutral in politics. I complained a lot about Obama.

13   Monitor your traded stocks

After buying or shorting a stock, actively monitor its performance and any new developments. Here's how:

1. **Use Stop Orders**: Protect your portfolio with stop or trailing stop orders, especially for rising stocks.
2. **Stay Informed**: Read articles about your stocks using platforms like Finviz, Seeking Alpha, or MarketWatch.
3. **Organize Watchlists**: Create multiple watchlists for different strategies (e.g., long-term value stocks vs. short-term momentum stocks).
4. **Track Performance**: Monitor your stocks' performance and sector diversification to avoid overexposure.

More notes:

- Categorize the stocks by sectors, and check the performances of these sectors.
- Keep track of the holding days for better tax treatments of long-term capital gains in taxable accounts. You may sell short=term losers in taxable accounts.
- To generate income, use covered calls.
- Market timing and sector timing.

Final Thoughts

Investing is both an art and a science. While no strategy is foolproof, staying disciplined, informed, and adaptable can help you navigate the market's ups and downs. Regularly review your portfolio, learn from your mistakes, and don't fall in love with any stock.

Section IV: Other sources

Investing, like health, requires discipline, research, and action. Use tools like Seeking Alpha and Fidelity to stay informed, but always be cautious of market noise and overhyped strategies. Diversify your portfolio, monitor market conditions, and apply what you learn to make better investment decisions.

14 Lessons from a popular book?

I recently read a popular book on how to make money in the stock market. While the strategies worked for the author, they may not work for you. Here's why:

- **Overuse of Strategies**: The book has been read by tens of thousands of people. When a strategy becomes widely adopted, it often loses its effectiveness. If you follow the same approach, you'll likely end up with the same stocks as everyone else, reducing your chances of outperforming the market.
- **Buffett's Philosophy**: The book is based on Warren Buffett's investment philosophy. While some of Buffett's strategies work, others don't, and some opportunities are inaccessible to retail investors. Given Buffett's mediocre returns in recent years, blindly following his approach might not be the best use of your time and money.
- **Lack of Diversification**: The book doesn't emphasize diversification, which is crucial for managing risk. Even good stocks can lose half their value unexpectedly. If you have $50,000 or less, consider holding three stocks across different sectors, with one being an ETF.
- **Ignoring Market Timing**: The book doesn't address market timing, which can be critical during market crashes. Without considering market conditions, you could lose significant value in your portfolio.
- **Value Traps**: The book suggests finding stocks at a 50% discount, but such opportunities are rare in a bullish market. When you do find them, be cautious—there's usually a reason for the steep discount. These opportunities are more common during market recoveries.
- **Margin of Safety**: The concept of a "margin of safety" is often highlighted, but my limited testing shows it's not a reliable predictor of stock performance.

- **Reading Annual Reports**: The book emphasizes reading annual reports, which can be useful. Here's a helpful video on how to do it: How to Read Annual Reports.

15 Using Seeking Alpha effectivley

Seeking Alpha is a valuable resource for investors. Here's how to make the most of it:

- **Portfolio Function**: Use the portfolio feature to track stocks you own or are interested in. You'll receive alerts for news and articles related to those stocks. This function is similar to Finviz and some broker platforms, though smaller stocks may not be covered.

- **Quality Articles**: The site offers many insightful articles. Focus on those written by authors you follow, especially if their strategies align with yours (e.g., dividend investing).

- **Market Insights**: The "Market Performance via ETFs" section shows trending sectors, while "Wall Street Breakfast" provides a daily summary of market events. These tools are useful for sector rotation and identifying momentum stocks.

- **Watch Out for Pitfalls**:
    - **Promotions**: Seeking Alpha is a business, so some content is promotional. Be discerning about what applies to you.
    - **Pump and Dump Schemes**: Be cautious with reviews of small or low-volume stocks. For example, one short-seller made negative comments about EBIX, a stock I owned, but it gained 150% in a year.

Filler

Here is a good article: 60 Value Resources.
http://seekingalpha.com/article/3485446-60-best-value-investing-resources-youd-be-crazy-to-miss

16 Making sense of health and investing

I read Dr. Campbell's *The* China Study, which advocates a whole-food, plant-based diet to prevent diseases like heart disease and cancer. While this may seem unrelated to investing, there are striking parallels between the two disciplines:

- **Statistics**: Just as a plant-based diet leads to better health outcomes over time, a well-tested investment strategy with more winners than losers will outperform the market in the long run. Statistics don't lie.
- **Market Noise**: The health industry is influenced by big corporations like meat producers and fast-food chains, much like how stock promotions and TV business programs are driven by advertisers. Always do your own research.
- **Action Matters**: Many people read books but fail to apply the lessons. I recommend paper trading to practice what you learn from investment books.

Dr. Campbell's book can make you healthier, and my insights aim to make you a better investor.

17 Leveraging Fidelity's Research Tools

Fidelity offers extensive research tools for free, even without an account balance. Here's how to use them effectively:

- **Equity Summary Score**: This score has proven useful. I prefer buying stocks with a score of 8 or higher for long-term holds and shorting those with a score of 4 or lower. However, use caution—scores can sometimes be misleading. For example, in June 2020, ZM and SHOP had high scores despite poor long-term metrics.
- **P/E Ratios**:
    - **5-Year Average**: Compare a stock's current P/E to its 5-year average to identify bargains. Be cautious if the P/E is zero or negative. I prefer using forward P/E (estimated earnings).
    - **Industry Average**: Compare a company's P/E to its industry average for better context.
- **Environmental, Social & Governance (ESG)**: Useful for socially conscious investors.
- **Research Reports**: Access reports under the "Analyst Opinions and Reports" tab. Focus on those with high StarMine Relative Accuracy. Experienced investors should also review Form 10-Q and balance sheets.

- **Momentum Analysis**: Available under the "Technical Sentiment" tab, this tool compares short-term, mid-term, and long-term momentum to indicators like SMA-20, SMA-50, SMA-200, and RSI(14).
- **Top-Down Approach**: When the market is up, select the best stocks in the best sectors or industries using the "Comparisons" tab.

An example

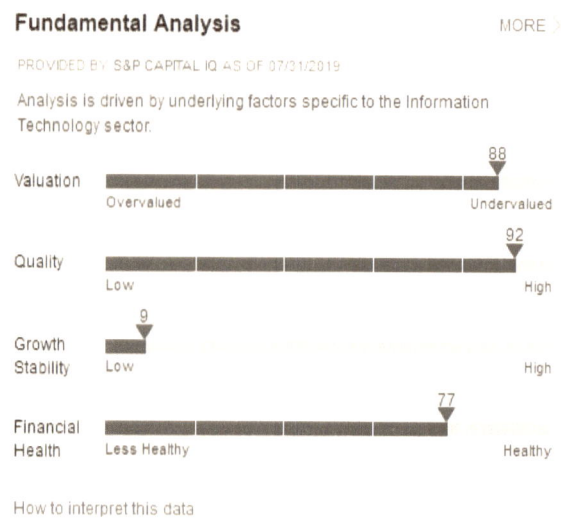

Most stock research sites group the related metrics, weigh them and have a score. The following is my guess only and over-simplified. Basically, they should have 3 scores: Valuation (for long-term trades), Momentum (for short-term trades) and Combined (Valuation + Momentum). Safety or Financial Health is whether the stock is safe (i.e., the chance to go bankrupt).

Valuation. Forward P/E. Insider Transactions.
Quality. ROI, P/E and Debt/Equity.
Growth Stability. Q-Q Earnings.
Financial Health. Debt/Equity. Earnings.

Links
Platform tutorial: https://www.youtube.com/watch?v=fxE5577LaxE
Fidelity index funds: https://www.youtube.com/watch?v=xdEunmLrhb4
Investing tips: https://www.youtube.com/watch?v=twMNKMhL_KY

Section IV: Finding stocks

18 Where the websites are

- **Free and simple screen sites**

    They are described in this article or type the following
    http://stocks.about.com/od/researchtools/a/071909screenlist.htm

    o   Yahoo!Finance.
        Click here or type
        http://screener.finance.yahoo.com/stocks.html

    o   Finviz.
        Click here or type
        http://Finviz.com/screener.ashx

        How to scan using Finviz (YouTube).
        https://www.YouTube.com/watch?v=aQ_0FTg9Cfw

        Screening using technical indicators (particularly useful for momentum stocks).
        https://www.YouTube.com/watch?v=RZRP2NeSX0s

    o   Your broker.
        Fidelity's screens are more sophisticated than most.

    o   More options: Google, CNBC.com and Moringstar.com.

    Here is a list.
    http://stocks.about.com/od/researchtools/a/071909screenlist.htm

- **Sophisticated screens (usually not free)**

    Most of them are more complicated and need time to learn. Both VectorVest and Stock123 provide historical databases for backtesting your screens. Zacks has an earnings revision database at extra cost. GuruFocus has an easy-to-use but powerful screen function.

AAII provides screened stocks from various screens in its low-priced subscription. Both AAII and Value Line take care of some specific industries, but they provide no historical database at least for regular subscriptions. AAII provides historical performance summaries of their screens included in its subscription.

Afterthoughts

Here are the links to screens provided by MarketWatch and NASDAQ.
http://www.marketwatch.com/tools/stockre...
http://www.nasdaq.com/reference/stock-sc...

How to find quality stocks.
http://seekingalpha.com/article/2381395-how-to-identify-quality-stocks-and-is-there-really-alpha-to-be-had

Filler
"Sell in May" could be a self-fulfilled prophecy. I prefer to sell on April 1 and come back on Oct. 15 to avoid the herd.

19   Fidelity

Fidelity offers a strong screen function. The most unique feature is incorporating its Equity Summary Score (used to be Analyst's Opinion) and some outside researches such as Zacks and Ford.

From the main menu, select "News and Research", "Screen and Filter" and then "Start a screen".

The following example selects stocks with the following criteria: Security Price (2 to 250), Market Cap. (300 and above), Equity Summary Score (8 and above), Zacks (Strongest) and Ford (Strongest).

It displays the 10 stocks. Research each stock. Read the News about each stock. You may want to use Finviz.com, Yahoo!Finance and other sources to double check.

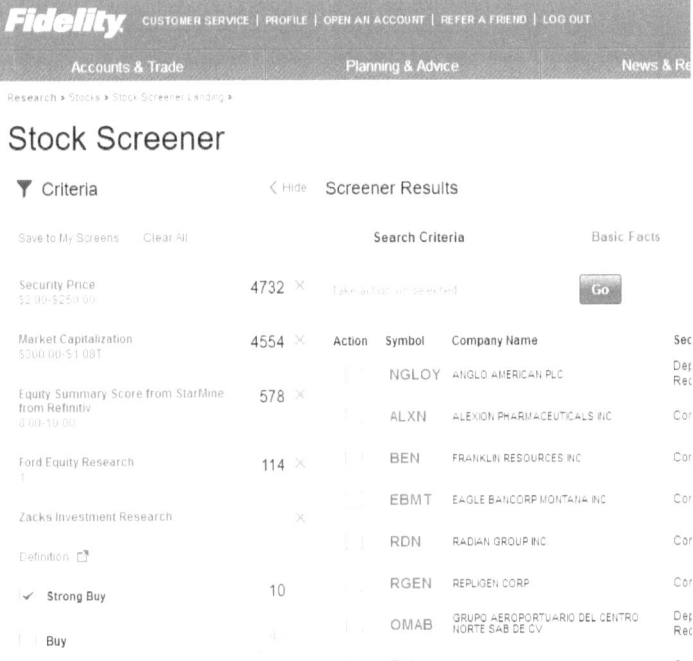

The following describes some of the features.

- Equity Summary Score. It is one of the major metrics I use in my proprietary scoring systems. They are not available to many small stocks. From my limited database in 7/2015 and for short durations, the results are:

Short Term: (7% return for the average)

Metric	Parm. 1	No. of Stocks	%	Parm. 2	No.	%	Predictability
Fidelity Analyst	Buy	150	10%	Sell	279	3%	Good

Long Term: (8% return for the average)

Metric	Parm. 1	No. of Stocks	%	Parm. 2	No.	%	Predictability
Fidelity Analyst	Buy	90	17%	Sell	208	4%	Good

It has its own limits, but they are very minor to me.

First, it does not have a historical database for verifying the screen performance such as the return after a year. However, I do not know any site that provides this function free. To work around this, I save the results in a spread sheet and update the performance.

Secondly, it does not provide many other filter criteria that can be found in other systems such as technical indicators or insider transactions found in Finviz.com. I use other sites for further evaluation.

Most investors should find that this screening is a very good tool and very easy to use.

20   Finviz.com screener

You should use fundamental metrics for fundamental stocks, growth metrics for growth stocks, momentum metrics for momentum stocks, or a combination. Basically you want to keep the fundamental stocks longer so the market would realize their values.

Finviz.com provides a screening function incorporating both fundamental and technical metrics and is one of the best free sites. Bring up Finviz.com in your browser and select screener. You have 4 tabs: Descriptive, Fundamental, Technical and All. It has the following features:

- The criteria specified can be saved but the number is limited.
- The searched stocks can be saved in a portfolio (for paper trading and performance monitoring).
- Technical indicators.
- For an extra fee, you can have a historical database. This would help you to test your strategies. The historical database is quite limited for some technical parameters only.
- Some advanced technical indicators work well especially useful in momentum trading.
- Use technical patterns. My favorites are Head and Shoulder and Double Bottoms (Peaks).
- Combine fundamental metrics and technical metrics to narrow down your selection.
- Combine fundamental metrics and technical metrics to narrow down your selection.
- Add Insider Trans (> 5% for me), Short Squeeze (> 20%), etc. for specific purposes.
- Candlesticks is hard to master. You need to read a book dedicated to it.

http://www.investopedia.com/terms/c/candlestick.asp
https://www.youtube.com/watch?v=FsqoV1aVrUc&list=WL&index=56

Finviz's screener lacks the following features:

- Stocks with prices trending up in the last several weeks (such as increasing X% in the previous week).

- Using exponential moving averages that supposedly have better predictive power than simple moving averages for momentum investing.
- Selecting ranges such as selecting all three major exchanges and market cap ranges.
- P/E for an ETF. It can be obtained from other sources such as ETFdb.com.
- When the earnings (E) is negative, you may have the wrong values for P/E and the metrics using E. For example, if you want stocks with P/E less than 20, the screener returns you stocks with negative earnings.
- Combine fundamental metrics and technical metrics to narrow down your selection.

All of these missing features can be worked around. The paid version may provide better functions.

Links:

Investopedia.
http://www.investopedia.com/university/features-of-Finviz-elite/other-chart-features.asp

How to scan using Finviz (YouTube).
https://www.YouTube.com/watch?v=aQ_0FTg9Cfw
https://www.youtube.com/watch?v=tHtovnCY6uY&list=WL&index=96
(Recommended)

Finviz's screener tutorial.
https://www.youtube.com/watch?v=glMtwB7OVf4&list=WL&index=56

Swing trading
https://www.youtube.com/watch?v=M8sNMhPJINU&list=WL&index=55

Screening using technical indicators (YouTube).
https://www.YouTube.com/watch?v=RZRP2NeSX0s

21 Common parameters

Different styles of investing use different parameters for screening stocks. Here is my suggested parameters in using Finviz.com. Vary them to your risk tolerance and market conditions. Finviz.com is not complete in all functions, but it could the best free screener that incorporates both the fundamental and the technical criteria. The first table is for Value and the next one for Growth. The last one is for finding stocks that the institutional investors are trading.

Screening value stocks

Value Screens	Common	Penny	Micro Cap	Dividend
General				
Market Cap (M)	>500 M	<50 M	50 -200 M	+Mid(>2B)
Price	>5	< 5	1-15	>5
In all 3 Exchanges	In	Not In	Most are In	In
Avg. Volume	>100K	>5K	>10K	>100K
Country	USA	USA	USA	USA
Dividend%				>3%
Float Short	<10%	<10%	<10%	<10%
Analyst Rec	Buy or +	Buy or + if avail.	Buy or +	Buy or +
Fundamental				
Forward P/E	<20	<20	<20	<25
ROE	>10	>10	>5	>15
QQ earning	>0			>0
QQ sales	>0			>0
PEG	<1	<1	<1	<1.2
Payout%				20-50%
P/S	<10	<10	<10	<10
Technical				
Price above 200 SMA	Yes	Yes	Yes	Yes
RSI(14)	< 70	< 70	< 70	< 70

There may be no analysts or very few following penny stocks and micro-cap stocks. QQ is quarter to quarter.

Screening Growth Stocks

Growth Screen	Common	Technical	Momentum
General			
Market Cap (M)	>50	> 1,000	>500
Price	>1	>10	>5
Exchanges (Major 3)	In	In	In
Avg. Volume	>50K	>200K	>100K
Fundamental			
Forward P/E	<30	<30	<30
Return of Equity	>5	>0	>0
QQ earning	>10%	>15%	>20%
QQ sales	>5%	> 5%	>10%
PEG	<1	<1	<1
Analyst recs.	Buy or +		
Technical			
Price above 200 SMA	Yes	Yes	
50 SMA	Yes	Yes	Yes
RSI	< 75	< 75	

Short-term trends are important for momentum stocks.

Explanation

The above are suggestions only. Adjust them to your personal preferences and risk tolerance.

- Finviz screener lacks ranges, such as market cap and multiple of exchanges. Most Finviz's parameters do not have a range option such as Exchanges, so you need to run the screen three times, one for each of the three major exchanges.

- Average Volume. When the price of the stock is less than $3, double the average volume requirement. In most cases, 10K is quite acceptable to me. When the volume is small, you may have to pay more (a.k.a. spread) to trade.

- There are many fundamental metrics such as Debt/Equity and Price/Free Cash Flow that are not included here, but they should be included in your further evaluation. Each industry sector has different thresholds. For example, the P/S is very different for a supermarket rather than a high-tech company. Compare the company to the average value of the companies in the same sector. Many sites including GuruFocus.com and Fidelity.com have the average values displayed.

- For momentum stock, you can ignore most of the fundamentals and concentrate on the price trend such as SMA-20 (Simple Moving Average for the last 20 trade sessions) and SMA-50. The higher the percent, the higher it is away from its own average. You do not want to hold momentum stocks too long (max. 3 months unless the momentum is still uptrend); personally my max. is 1 month.

- For growth stocks, ensure the PEG (P/E growth), quarter-to-quarter earnings and quarter-to-quarter sales are above the averages in its own sector and/or the market.

- Technical analysis favors large cap stocks with large volumes. I prefer stocks with positive earnings and they are fundamentally sound.

- When the SMA-20, SMA-50 and SMA-200 are all positive, they should be in an uptrend.

- RSI(14) indicates whether the stock is oversold (>65) or under bought (<30). The range is my suggestion only.

- You may want to check out your strategies using a virtual account from your broker.

A general guideline for Institutional investors

Criteria	Value
Description	
Relative Volume	Over 2 M
Country	USA usually
Institution Ownership	Over 50%
Technical	
SMA-200	>10%
Volatility	Week – Over 3%
RSI(14)	>40%

Fundamental	
Market Cap	>1B
ROE	>10%

- Again, these are my suggested metrics. I prefer USA companies and many are global companies. If you use foreign countries, ensure they are larger companies and/or in countries that have regulations similar to our SEC's.
- For value investors, select Forward P/E less than 20 (25 for high-tech companies) and their Earnings are positive.
- Check out how many analysts are following the stocks that you are interested in.

To illustrate, I find 12 stocks. I narrow them down to 3. First, I skip all stocks that already have had more than 10% rise recently. They may have risen too high already.

Select profitable stocks with forward P/E less than 25. "Debt/Equity" is less than .5 (50%). Then, ROI is higher than 25%. Stop when you have reached the optimal number of stocks (3 for me in this example).

If you find too many stocks, tighten the criteria and vice versa. Save the criteria and the selected stocks in a portfolio for paper trading.

Filler: Irresponsible is my best defense

I told my date that I would not be responsible after the second drink due to the lack of an enzyme.

#Filler:
Many farmers have gone bankrupted as the banks do not loan them money to buy seeds for the next year. Our storage is over-flowed. Soybeans and pork are rotting. Trump's subsidies will not help a lot for farms who have small farms and he is going to lose all the votes from these farm states.

Overview of Finviz.com

This article is written by DeepSeek (AI).

Finviz.com (short for Financial Visualizations) is a powerful and user-friendly financial visualization tool that provides investors with a comprehensive suite of tools for stock screening, market analysis, and portfolio management. It is widely used by both individual and professional investors to make informed investment decisions.

Key Features:
1. **Stock Screener**:
    - **Customizable Filters**: Finviz offers a highly customizable stock screener with over 60 filters, including fundamental metrics (P/E ratio, EPS, dividend yield), technical indicators (SMA, RSI, MACD), and descriptive criteria (sector, industry, market cap).
    - **Predefined Screens**: Users can choose from a variety of predefined screens such as "Most Active," "Top Gainers," "Top Losers," and "Unusual Volume."
    - **Visualization**: The screener results can be displayed in a table, chart, or heatmap format, making it easy to spot trends and patterns.
2. **Market Overview**:
    - **Real-Time Data**: Finviz provides real-time data on major indices, futures, and forex markets.
    - **Heatmaps**: The heatmap feature visually represents the performance of stocks and sectors, allowing users to quickly identify the best and worst performers.
    - **Charts**: Interactive charts for indices, sectors, and individual stocks are available, with various technical indicators and drawing tools.
3. **Portfolio Management**:
    - **Portfolio Tracker**: Users can create and manage multiple portfolios, track performance, and receive alerts on price changes and news.
    - **Performance Analysis**: Detailed performance metrics and charts help users analyze their portfolio's strengths and weaknesses.
4. **News and Analysis**:

- **Latest News**: Finviz aggregates news from various sources, providing the latest updates on stocks, sectors, and the overall market.
- **Insider Trading**: Information on insider transactions is available, helping users gauge insider sentiment.
- **Analyst Ratings**: Analyst recommendations and price targets are provided for individual stocks.

5. **Advanced Features**:
   - **Backtesting**: While Finviz does not offer full backtesting capabilities, users can manually test strategies by saving screener results and tracking performance over time.
   - **Alerts**: Customizable alerts for price changes, volume spikes, and other criteria help users stay informed without constant monitoring.

User Experience:
- **Ease of Use**: Finviz is designed to be intuitive and user-friendly, with a clean interface and easy navigation.
- **Free and Elite Versions**: Finviz offers a free version with robust features and an Elite version ($39.50/month or $299.50/year) that includes additional features like real-time data, advanced screening options, and more frequent updates.

Benefits of Using Finviz.com:
- **Comprehensive Data**: Access to a wide range of financial data and analysis tools in one platform.
- **Visualization**: Heatmaps and charts make it easy to interpret complex data and identify trends.
- **Customization**: Highly customizable filters and screens allow users to tailor the tool to their specific needs.
- **Efficiency**: Saves time by consolidating data and tools that would otherwise require multiple sources.

Limitations:
- **Historical Data**: Finviz does not provide extensive historical data for backtesting strategies.
- **Survivorship Bias**: The platform does not account for delisted or bankrupt companies, which can affect the accuracy of performance analysis.

Conclusion:
Finviz.com is a versatile and powerful tool for investors looking to enhance their market analysis and stock screening capabilities. Its comprehensive data, customizable features, and user-friendly interface make it an invaluable resource for both novice and experienced investors. While it has some limitations, its strengths far outweigh them, making it a go-to platform for financial visualization and analysis.

22   A simple tutorial

From your browser, bring up Yahoo!Finance's screener by clicking here or type http://screener.finance.yahoo.com/stocks.html.

Select the following to select stocks with share price > $5, market cap > 250 mil, P/E < 15, Est. Earning Growths up to 20% for 1 year and up to 5% for 5 years, and Buy Rating = 1.

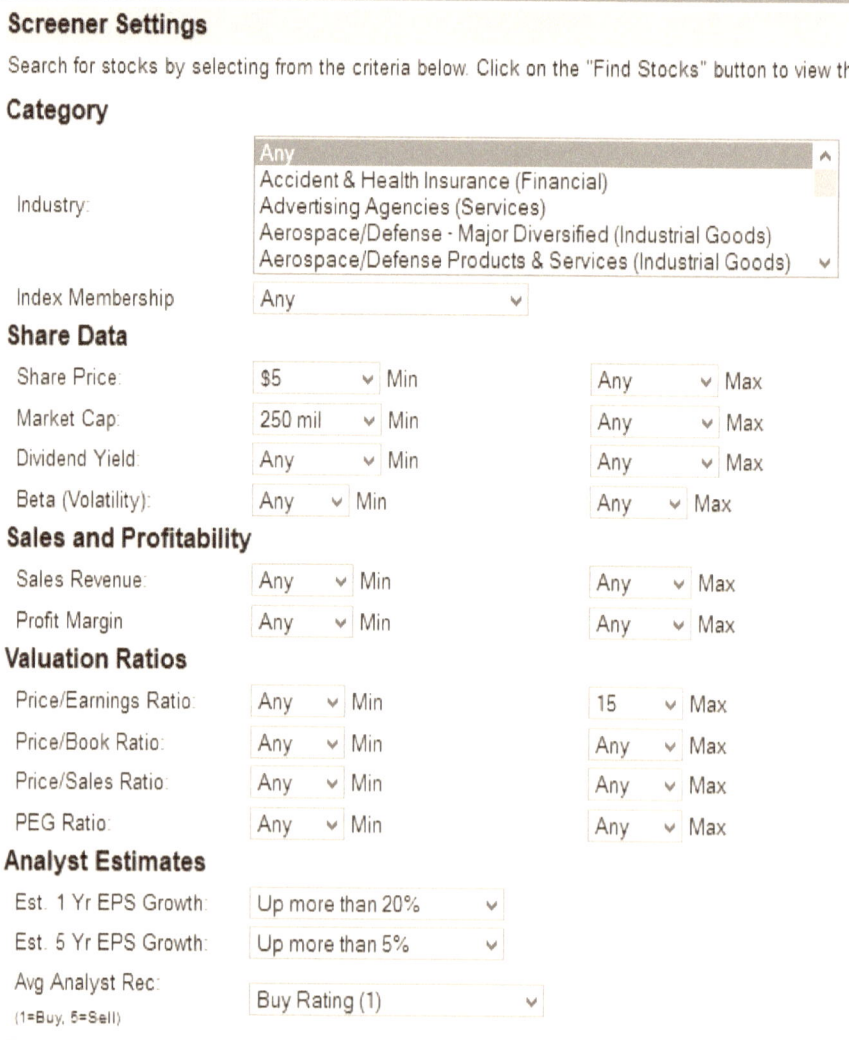

Click on Find Stocks.

As of 9/21/2013, you cannot find any stocks based on these criteria. Relax the filter by taking out the Est. 1-Yr Growth and the 5-Yr Growth. Click on Find Stocks again. You should find several stocks.

The stocks with '.xx' at the end could be the stocks you may not want to consider. They could be foreign stocks in foreign exchanges, listed in pink sheets, etc. That's why most screens allow you to select Exchanges. The exception is on the Pink Sheets for our penny stocks.

One common problem with this screen is that it may not handle negative or zero earning. So, you may want to select stocks whose earnings are greater than zero.

#Filler: Free Loaders

We have to limit free loaders. The mentally retarded and the REAL disabled are not free loaders so are not those who lose jobs.

The addicts are, the lazy folks are, the three-generations of teenage mothers are, the young folks tuning the motor bikes all day long are, the 'falsely disabled' are...

When the illegals become legal, how many of them will quit their jobs and become free loaders?

Filler: We're victims of our own success

A higher living standard means higher wages, more protections for our workers and more regulations for our environment. All these will make us less competitive.

23 Sectors to be cautious with

There are many reasons to be very cautious when investing in the following sectors. However, Technical Analysis (a.k.a. charting) would give you more hints than the fundamentals for stocks in these sectors.

Loan companies/banks
The financial statements do not show the quality of their loan portfolios. Banks should make easy money when you compare the CD rates to the mortgage rates. However, they could lose money in the following: 1. Default of loans / mortgages that happen frequently during recessions. 2. Banks are making risky investments that fail such as Bitcoins. 3. Investing in losing vehicles, such as the 'safe' Treasuries during rapid interest hikes (happened in 2023). 4. Poor management and/or frauds. Following this advice, you may be able to skip the banks that melted down in 2007. The peak of Citigroup was $550 and several banks including Lehman Brothers went bankrupt.

To protect ourselves, do not have one bank account with our assets over $250,000, which is protected by FDIC. Be careful on foreign banks, especially the small ones and those that are not protected by FDIC.
https://www.youtube.com/watch?v=qmpVABboOKQ

Failure of Silicon Valley Bank in 2023. If Biden did not mention about paying deposits back in full (many companies have deposits more than the insured amount), it would have shaken our financial system and the entire economic system. The failure is partly due to the rapid interest rates hikes and partly due to the loss of the loans from startup companies in a slowdown in the tech sector. Any unlawful insider trading? Be cautious on small banks; in 2008, about 1/3 of the small banks failed. I expect money from small banks would move to precious metals and larger banks.
https://www.youtube.com/watch?v=atIyLIP9sFs

Drug (generic is ok)
Understanding the complexities of the drug pipelines, its potential profits for new drugs and the expiration of its current drugs may not be worth the effort for most retail investors. In addition, a serious lawsuit and / or a serious problem with a drug could wipe out a good percentage of the stock price. When a drug shows unpromising sign(s) in any trial phase, the stock could plunge and vice versa.

Miners
It is extremely difficult to estimate how much ore (sometimes a miner owns several different types of ores and/or of different grades in the same or different mines) that the company has. It is further complicated by the complexities to

extract and transport them. When the total of these costs is greater than its production price, the company will not be profitable. Understanding the market for ore futures is another discipline.

Many mining companies are in foreign countries such as Canada, Australia and countries in South America. Their financial statements of Canada and Australia are more trustworthy than those from most other emerging countries.

One potential problem of mining companies from many emerging countries is nationalization.

Mining rare earth ore is extremely risky when the profit depends on how China, a major producer of these ores, will price its ores. After China announced the export restrictions on rare earth elements, several non-Chinese companies announced to reopen their mines for rare earths but few have made any profits as of 2013. Developed countries have stricter environmental regulations. Coal suffers from the rising use of cleaner oil and gas.

Insurance companies
Insurance companies profit by:

1. The difference between the total premiums received and the total claims minus expenses in running the company.
2. How well they invest your premiums; you pay your premiums earlier than you may collect from the claims.

They can protect the profits in #1 by restricting claims by natural disasters such as earthquakes and by re-insuring. However, a bad disaster could wipe out a lot of their profits.
Even if the insurance company shows you its investment portfolio, most of us, the retail investors, do not have the time and expertise to analyze it.

Emerging countries (not a sector)
Their financial statements especially from small companies cannot be trusted and many countries use different accounting standards. Emerging countries are where the economic growth is. I trade FXI, an ETF, rather than individual Chinese companies. I have lost a lot in small Chinese companies due to fraud. To check out whether the stock is an ADR, try ADR.COM.
https://www.adr.com/

Stocks with low volumes (not a sector)
Most likely you pay a high spread to trade these stocks. They can be manipulated easier. I remember when I had a hard time trying to sell a stock of this kind. The majority of this company is owned by one person.

For simplicity, I trade stocks with the average daily trade volume over 6,000 shares (double it if the price is $2 or less). A better way could be in calculating the percent of your trade quantity / average daily trade volume to reduce the effect of penny stocks that have larger volumes due to the low prices. You need special skills to trade these stocks but it could be very profitable.

Good business and bad business
Banking is a good business. My deposit in them makes virtually zero interest, and they loan the same money making 3%. If they are more selective in loaning my money, they should make a good profit.

Restaurant is an easy business to open/run, but it is very hard to make good money. With the rising of minimal wages, it will get even tougher. That could be the reason for so many coupons today. The high-end restaurants are doing better due to the rising stock market. As of 8/2014, the newcomers Noodles & Company (NDLS) and Potbelly (PBPB) are not doing very well.

Retailing is a tough business. Looking at the top 10 retailers 15 years ago, I can only find two including Macy's that are still surviving. Most are either bankrupt or being acquired. Even Macy's was at one time in financial trouble.

Airlines are a tough business. You can tell by the average increase in fares in the last 10 years. It cannot even beat inflation. They have to charge you for everything. The next frontier charge is the restroom (especially for long-distance flights). Now I understand why they call themselves "Frontier Airline". As of 2014, it is quite profitable due to mergers and lower fuel cost.

There are several software companies that produce software such as virus detecting programs and tax preparation software. The customers faithfully buy new versions every year. That's great business.

Afterthoughts
As of 8/2013, is the emerging market oversold?
http://seekingalpha.com/article/1658252-have-emerging-markets-gotten-oversold
When an index of an emerging market is up by 10% and the currency exchange rate to USD is down by 20%, then it is not profitable.
Links
Nationalization:
http://en.wikipedia.org/wiki/Nationalization
Spread:
http://en.wikipedia.org/wiki/Bid-offer_spread
Insurance:http://seekingalpha.com/article/1239671-property-casualty-insurance-and-reinsurance-what-you-need-to-know

Book 4: Technical Analysis (TA)

Technical analysis (TA) is the analysis of the price movements and the short-term trend and possible reversal, while fundamental analysis focuses on metrics such as price/earnings ratio and debts. TA assumes the future stock price behavior can be determined by the patterns of past price behavior – it is true more times than untrue. Traders use TA a lot and can profit by shorting stocks. Investors can use them to find the entry points and exits points and some investors only buys stocks with positive long-term trend (using SMA-200).

Many times stock analysis based on fundamentals fail when the evaluation is solely based on fundamentals. Technical Analysis (TA) has the following characteristics:

- Most of the time, TA is profitable in the short term (less than 3 months). The weather man is more accurate in tomorrow's weather rather than a month away. TA can also signal the reversals.
- It is too many signals if you have more than three TA parameters. To start, use SMA (Simple Moving Average) and RSI(14); both are available in Finviz.com without charting.
- You can combine TA with fundamentals such as a rising SMA50 with increasing Insider Purchases. In addition, you can use more than one TA indictors.
- For market timing, TA is a huge part, but many fundamentals should be considered too. You can use similar techniques to time the market and time stocks and/or sectors such as Golden Cross / Death Cross.

Technical analysis wins for the following reasons:
- Information such as a new product or a major lawsuit pending is not reflected timely in fundamentals, but rather in technical analysis. It gives us guidance in understanding the trend of a stock or even the entire market.
- Most TAs are based on accumulated data. For example, if RSI(14) is greater than 65, most likely this stock is overbought. If there is no reason for this condition, you may consider to sell it.
- When too many investors follow TA, it would become self-prophecy.
- Do not act against the trend. The fundamentalist may buy a stock when it loses 50%, the TA investor most likely will not buy it. Many times the losing stocks will lose another 25% or so. The TA investor most likely buys it on the way up only or short it on the way down.

An example. NVRO (a stock symbol) has appreciated about 100% from mid Feb. to Oct. in 2016 despite its poor fundamentals. It has a new product that could revolutionize physical healing and eliminating pain that will not be shown in the fundamentals except by the eventual Forward P/E. Technical chart can inform us of the uptrend.

Volume is the confirmation. Institution investors drive the market. When the market (esp. the S&P 500 stocks) is down and the volume is up, there is a good chance institution investors are dumping their holdings. It is obvious when most of the indicators are up but the volume is small.

Filler: A nightmare?

I got a call from Buffett asking me to lead their stock research.
I asked him why for a nobody; you may be asking the same question. No kidding.

He told me that he should have read my book Scoring Stocks to buy Apple instead of IBM in May, 2013. It would save his company millions of dollars minus $10 for my book. Not to mention the market timing technique that had worked in the last two major market plunges.

I told him, "OK, I'll beat your mediocre returns of the last 5 years."
He said, "You can do better than that and at least beat SPY. If you do so, no one will be that stupid to leave my fund and pay the hefty capital gain taxes."

I told him, "I cannot beat the market as you are the market especially after your expensive fees. In addition, I do not know how to avoid day traders from riding my bandwagon in trading. Also most of my big profits were made in small stocks that your fund cannot trade besides owning the company."

I woke up trembling. I'm glad it is only a nightmare.

1   Technical analysis (TA)

The basics
Technical analysis (a.k.a. charting) is easier to learn than you might expect. It represents the trend of the market (a stock or a group of stocks) graphically. If more investors are in the market, the market would move upwards until it changes direction. We divide the trends into short-term, intermediate-term and long-term.

The chartists usually do not consider fundamentals as they believe they have already been priced into the stock price and some fundamentals are not available to the public. To illustrate, a new drug has been discovered, the stock price of the company jumps initially by insiders purchases and the informed. Its fundamental metrics do not demonstrate this right away, but many investors are buying to boost up the stock price as evidenced by the technical indicators such as SMA for 20 or 50 days.

The volume is a confirmation. When the stock moves up or down by 10% with a low volume, the trend is not yet confirmed.

The trend of the stock price is not a straight line in most cases. Hence a trend line is usually drawn to indicate the direction of the stock. Many investors believe the stocks fluctuate in certain ranges (i.e., channels) and the chart draws the upper value (the resistance line) and the lower value (the support line). In theory, the price of a stock fluctuates within the resistance line (ceiling for understanding) and support (floor). When it reaches its support, it becomes a buy and vice versa for a sell. Most charts including Finviz.com would display these lines.

When the price passes out of the channel, it is called a breakout. Darvas, one of the oldest and most successful chartists, profited from the breakouts of the resistance line and believed the stock was close to the support line of the new channel. Hence it would be a long way up in theory.

If it were so simple, there will be no poor folks
It works most of the time, but do not place all your money on it. For chartists, 51% is great (the same for playing Black Jack). Some trends reverse very fast such as the bio drug stocks in 2015. You need to hedge your bets such as placing stop orders. Most do not want to spend their lives watching the trend from a big screen.

Most novices use too many technical indicators and lose in their performances to the professionals. Recently, most chartists were not doing all that great and I did not find many books on their success than a decade ago. It could be due to too many followers in similar setups. I verified it with my recent testing using Finviz.com.

Simple Moving Average
The basic technical indicator is SMA-N. It is the average of the last N trade sessions. To illustrate, if N is 15 and the exchange is open during this period, you need 3 weeks (21 days) of data. When N is 20 (or SMA-20), we classify it as short-term. Similarly, SMA-50 is an intermediate-term and SMA-200 is long-term. Assuming 5 trade sessions per week, 20, 50 and 200 can be translated to 4, 10, and 40 weeks respectively. I prefer the default 50, 100 and 250. Day traders and swing traders can change to shorter durations such as 5, 10 and 50.

This trend duration is important. For example, do not want to place long-term purchases using the short-term SMA-50. There are many modifications to SMA such as giving more weight to recent data, but I have not found them any better. Finviz.com includes this information without charting (SMA-20, SMA-50 and SMA-100 in percentages).

Defining the trend periods is rather arbitrary. I use SMA-350 to detect the market plunges and SMA-100 for stocks. Weighted Moving Average weighs more weight on recent price data.

It can be used to determine whether we are in a bull, a bear or a sideways market using SMA-50 (or SMA-200 for longer term) for the market (using SPY), the sector (using an ETF for the sector and the specific stock. The trend is up when the price is above the SMA and the reversal of the trend.
https://www.youtube.com/watch?v=jdYNaE5GJ0k

The trend is your best friend
Most traders use TA for trending in a short duration. Investors can also use TA to time the entry and exit points for better potential profits. Value investors are usually patient and they do bottom fishing and they search for 'oversold' conditions using RSI(14). Again, high volume is a confirmation.

Many sites provide charting free of charge such as Yahoo!Finance. Finviz.com provides a lot of technical indicators without charting such as

SMA% and RSI(14). It also provides screen searching for stocks that meet your technical analysis criteria.

Hands on
Bring up Finviz.com and enter any stock symbol such as AAPL. You can see the daily prices of AAPL from about nine months ago to today. Three SMAs (Simple Moving Average) are displayed as SMA-20, SMA-50 and SMA-200. The first two are for short-term trends. When the price is above the SMA, it is expected to be trending up. Again, the trade volume is used as a confirmation.

You can also see the resistance line and the support line drawn. In theory, the stock will trade within these lines. When it exceeds its resistance line, it is called a breakout, and vice versa for a breakdown. Sometimes it displays some technical patterns such as Cup and Shoulder and Double Down (both are positive patterns).

Select Weekly data. The Candle chart is better described than the Daily chart. Candles give us better descriptions of the price: open, close, high and low. The green color indicates the price is up for the period (a week in this example) and the red color indicates a down period.

In addition, Finviz.com includes some technical indicators in the metric section such as RSI. Most other chart sites are similar in the basics. Use Finviz's Help and select Technical Analysis for more description. Investopedia has enhanced descriptions on this topic.

TA patterns
There are many TA patterns such as Bollinger Bands and MACD. The patterns are based on the stock prices and many times they prove to be correct predictions especially on stocks with high volume and high market caps. Patterns have been repeating themselves many times as they are driven by investors.

Sites for TA
There are many free sites for charts with explanations of their technical indicators. Popular ones include BigCharts.com, SmallCharts.com and Yahoo!Finance. Fidelity includes some unique features in its charts such as P/E.

Why I do not use TA as a primary tool for stock picking
My investing style is different from a day trader. I prefer to 'Buy Low and Sell High' instead of 'Buy High and Sell Higher'. I try to find the real bottom

price. TA will not find the bottom very easily but it tracks the trend better. As a bargain hunter, I do not expect the stock will rise fast as I'm usually swimming against the tide. However, value stocks could stay in the low price for a long time (i.e., value trap). I like to select stocks that turn around as evidenced by the SMA-20 and SMA-50.

With that said, my momentum portfolio has appreciated consistently and usually has the best performing stocks among all my portfolios. It is based on the timely grade from my subscriptions plus the metrics on TA timing.

Most chartists would also tell you to buy the stocks that have broken out (i.e., higher than the resistance line) and/or stocks at their highs. Contrary to value investing, you should exit when the trend reverses. The reversal could happen very fast and hence protect your portfolio by setting up stop loss (preferably with trailing stop) orders.

My opinion
I do not want to argue whether TA is good for you or not. You need to find that out. Most likely, the day traders and very short-term traders will profit more from TA than the investors seeking value stocks for the long-term gains.

Random remarks
Even if you do not use technical analysis, you should spend some time learning it. It is better to marry fundamentals and TA. My random remarks are:

- The Institutional investors (insurance companies, pension funds, mutual funds, etc.) use TA and they MOVE the market. A lot of times it becomes a self-fulfilling prophecy. It is better to join them as most of us cannot beat them.
- Day traders take advantage of the institutional investors by spotting their trends and jumping on the bandwagon.
- Most TA stocks should be good sized and have large average daily volumes. I prefer to use TA on value stocks to prevent long-term losses.
- I do know some folks making big money using TA, but I know more making good money using fundamentals. Since TA predicts the market better in the shorter term, its practitioners may have to pay higher taxes (in today's tax laws) in taxable accounts.
- Our objective should be making money with the least risk. Once you claim to belong to a certain group of either Fundamental or TA, you will be biased and forget your primary objective in investing.

- TA tracks the last two big market plunges (2000 and 2007) pretty well. The chart will not warn you right away for the upcoming plunge (as it depends on past data) to avoid the initial losses, but they will warn you to avoid bigger losses.
- You can use TA to short the stock, the sector, the country or the market.
- Risk management (with stops to reduce losses and trailing stops for rising stocks) and trade positions (more positions on stocks with better potential) could make you a fortune, even if you have only 50% correct.
- Your desire, passion, discipline, knowledge and hand-on skill (including learning from your successes and failures) are the keys to success. A well-tested strategy and TA tools to time the trend of a stock, sector and the market are the tools.

Afterthoughts
Besides searching for stocks that have potential breakouts, we should check the stocks we own for potential breakdowns.
Technical Analysis tutorial.
https://www.YouTube.com/watch?v=GENBVwV8PMs
SMA tutorial.
https://www.YouTube.com/watch?v=Na-ctpPsnks

Links
Fidelity video: Technical Analysis
https://www.fidelity.com/learning-center/technical-analysis/chart-types-video

2   Examples of using TA

I have outlined how we can spot market plunges using TA and I use it to monitor the market every three months or so (I recommend to do it every month and even more frequently when the market is risky). Here is an example of how to use it to trade individual stocks.

I have to admit I do not use TA that much on individual stocks and clearly I am not an expert in TA. If this article stirs up your interest, read more books or attend seminars / classes on TA. However, this book describes the basic and most useful technical indicators. There are many good and free articles from Investopedia on this topic. Personally I prefer to seek fundamentally sound companies at bargain prices and wait for their full appreciation. It has been proven to me many times over.

TA is very useful for momentum and day traders. With the rising volume, you can detect that the stocks are traded by managers of mutual funds, hedge funds, insurance companies and pension funds, and you profit by riding on their bandwagons.

Some stocks are good for TA. Usually they are larger companies with above-average volumes and are fundamentally sound. Avoid the stocks that are trending downwards unless you're bottom fishing. Let me pick CSCO (a cyclical stock) for an illustration. I bought it several times in 2012. I sold some in 2013 and 2014 making good profits. This is quite different from what short-term traders would use during the following:

The green line is a 50-day simple moving average (SMA) for the following chart using one year data.

If it does not display clearly on a small screen, type the following on the browser in your PC.

http://ebmyth.blogspot.com/2013/05/chart-for-ta-example.html

Buy the stock when it is above its SMA and sell when it is below. Following the chart would make good money based on this simple rule. Also, practice the strategy "Sell on May 1, Buy back on Nov. 1".

Not all stocks follow this profitable pattern. Fundamentalists may try to pick the bottom in late July while chartists enter positions on its upward trend. The chartists have an advantage to stay away from stocks in their downward trend.

Exponential Moving Average has better predictable power as it weighs more on recent prices. Some indicators / patterns work better in specific market conditions – all markets are different.

Volume is important as a confirmation. If the price of a stock is up with thin volume, the rise is questionable and it could be manipulated.

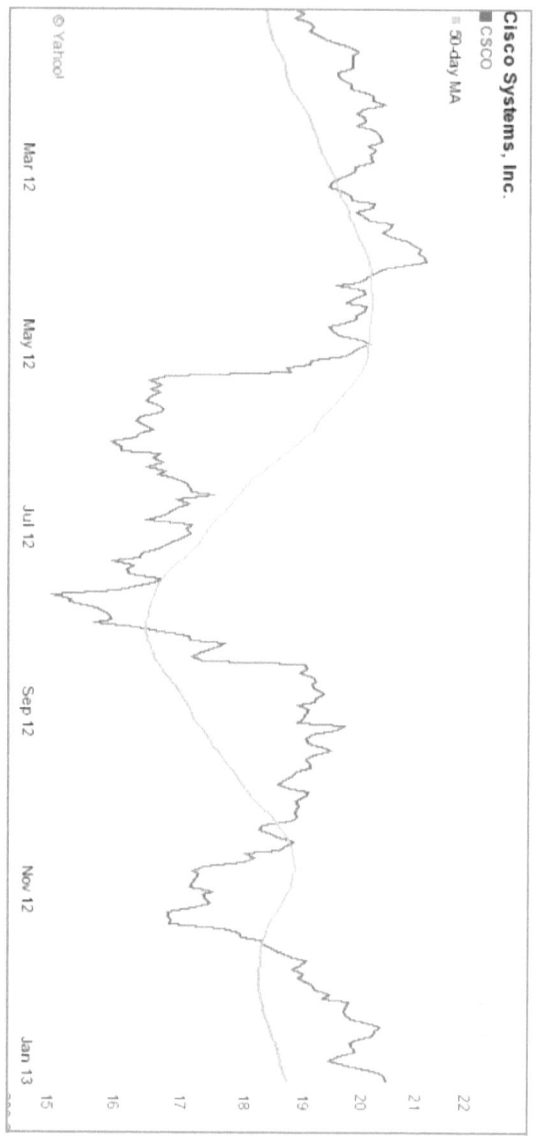

Table: CSCO 50-day SMA   Source: Yahoo!Finance

We can improve the trades by:
- Use different moving average in the number of days (50 in this example) and other indicators such as EMA (a moving average that weighs higher on more recent data). It may improve prediction accuracy and/or cut down on the number of trades. RSI(14) suggests overbought / oversold conditions.

- Instead of selling the stock for cash, consider selling the stock short. Selling short is definitely not for beginners.

- The accuracy is usually improved by a separate chart for the sector the stock belongs to and another one for the market. For CSCO, you can use an ETF for network companies and SPY (or a similar ETF) to represent the market.

   In theory and in theory only, when both the stock, the sector that the stock is in and the market all move down, the stock price has a high chance that it would move down, and vice versa.

   We use the 50 days (in SMA) for short-term holding of stocks (20 for even shorter holding period and 200 days for longer holding period). Personally I use 30 days for the sector ETF. Again, 'Days' is actually 'Trade Sessions'.

TA is not for most fundamentalists but it should be used

For a bargain hunter like me, TA would not benefit me a lot for picking stocks at their bottoms. I would try to pick up CSCO with prices ranging from 15-17 and all well below the moving average line, but TA would not show me a Buy signal. However, for short-term swing traders TA is a Godsend.

To me, TA is a good indicator for growth, momentum and for short-term trading. Some fundamentalists may use TA for entry and exit point is. Some recommend buying the stock when the price is above the SMA-200 (same as when SMA-200 is positive and that can be readily obtained from Finviz.com).

It is profitable for 'Buy High and Sell Higher' if you can protect your profits effectively. This is also called 'Buy at a reasonable cost'. One's opinion.

In selecting a tool, you have to understand how, and why to use it and whether it fits your investing style. I use TA for market timing for the entire market more than on individual stocks. When I have more time, I probably would use TA more frequently.

Most of us cannot spot the bottom of a stock; I have had some success but most likely they were due to luck. When a stock is moving up from the bottom, there is a good chance it will move further up. TA shows it and the volume confirms it.

Conclusion

Even a fundamentalist like me can benefit a lot by using TA. This book touches on the very basics of TA.

Besides monitoring the fundamentals of the stocks you bought once every 6 months, you should analyze their technical indicators more often (1 month to 3 months depending on your available time). When the market is risky (close to the SMA average), run the SMA chart more frequently (say once a week).

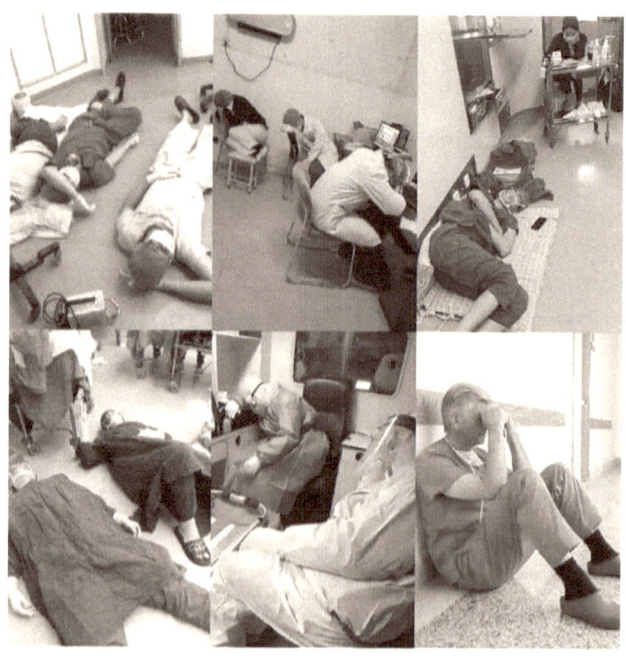

Not taken by me.
They are more important than ALL entertainers and athletes

3   Easy TA without charts

Bring up Finviz.com from your browser. Enter the stock you're evaluating. SMA-200 stands for Simple Moving Average of the last 200 trade sessions. RSI(14)% is the relative strength index for the last 14 trade sessions.

The following is just a suggestion with conservative parameters. Adjust the parameters according to your risk tolerance and requirements. Do not buy the stock with SMA-200 is < 0 (trending down), SMA-200 > 40 (peaking), or RSI(14)% > 65 (overbought).

Filler: Love is blind

The dividend lovers say that when their stocks drop by 50%, they are getting a 50% raise. There was a recent article on this STUPID logic - insulting my intelligence by just reading the title. When the company is bankrupted, they are getting a 100% raise. Should they check in the closest clinic to get their brains examined?

Love is blind and fools are fools and this cannot change the truths in our lives.

---

4   Simplest technical analysis

When the stock, the sector that the stock is in and the market are both above its SMA-n averages (Single Moving Average for n days), it is most likely trending up.

1. Bring up Finviz.com from your browser.

2. Enter SPY. Write down the SMA-200 (Single Moving Average for 200 days). Positive numbers indicate that the trend for the market is up.
However, the market could be peaking or overbought. Do not buy stocks when SMA-200 is over 5% and / or RSI(14) is over 65%. RSI is a metric in the same screen.

3. Enter the sector ETF the stock is in. Write down the SMA-50. Positive numbers indicate that trend for the sector is up.
However, the sector could be peaking or overbought. Do not buy stocks when the SMA-200 is over 10% and / or RSI(14) is over 65%. RSI is a metric in the same screen.

4. Enter the stock symbol. If your average holding period of the stocks is 50, use SMA-50 and so on. I recommend SMA-200 for holding stocks long term. Write down the SMA-n for your stock. Positive numbers indicate that the trend is up.

However, the market could be peaking or overbought. Do not buy stocks when the SMA-200 is over 25% and / or RSI(14) is over 70%. RSI is a metric in the same screen.

If the above three criteria and the fundamental criteria are satisfied, most likely it is a good buy. If you buy sector ETFs or mutual funds only, you can skip step #4.

Filler: The Ten Commandments of Investing.
http://www.investopedia.com/articles/basics/07/10commandments.asp

- Set goals. * Personal finances in order. * Ask questions. * Do not follow the herd. * Due diligence. * Be humble. * Be patient. * Be moderate. * No unnecessary churning. * Be safe. * Do not follow blindly.

- My additions: * Diversify. * Study market timing. * Protect your losses and profits. * Monitor your screens and your metrics. * Be emotionally detached from investments. * Learn from mistakes. * Stay away from bubbles. * Be socially responsible.

#Filler: Objectives in life

There are more important objectives in life than seeking wealth such as happiness, health, relationship… With wealth, a wise man can make the other objectives easier to obtain but an unwise man can do the opposite. When you lose a lot of money, you're still smiling then you're a winner.

My friend's friend died of worrying about losing most of his life saving in the stock market. Eventually the market returned, but he was dead already. We have to be emotionally detached to our wealth.

5   Bollinger Bands

Bollinger Bands have been proven useful for traders. In theory, the stock is traded between the upper band and the lower band forming an envelope. For more info, click the following link.

http://www.investopedia.com/terms/b/bollingerbands.asp

The following chart was drawn by Yahoo!Finance for CSCO from 8/7/2012 to 8/7/2014 selecting Bollinger Bands for the 50 days as a parameter. If you trade more often, use 20 days. If the chart is too small to display on your screen, enter the following in your PC's browser.
http://ebmyth.blogspot.com/2014/08/screen-csco-bollinger-bands-50.html

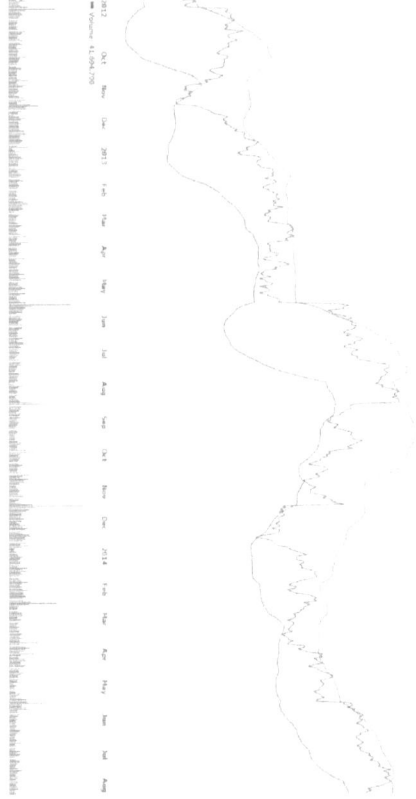

Bollinger Bands 50 Days.   Source: Yahoo!Finance

You buy the stock when the price is close to the lower band and sell the stock when it is close to the upper band.

When the stock price passes the upper band, it is called a breakout. Similar for the stock falling below the lower band.

From the above, we should make some good money.

It is advisable to use at least one more technical indicator. I recommend the RSI(14), which is also accessible from Yahoo!Finance or similar sites. When it is above 70, it is overbought, so I recommend selling the stock. When it is below 30, it is oversold, so I recommend buying the stock. However, fundamentals have not been considered. Some stocks just go to zero and some just surge.

6   MACD

MACD, Moving Average Convergence Divergence, is an effective momentum (i.e. short-term) indicator used by most traders. When the stock price is crossing above the zero line, it is a buy and vice versa. It may give false signals in sideways fluctuation.

###
Again, try to master SMA and RSI(14) first. Using too many indicators usually harms you more than helps you. You can use Finviz.com to search stocks with technical indicators.

7   Other TA indicators/patterns

They are briefly mentioned here. Click on the links or use Investopedia for more descriptions.

Double Bottom is a bullish pattern as the support line is stronger than the resistance line.
Double Top is the opposite and is a bearish pattern. I prefer the price of the second top is less than the price of the first top. It seems there are no enough investment in this stock to break out of the second top.

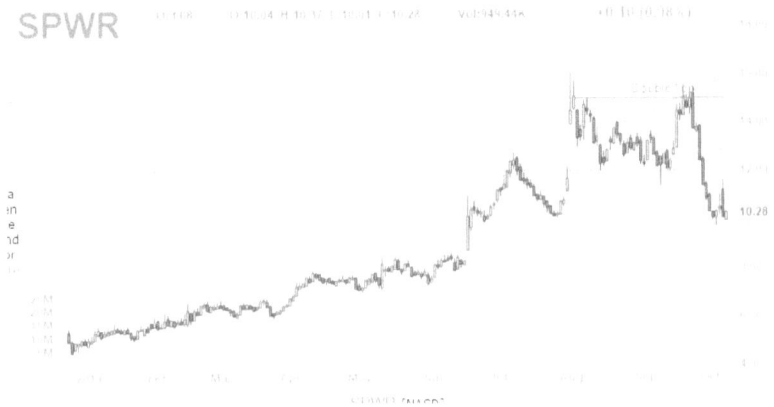

Resistance and Support. The stock is supposed to fluctuate between an imaginary zone of resistance and support. Short-term traders may sell when the price is close to the resistance line and close any short positions when it is close to the support line. However, breakouts from this zone are possible and many traders trade stocks on breakouts. It is a little similar to 52-week highs and lows. The trend line indicates the trend of the stock.

Cup and handle is a bullish pattern. The stock price peaks and then forms a shape of a cup and handle.

Head & Shoulder is a bearish pattern while the reversed Head & Shoulder is a bullish pattern. It signals that the peak (the head) has been reached and the second top (the shoulder) has failed to reach the previous peak.

Stochastic Oscillator. It is similar to RSI(14). Many traders use this indicator. If it is above 65, it is overbought. If it is below 30, it is oversold. In general, I would trade on an uptrend when the stock is moving from 60 to 85; it depends on how volatile the stock is. It is better to use with other indicators and as a reference.

To illustrate when to buy, one suggestion is to buy when this indicator changes to an uptrend while the price is still going down.

Many traders follow these technical indicators and SMA. They could become "self-fulfilled" prophecies.

Link

Chart patterns. https://www.youtube.com/watch?v=o6hZma0bajE

8   Simplest technical analysis

When the stock, the sector that the stock is in and the market are all above its SMA-N averages (Single Moving Average for the last N sessions), most likely the stock is trending up.

5. Bring up Finviz.com from your browser.

6. Enter SPY. Write down the SMA-200 (Single Moving Average for 200 sessions). Positive numbers indicate that the trend for the market is up.

   However, the market could be peaking or overbought. Be careful when SMA-200 is over 5% and / or RSI(14) is over 65%. RSI is a metric on overbought / underbought.

7. Enter the sector ETF the stock is in. Write down the SMA-50. Positive numbers indicate that trend for the sector is up.

   However, the sector could be peaking or overbought. Be careful when the SMA-200 is over 10% and / or RSI(14) is over 65%.

8. Enter the stock symbol. If your average holding period of the stocks is 200, use SMA-200 and so on. I recommend SMA-200 for holding value stocks long term and SMA-50 for momentum stocks. Write down the SMA-N for your stock. Positive numbers indicate that the trend is up.

   However, the stock could be peaking or overbought. Be careful when the SMA-200 (or SMA-50) is over 25% and / or RSI(14) is over 65%.

If the above three criteria and the fundamental criteria are satisfied, most likely it is a good buy. If you buy sector ETFs or mutual funds only, you can skip step #4. In any case, use stop loss to protect your investment.

#Filler: The Ten Commandments of Investing.
http://www.investopedia.com/articles/basics/07/10commandments.asp

- Set goals. * Personal finances in order. * Ask questions. * Do not follow the herd. * Due diligence. * Be humble. * Be patient. * Be moderate. * No unnecessary churning. * Be safe. * Do not follow blindly.
- My additions: * Diversify. * Study market timing. * Protect your losses and profits. * Monitor your screens and your metrics. * Be emotionally detached from investments. * Learn from mistakes. * Stay away from bubbles. * Be socially responsible.

9 More on technical analysis

This chapter describes some TA indicators that can help us. Click on the following links for a better description.

- Finviz.com.
  It has SMA20%, SMA50% and SMA200% to represent the short-term, intermediate-term and the long-term indicator. SMA stands for Simple Moving Average and n for days for the duration of the average (for example, 20 days for SMA20%).

  If you are a long-term investor, use SMA-200 (or SMA-350%). Using SMA-20 would cause a lot of sells / reentries, which costs more in trading fees.

  Buy when the price is above the Moving Average line and sell when the price is below it. Finviz.com provides the percent of moving above the moving average to indicate just how much the price deviates from the average.

  If you hold the stock for an average of 50 days, use SMA50%, and so on. If you hold stocks for an average of 90 days, you have to create your own SMA using one of the many websites including Yahoo!Finance and specify 90 days for the period.

  Try other similar technical indicators such as EMA, which is supposed to weigh more on the more recent data. A weather man can predict tomorrow's weather better than the weather a week away.

- RSI(14) indicates whether the stock is overbought or oversold. RSI oscillates between zero and 100. Traditionally, and according to Wilder (the author of this method), RSI is considered overbought with a value above 70 and oversold with a value below 30 as described in the article.

  When it is oversold, most likely the stock will fall, and vice versa.

  (http://stockcharts.com/school/doku.php?id=chart_school:technical_indicators:relative_strength_index_rsi)

  Click here for another article.

(http://financial-dictionary.thefreedictionary.com/Relative+Strength+Index)

- Cup and handle is a popular indicator of when the stock price would surge.
  (http://www.investopedia.com/terms/c/cupandhandle.asp)

- Double bottom indicates that the stock will move up.
  (http://stockcharts.com/school/doku.php?id=chart_school:chart_analysis:chart_patterns:double_bottom_revers)

  It shows a double bottom for Apple in 2013.

10   Using Fidelity

Click "Research and News" and then "Stock". Simple charting and advanced charting are both provided.

Hints:
- Fidelity provides suggested stops.
- Click on the Support and Resistance under Technical Analysis to display the Resistance Line (upper limit). Click on the Resistance Line and you can get the Support Line (lower limit).
- Click on Advanced Chart and then click on "learn how to use the chart". Under Advanced Chart, select Draw and Trend Line. Select the upper line by touching the highest points and do the same for the lower line.

11   The power of market timing

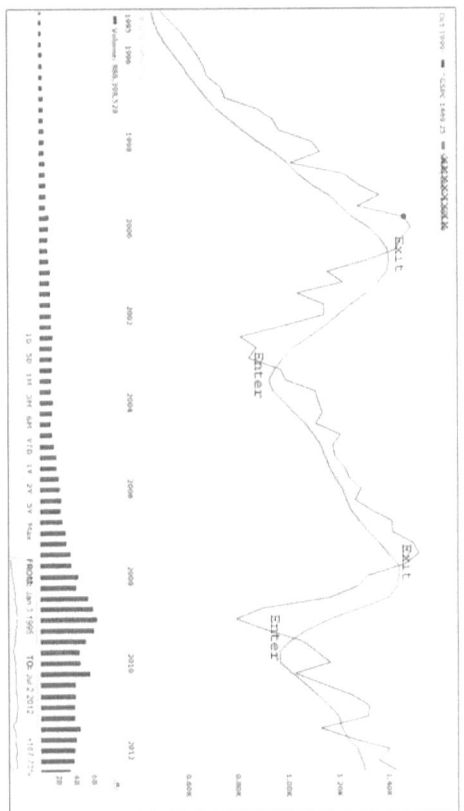

Most e-book readers allow you to select the graph to make it fit entirely on your screen. I use SPY, an ETF simulating the market. Detecting market plunges as seen in this graph indicates the exit points and reentry points also from 2000 to 9-2009 as follows.

Market Plunge	Peak	Bottom	Indicator Exit	Indicator Reenter
2000	08/28/00	09/20/02	10/01/00	06/01/03
2007	10/12/07	03/06/09	02/01/08	09/01/09
			08/01/11	11/01/11

Table: Vital Dates

For simplicity I skipped a few brief exits and reentries since 2011. You can run the simple chart once a month. When it indicates a potential market plunge is close, run the chart once a week. The last row represents a false signal.

This is based on stock prices so it may not identify the peaks and bottoms precisely, but so far it has not failed to avoid big losses and ensure big gains by reentering the market. I hope the next market plunge would give us enough time to act as these two did.

Unbelievable return with market timing

Calculate how much you made if you followed the above exit points and reenter points from 2000 to today. I bet you would have made a good fortune.

I compared the above returns with the SPY without market timing from 1-2000 to 9-2013.

There are many assumptions. Dividends and compounding are not considered. My return should be substantially better if I include buying contra ETFs during the exits and selling them during the reentries. I was shocked by the incredible return by using this simple market timing. Again, past performance does not guarantee future performances.

Summary info:

S&P 500 1-2000 to 9-2013	With Market Timing	Without Market Timing
Better	500%	
Gain	1,000	167
Gain %	68%	11%
Annualized gained	5%	1%
Days	4,959	4,959

Calculations:

S & P 500	With Market Timing	Without Market Timing
1-2000	1,469[1]	1,469[1]
Exit 10/01/00	1,041[2]	1,041
Enter 06/01/03	1,041	964[4]
Exit 02/01/08	1,489[3]	1,379[4]
Enter 09/01/09	1489	1,020[5]
Exit 08/01/11	1,888	1,293
Enter 11/01/11	1,888	1,251
09/03/13	2,469	1.638
Gained	2,469 – 1,469=1,000	1,638-1,469=167
Gain %	1000/1469 = 68%	167/1469 = 11%

Annualized gained	68% * 365/4959=5%	11%*365/4959=1%
Better	(1,000-167)/167 = 500%	

Portfolio with Market Timing:

[1] Both start with S&P 500 of 1,469 on 1-3-2000.
[2] 10/01/00
The market timing portfolio exits the market and remains the same value of 1,041 until 6/1/00.
[3] 02/01/08
The market timing portfolio exits the market and remains the same value of 1,489 until 9/1/09.

'1,489' is calculated as follows:
1,041 * (1 + Rate) = 1,041 * (1 + 1,379-964)/964) = 1,489
where the S&P 500 is 964 on 6/1/00 and 1,379 on 2/1/08.

The other calculations are based on the S&P 500 at 1,020 on 9/1/9, 1,293 on 8/1/11, 1,251 on 11/1/11 and 1,636 on 9/3/13.

Portfolio without Market Timing:

[1] Both starts with the S&P 500 of 1,469 on 1-3-2000. We could use the 9/3/13 the S&P 500 value, but it would not account for some compounded interest considerations.

[4] S&P 500 is 964 on 6/1/00 and 1,379 on 2/1/08.

[5] 02/01/08. The portfolio value is calculated to be 1,020 as follows:
1,379 * (1 + Rate) = 1,379 * (1 + (1020-1379)/1379) = 1,020
where S&P 500 is 1,379 on 2/1/08 and 1,020 on 9/1/09.

The other calculations are based on the S&P 500 at 1,293 on 8/1/11, 1,251 on 11/1/11 and 1,636 on 9/3/13.

I cannot believe the shocking return with market timing. I checked my calculations and there was nothing wrong that I could find. If you find something wrong, send your findings to me (pow_tony@yahoo.com).

12 Simplest market timing

Why market timing
Before 2000, market timing was a waste of time. However, after that, we have had two market plunges with the average loss of about 45%. It sounds harder to time the market than it actually is. We have a simple technique to detect market plunges and when to reenter the market. Our objective is reducing the loss to 25%.

Market timing depends on charts; the following describes how to use chart information without creating charts. Most charts will not identify the peaks and bottoms of the market as they depend on data (i.e., the stock prices). However, it would reduce further losses. It is simpler than it sounds. Just follow the procedure below.

The first part of this technique detects potential market plunges, and the second part advises you when to start reentering the market. It applies to individual stocks too. It also works to detect the trend of a sector (entering an ETF for the specific sector instead of SPY) and a specific stock.

Step-by-step procedure
When the market timer indicator (Death Cross) described next tells you to exit the market, sell SPY (an ETF simulating S&P 500). Do not forget to buy back SPY or similar ETF such as RSP, when the indicator (Golden Cross) tells you to return.

My experiences in 2000s
Basically I did the same as the above with some adaptations. I worked for a mutual fund company and they did not allow me to trade stocks effectively. However, I was allowed to trade sector funds offered by the company. Every two months, I switched to the sectors with the best performances for the last month. When most sectors were down for the last month, I rotated them to the money market fund. In March or April, 2000, I switched to traditional sectors from high-tech sectors (better to switch to market money funds). During that time, I bought stocks that had enough cash to last more than two years judging by their burn rates. The indicators should do a better job.

How to detect market plunges without charts (similar to <u>Death Cross</u>)
1. Bring up Finviz.com.
2. Enter SPY (or any ETF that simulates the market) or RSP, equally-weighted SPY.
3. If SMA-200 is positive, it indicates that the market plunge has not been detected and you can skip the following steps.

4. The market is plunging if SMA-50 is more negative than SMA-200. To illustrate this condition, SMA-200 is -2% and SMA-50 is -5%.
5. Another hint: B/S (buy sell ratio) is negative, specially it is more negative than last week.
6. Conservative investors should sell most stocks starting with the riskiest ones first such as the ones with negative earnings, high P/Es and/or high Debt/Equity. Obtain this info from Finviz.com by entering the symbol of the stock you own.
7. Aggressive investors should sell all stocks. Extremely aggressive investors should sell all stocks, buy contra ETFs such as PSQ, and even short stocks. I do not recommend beginners to be aggressive.

Example
As of 2/12/2022, the following are from Finviz.com.

ETF	SMA-200	SMA-50	SMA-20	Death Cross?
SPY	-0.8%	-4.2%	-1.7%	Yes (Step #4)
RSP	-0.5%	-1.9%	0.4%	Yes (Step #4)

Both ETFs indicate the market is a confirmed crash from my indications using a technique similar to Death Cross. However, they are quite close, and we should keep an eye on these numbers. In this case, SMA-20 has not been used. If it is a false alarm, the Golden Cross would indicate it and you should return to equity; it could be quite common in volatile markets. The futures indicate that on Monday (2/14/22) the market would plunge further. Another test is using SMA-350: When the current price is below SMA-300, it is a crash. SMA-20 has to be more negative than SMA-50 and it has not been used here.

Simple chart example. Bring up StockCharts.com and enter SPY. It indicates Death Cross occurred on about March, 14, 2022.

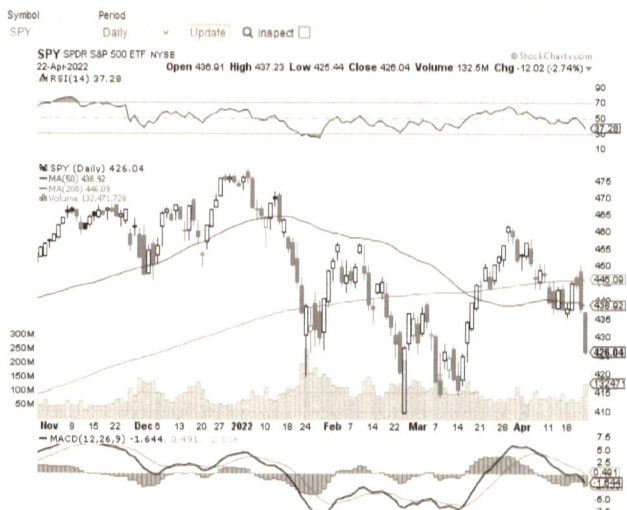

When to return to the market (similar to Golden Cross)

Use the above in a reversed sense to detect whether the market has been recovering. However, when the SMA-200 turns positive, I would start buying value stocks (low P/E but the 'E' has to be positive, and/or low Debt/Equity).

1. Bring up Finviz.com.
2. Enter SPY (or any ETF that simulates the market).
3. If SMA-200 is negative, the market is not recovering, and you can skip the following steps.
4. Sell all contra ETFs and close all shorts if you have any.
5. Market recovery is confirmed when SMA-50 is more positive than SMA-200. To illustrate this condition, SMA-200 is 2% and SMA-50 is 5%. Commit a large percent of cash (or all cash for aggressive investors) to stocks. If you do not know what to buy, buy SPY or an ETF that simulates the market.
6. Another hint: B/S (buy sell ratio) is positive, specially it is more positive than last week.

How often should you check the market timing indicators?

Do the above once a month. When the SPY price is closer to SMA actions percentage, perform the above once a week. The charts and data for market timing described in this book are based on SMA-350 (Simple Moving Average) that is more preferable than this simple procedure, but it requires some simple charting.

Nothing is perfect

If the market timing is perfect, there would be no poor folks. The major 'defects' are:

- It does not detect the peak / bottom as it depends on past data. However, it would save you a lot during the crash.
- It is hard to determine whether it is a correction or a crash.
- From 2000 to 2010, there was only one false signal. The indicator tells you to exit and then tells you to reenter the market shortly. In most cases, you do not lose a lot. After 2010, we have more false signals.
- The market may not be rational or may be influenced due to specific conditions such as excessive printing of USD. If you do not mind charting, use SMA 350 (or 400) using SPY. Buy when the price is above SMA-350 (or SMA-400), and sell otherwise. SMA-400 reduces the number of false signals, but it is not nimble.

13   Why the market fluctuates

The following chart uses SPY (simulating the market) with SMA-350 for the year of 2020 using Fidelity's charting function. It will be used to demonstrate how SMA-350 worked for 2020; the dates may be several days off. This article is written on 1/1/2021.

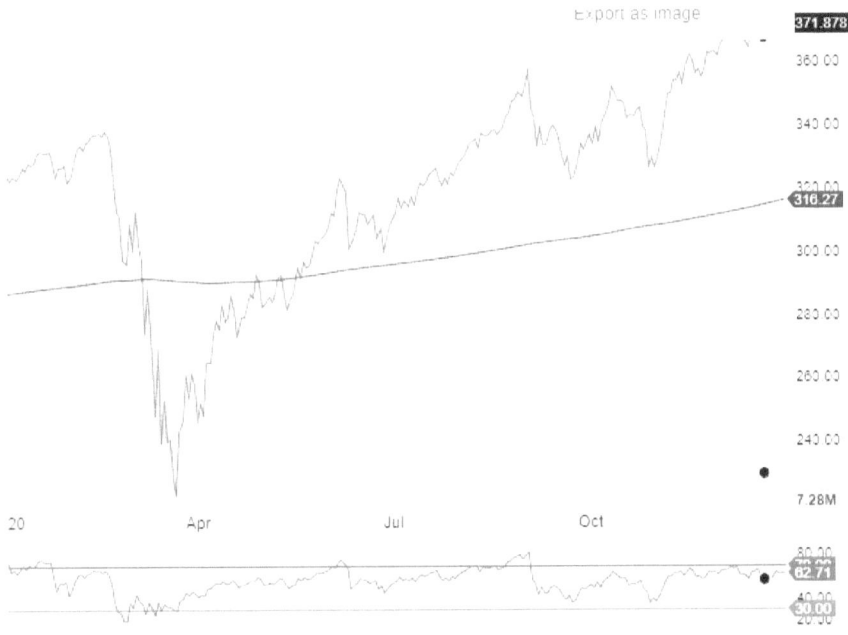

Market Timing

SMA-350 (Simple Moving Average for the last 350 sessions), described in one of my books, worked fine in 2020. It told us to exit the market on about 3/11/2020 and return on about the beginning of June. There were two false signals (on about 4/28 and 5/8) that told you to exit but return to the market shortly.

The other indicators are RSI(14) and P/E. Fidelity's chart uses 80 for overbought and 30 for under-bought for RSI(14). The market has been overpriced for a long while. In this case, technical analysis (SMA-350 I used in my example) works better than fundamental (P/E as one of the metrics); It has been sold for the entire 2020.

Why there is a big drop in late March and why it comes back
The trigger is the pandemic.

The market came back for many reasons:
- We understood the pandemic better.
- A lot of money in the sideline.
- The government supplies more money by printing it excessively.
- The government lowers the interest rate (almost to zero).

2021 prediction
It is quite hard to predict the market. Here are my thoughts. The market is not rational (fundamentally speaking).

For:
- The government keeps on excessively supplying money.
- With easy credit, the rising housing market leads to many profitable sectors such as furniture.
- Due to easy credit and recovering, many companies buy back their own stocks.
- Low margin interest rate usually boosts the stock market.
- If the vaccines can control this pandemic, many sectors will recover. As I demonstrated before, we have to wait one more year for some sectors such as airlines, restaurants and cruise lines.
- Trade war with China could be reduced under Biden.

Against:
- The pandemic has not been stopped.
- Unemployment is breaking previous record.
- Small businesses continue to go bankrupt.
- Complete decoupling with China.
- The government tools do not work anymore such as lowering interest rate.

- Super inflation is due to ample supply of money chasing a fixed amount of assets (stocks for example). The status of the USD as a reserve currency would also be shaken.

As in any market, there are two camps opposite to each other. Need to watch the market like a hawk and take actions accordingly (talk to your financial advisor first). I expect the plunge would cause the market to lose about 40% if it happens.

#Filler: Glad to be an investor

After watching the following YouTube video, I am glad my parents did not push me to play piano and also glad I do not have any musical gene. How can I compete with this kid?

https://www.youtube.com/watch?v=yf0B4rVoq44

Also, glad not into some life-threatening professions such as surgical doctors, soldiers, fire fighters, etc. I can make mistakes in investing from time to time without suffering from the consequences. With the uptrend market for most of the last 50 years, most investors should make good money. Thank God.

14   Market timing example

The market is making new highs. There are always two camps of market timers. One camp predicts a crash is coming while the other predicts it will continue making new highs. This article includes both arguments and suggests how and what actions you need to take to protect your investments.

Management summary

The market is fundamentally unsound evidenced by fundamental metrics but technically sound evidenced by technical metrics that both will be described in this article. The data were obtained on 09/22/2018. The market has not changed a lot as of 01/2020.

Suggested actions
No one predicts the market correctly and consistently. Otherwise there are no poor folks. Moving the risky investments such as most stocks to cash too early would miss the potential profits. Moving it too late would risk the loss of your stocks.

Your actions depend on your risk tolerance. If you are conservative such as a retiree, you may want to have a larger portion of your investments in lower risk such as CDs and bonds. You can take one of the following three actions or combine all of the three actions.

1. When the market turns to technically unsound, it is time to move your stocks to cash. The market timing indicators may give false signals. In this case, the indicator would tell you to move back to stocks. Most likely you do not lose much except dealing with the consequences of taxes in non-retirement accounts.
2. Move a portion of your risky investments into cash, laddered CDs and/or short-term bonds. Again, the size of the portion depends on your risk tolerance.
3. Use stops. The sell orders would be changed to market orders when the stocks dip below prices specified by you. I prefer to use SPY or other ETF to determine the market direction. Some sectors and some stocks move faster than others. In one crash, my energy stocks were still profitable while the market was tanking. Eventually these energy stocks caught up and fell fast. Today's highly profitable stocks are FAANG stocks as a group.

I propose and prefer 'manual stop orders' to prevent market manipulation. However, usually large ETFs cannot be manipulated easily. Manipulators try to profit from your stop orders. Set a stop order price in your `mind. When the stock falls to that specified price, sell it via a market order.

My friend confirmed my "manual stop order":

"High-frequency trading via Algo Trading Strategy can see exactly where pre-set trailing stops are and sweep across them (play them) like strings on a violin. Pre-set a trailing stop and it is bound to be triggered because Algo hunt them down. Then watch the market rip higher."

Analysis: Fundamentals and Technical
It consists of Fundamental Analysis and Technical Analysis. The former measures how expensive the current market is and the latter measures the trend of the market.

Many metrics were obtained from Finviz.com as of 9/22/2018 while others are obtained from other websites. With the exception of Fidelity.com, all websites described here are free and readily available. It also serves as a guide on how you can do your own market timing especially after a few months.

The following chart uses SPY to represent the market of the top 500 stocks. It is market cap weighted. It means the higher the market cap the stock is, the higher percent of the stock is represented in the index. It turns out most are riskier FAANG stocks.

Enter Finviz.com in your browser and enter SPY. I am not responsible for any errors.

Indicator	Pass	Current Value	Indicating
• Technical			
Death Cross[1]		SMA-50 = 2.3% & SMA-200 = 6.3%	Pass
Technical Analysis: 350 SMA%[2]	>0	Price above the SMA-350.	Pass
RSI(14)	<70	61	Pass
Duration (yr.)	<5	10	Fail
		Overall	**Pass**
• Fundamental			
Valuation			

P/E[3]	<15.7	25.4		High by 62%. Fail.
Shiller P/E[3]	<16.6	33.5		High by 102%. Fail
P/B[3]	<2.78	3.52		High by 27%. Fail.
P/S[3]	<1.50	2.33		High by 55%. Fail.
Oil price	30-100	70.71		Pass
Interest rate[6] T-Bill 1 months[7]	<5	2.05		Pass
T-Bill 3 months[7]	Yield	2.18		
T-Bill 30 years[7]	Curve	3.20		Pass
Flow to Equity[4]		-3.371M		Fail
Flow to bond[4]		7.206M		
Corporate debt/GDP[8]	<40	45%		High by 13%. Fail.
USD[5]		Strong		Fail
Gold		High		Fail
Bubble		Several		Fail
Market experts		Fear long term		Neutral
Politics		Trump		Fail
Misc.		Trade war		Fail
		Overall		**Fail**

[1] This is the market timing technique without using a chart.
[2] I tried to use SMA-400% to reduce false signals without success.
[3] Get it from http://www.multpl.com/ Same as CAPE.
[4] Get it from https://www.ici.org/research/stats. It is based on 09-12-18. "Flow to Equity" is based on domestic ETF estimate. Treat it as two phases in moving to equity. First phase of moving excessively to equity indicates the market is peaking. The second phase indicates the market is plunging when flow of equity is excessively negative.
[5] Global corporations will suffer in profits converted back to USD and hard to sell to foreign countries. [4] Get it from the above link.
[6] Rising interest is bad for corporations and high-ticket products, but good for lenders.

[7] Get it from https://www.treasury.gov/resource-center/data-chart-center/interest-rates/Pages/TextView.aspx?data=yield based on 09/21/18
[8] With the low interest rate, it may not be that critical. Corporations take advantage of the low interest rate.

Overall

Overall, technical is fine as the market is making new highs. Many aggressive investors exit the market on technical indicators only as the over-valued market could linger on for a long term such as from 2009 to 2017 so far.

Overall, fundamental is not sound. The increasing market price also is decreasing the fundamental metrics such as P/E, P/B and P/S. It is bad unless there is reason to support such as the fast earnings growth in 2009.

Many metrics are deteriorating

RSI(14) is getting closer to 65 (a passing grade specified by me).

Inverse yield curve (1.5 vs. 2.33) is about 61% apart from my interpretation and calculation. It is not a warning now but we should keep an eye on it. Most market crashes have occurred when it is 0% or negative. The theory is that in a normal case the short-term interest rates should be lower than the long-term interest rate.

Another source calculates it is 1.1% and that is very close to inversion since the last recession. From MarketWatch, the 30-year fixed interest rates is 4.66% and 1-year rate is 3.96% giving an inverse yield curve 18% apart, which is quite alarming.

Mathematically incorrect, today's full employment is at 4%. Most recessions are closely preceded by troughs in unemployment and the reverse for economy recovery.

GDP growth has been predicted from 1.8% to 3%. The 3% is from the White House for their obvious purpose. I predict it will pop up due to meeting the tariff deadlines, tax cuts and spending increases. It will then be declining to 2%. A healthy US economy should maintain 3% without special factors such as excessive immigration.

We have record debts: investors' margin, corporate debt and Federal debt. These are bubbles going to burst. Federal debt / GDP is about 95% (https://fred.stlouisfed.org/series/gfdegdq188S) today. It does not predict the market performance as this ratio was 53% and 55% before the last two market crashes. It will affect the long-term performance of the economy when we have to service the huge national debt.

We do have 10 years of stock growth at the expense of record Federal deficit. Thanks to President Obama from investors and no thanks from next generations who have to pay back our national debt. It is overdue for a correction. Hopefully it is not a crash which has an average loss of about 45%. We did have two recent corrections losing more than 10%: 2011-12 EU debt crisis and 2014-16 oil crash. The oil price has been rising from $30 per barrel to today's $70. It is still a long way from my warning of $120.

Potential triggers
Trade wars with China, Canada or EU will be the strongest trigger. Our most profitable companies are virtually all international companies. They need fair trade to prosper.

The other trigger is the possible impeachment of President Trump.

Check the validity of our charts
It seems some metrics vary. It could use after hour trading. It could be the "Days" may be "Sessions" – calendar day is different from trading session. I selected 10 years for most of the charts and StockCharts let me select only 5 years.

Here is a list of sites for charts.
https://www.stocktrader.com/2013/12/10/best-free-stock-chart-websites/
These are the three sites I use a lot: Fidelity (customers only), StockCharts and Finviz.com (missing some metrics).

As stated before, SPY may not be the best to represent the market. I prefer an ETF for 1,000 stocks and weigh the stocks evenly (i.e. not according to the market cap). Google "market timing 2020 (or current year)" for more expert info. Here is one.

Mid-year (6/15/2020) update
This is an update to my two articles: "Market timing example" and "Disaster of 2020".

Basically nothing significant has changed recently: The market is fundamentally unsound and technically sound after the recent rally. The only update is our national debt is skyrocketing. Today's "Debt/GDP" is similar to the market height in 2000 and we know what happened afterwards. That's why Buffett has accumulated a lot of cash now.

Even with the unlimited QE (i.e. printing money excessively), the high inflation and market crash predicted by many experts have not been materialized so far. This is my third prediction in "Disaster of 2020". The status of USD as a reserve currency will be shaken; I do not know when, as I do not have a time machine.

Why the market keeps going up while the economy is going down? The Fed has provided a lot of cash and the cash is chasing a fixed number of assets such as gold and stocks. It is the simple, proven theory of demand and supply. It will continue for a while as long as there is unlimited supply of money. At some point, it will pop. At that time, it could lead to a long recession, unless the economy improves as it did in 2009. The smart Fed chairman knows how it will harm the country by excessively printing money. However, he has to obey his boss who is seeking for reelection.

I expect we are in a prolonged period of low interest rates and even negative interest rates. When the rates are negative, our Treasury bonds are no longer marketable. The foreign central banks including China would dump our national debts if it has not been already started. The economy is dressed up nicely in an election year. Giving us free money is the easy way to buy votes, but the long-term effects are very harmful.

Using cheap money to buy back the company's stock would boost the stock price and hence make the management wealthier. It is a false sense of the stock value. When the company cannot pay back the debt obligations, the company would go bankrupted. If the U.S. were a company, she has gone bankrupted already.

As of 6/15/2020, QQQ (representing NASDAQ stocks) has been up 11% YTD and it is far better than DIA (representing DOW stocks) and SPY (representing the 500 large stocks in the S&P Index and losing about 5% YTD). QQQ has a lot of tech stocks while DIA has a lot of losers including Boeing. Most FAANG stocks are making record highs and QQQ is market cap weighed.

Most of the ETFs on chips have been up more than 40% in a year. I bought Amazon and two chip ETFs. I use trailing stops to protect my portfolio. Huawei is buying a lot of U.S. chips in the 120-day relaxed period. In September this year and if there is no extension, I would sell these chip ETFs fast.

I have used the strategy described in my book "Profit from the recovery of the pandemic" to take advantage of this volatile market. I used 5% as the threshold and I had too few trades; now I changed to 3%. Expecting a market crash, I weigh more on contra ETFs. As described in the same book, I bought a lot of contra ETFs, GLD and the stock of a gold miner. It is for insurance. ETFs on oil is my big mistake.

If the U.S.D. loses the status of reserve currency (not likely soon), it would bring prolonged depression and high inflation in the U.S. In this case, it is safer to invest in real estate, precious metals and profitable companies than in CDs and bonds that would lose values due to inflation.

Check out many articles on the status of the current market. Many have opposing views, so you have to make your own decision. In any case, play it safe with stops. Here is one article from MarketWatch.com.

Canary warning?

When I was working on my new book "Best stocks to buy for 2021" on Dec. 10, 2020, I found something really strange. I have never rejected so many stocks that have Fidelity's Equity Summary Score higher than 9. I rejected them as there were a lot of dumping from the insiders. Insiders know their companies better than most of us. Is it the canary telling us the market is over-valued?

Initially the following stocks have been screened by my value screens. Buy any one of the following stocks, **only** if you have good reason(s).

Symbol	Fidelity Score	Insider Purchase
BCC	9.9	-24%
GPI	10.0	-17%
HEAR	10.0	-75%
HIBB	9.4	-30%
HVT	9.5	-37%
HZO	9.5	-27%

A correction or a crash?

In Dec., 2018, the S&P 500 is about 15% down and a crash is about 45% down.

If a crash is coming, there should be additional 30% down. If it is a correction (15% average), then we have it already. Should we pick up bargains now? Or, are they bargains? It is a trillion-dollar question.

We need a trigger for a market crash like the financial crisis in 2008 and the internet bubble in 2000. Besides the record-high margin debt, the possibility of Trump's impeachment and a trade war, I do not see any.

Filler: CIA mistook it as a missile silo in China.

15   Market timing by calendar

The following predictions are based on historical data. You may have slightly different findings depending on when you start and when you end your testing.

You can load the historical data of SPY via Yahoo!Finance and check out how close you are or different from my own predictions. They are my predictions based on historical data. Use it as a reference only.

- Presidential cycle.
  Usually the market performs worse in the first two years after the election than the next two. During the 3rd year the president has to make the economy look rosy in order to buy votes. Statistically it is the best year for the market and is followed by a good year (the election year). The government may stimulate the economy, the stock market and employment by printing more money, lowering interest rates and lowering taxes. The market in the 100 days before the election should be positive and less volatile according to 40 years of data.

  Democratic presidents have better market performance statistically than Republican presidents. This is not too logical as though Republicans are more pro-business traditionally.

- Olympics.
  It has been proven that the host country has a better chance that its stock market appreciates the year after the Olympics. It could be due to the exposure from the Olympics and / or the huge expenses in preparing for the Olympics.

  The last two Olympics follow this pattern as of 12/23/2013:

Olympics Country / Year	ETF	Period	Return
United Kingdom / 2012	EWU	Jan. 3, 2013 - Dec. 23, 2013	11%
China / 2008	FXI	Jan. 3, 2009 - Dec. 31, 2009	43%

  Greece could be an exception. It is too small a country to host this world-class event and it has wasted too many resources by building too many white elephants that the country can never justify. Brazil depends on its export of natural resources to China, so I do not count on the Olympics effect there.

Winning a lot of Olympic medals has no prediction for the stock markets. Both the Russian Empire and E. Germany were winners but disappeared in their original forms afterwards.

- Seasonal.
  Best profitable investment period is: Nov. 1 to April 30 of the following year. It is similar to the saying 'Sell in May and Go away'. It did not work since 2009 as it was an Early Recovery (defined by me) in the market cycle.

  The market does not always happen as predicted. However, when more folks follow this, it becomes a self-fulfilling prophecy. I prefer "Sell on April 15 and come back on Oct. 15" to act before the herd. The more practical strategy is to start selling in April 1 and become more aggressive (selling at closer to the market prices) when it is close to May 1. For the last five years, I did not find this prediction reliable.

  The explanation of the 'summer doldrums' could be that the investors cash their stocks for vacations and college tuition in the fall. Buying quality companies at the dips could be profitable.

- The worst month: September.
  The next worst month is October. However, if there is no serious market crash during October (and this month has more than its shares of crashes), it could be the best month to buy stocks.

- The best month for the bull: November.
  However, several market bottoms occurred in October and November. The next strong month is December.

- Best 30 days: Dec. 15 to Jan. 15, next year.
  It was correct for the period of 2012-2013.

- Window dressing.
  Institutional investors sell their losers and buy winners around Nov. 1. From my rough estimate and on the average, the winners have a 2% percentage point gain better than the market and the losers have 1% worse than the market.

I recommend that you evaluate the top 10 winners from the last 10 months or YTD in Oct. 15 and sell them at 3% gain or two months later.

I recommend that you buy in Dec. and sell them 3 months later. Include the stocks with more than 30% loss for the last 11 months or YTD, sort them by Earning Yield in descending order and evaluate the top 10 stocks.

In both cases, do not buy foreign stocks and stocks with return of capital. Ignore stocks not in the three major exchanges, with low volumes and stock prices less than $2. Do not buy in losing years such as 2007 and 2008. I have my tests with my own assumptions and I use tools not available to most readers.

This is a guideline only. Do not buy any stocks during market plunges. Current events should be considered first such as a potential war and the hiking of interest rates.

Afterthoughts

- I predict it will be a sideways market in the later part of 2013. I am following the sideways strategy: Buy on dips and sell when the market is ups. One's prediction.

- Why September has a bad reputation?
  http://www.marketwatch.com/story/betting-on-septembers-terrible-odds-2013-08-27?dist=beforebell

  The September of 2013 (2 days away at the time of this writing) will have more problems. Check it out how many of the following are correct on Oc. 1, 2013. Use it as a future guideline to predict the next September using the current market conditions then:

  1. The market is not excessively expensive, but it is not cheap. It is due for a 5% correction.
  2. Unrest in Syria (check any unrest in your next prediction on September).
  3. High oil prices due to Syria.

4. September is statistically a bad month for the stock market. However, it could be an opportunity to invest after the correction if any.
5. Interest rates is rising.
6. All the above indicate the market will dip. However, the rosier outlook is that the global economies are improving even slowly.

- January effect.
  The performance of January may determine how the entire year performs. I cannot find any rationale but it has been proven right statistically.

- Earnings period announced in Jan., April, July and Oct. would cause big swings in stocks when they have surprises. Earning revisions could be a good predictor.
  http://www.investopedia.com/terms/e/earningsseason.asp

Links
Presidential Cycle:
http://www.investopedia.com/articles/financial-theory/08/presidential-election-cycle.asp

Calendar-based market timing:
http://stock-chartist.com/2010/10/calendar-based-market-timing/

Calendar market timing for 2013:
http://www.investorecho.com/archives/8047

Filler: Golden Gate

Just minutes ago, my mail system asked me to sign in. I did and repeatedly they asked me to sign in again and again. I closed down everything and followed Gates' golden rule: If everything does not work, just power down everything and power it up again. I did this and prayed too. It works. Thanks Gates for fixing my problem.

There is NO one doing BASIC quality control. If it happened in my generation, many guys would be fired. Mediocrity is the new norm?

16   Profitable Early Recovery

I had an 80% return in 2009 in my largest taxable account. I did not include it in my other books before as I just found the statement. Early Recovery, a phase of the market cycle defined by me, is the best time to make a profit. My chart told me to start to move to equity in September, 2009. I did in March, 2009 for other reasons. It could be luck, technique or both.

I did dip into the credit line of my equity loan (not recommended to most) due to lower interest rates than a margin interest. I paid back the loan right after I sold some stocks. The turnaround was high until I exhausted my short-term losses (tax loss harvest). The strategy is bottom fishing. Some sectors described are better in this stage of the market cycle.

I had similar success in 2003. I did not have a defined bottom fishing technique at that time. I expected the market to fully recover in two years. From Value Line, I selected stocks with high "Projected 3-5 year returns" and the short-term assets can last for two more years (judged by the burnt rates).

As the stocks are recovering earnings (E), the trailing P/E may not be a good indicator, but the Forward P/E may be. Most sites on evaluating stocks such as Fidelity have a value grade. Also look for candidates for acquisition. From the last recoveries, I spotted at least one such candidate. They are usually small companies (50 to 300M market cap) and have valuable assets such as customer base and patents. Aggressive investors should buy stocks with the worst timing grades and this the only time to do so; these beaten-up stocks could be big winners.

An article stated that the entire company of an internet company can fit into the conference room of Exxon, and it had the same market cap as Exxon if my memory serves me right. In early April, 2000, I switched all my tech mutual funds in my annuity into traditional sectors (better to cash in hindsight) to avoid the crash. Fishing in the market bottom is risky but very profitable. The Golden Cross could miss the bottom as it depends on past data. Other hints are Buy / Sell ratio is less than 0.2, RSI(14) for SPY is less than 25 and the market has more than 40% lower from the peak.

The stocks that have been beaten down badly and have poor timing scores could be the stocks that have the highest appreciation potential. It is different from the traditional evaluation. I prefer those stocks with positive earnings or at least not losing a lot. The appreciation periods for most of these stocks may not last long. Hence, I recommend using trailing stops (and reviewing the stops periodically) for appreciating stocks. To illustrate, you do not want to lose more than 10% from the peak of a stock and do not take profit prematurely.

My predictions for 2023. If the market recovers in 2023, it could be the beginning of a new cycle. We can use the market timing indicator to confirm it. If there is a serious recession, all bets would be off.

I invested a lot of defensive stocks such as consumer staples, healthcare and utilities. The stocks I recommended in 79% or my book "Best stocks for 2022" has a return of 4% beating RSP by 153% from Dec. 15, 2021 to Dec. 1, 2022. Not counting market timing and the acquired USAK that gained 79% and annualized to 105%.
http://tonyp4idea.blogspot.com/2022/12/best-stocks-series.html

During market recovery, usually the beat-up stocks recover first. Usually the small stocks gain larger profit in the short term and then the large caps. Ensure the stocks are profitable or at least Forward P/E is positive.

Links:

Bottom fishing: https://www.youtube.com/watch?v=hANAn9szRBA
Recommended stocks for Q3 2022. Understand why.
https://www.youtube.com/watch?v=4IxS7pfGukM

17 Market cycle

"Bull markets are born on pessimism, grow on skepticism, mature on optimism, and die on euphoria" - Sir John Templeton

The stock market has cycles as our practical interpretation of the above. It is about five years apart, but it fluctuates widely. I divide it into four stages: Bottom, Early Recovery, Up and Peak.

My defined four stages of a market cycle

We need to apply the right investing strategies to each of the four stages of the cycle.

- **Bottom**

    I would not invest for at least the first six months (or even a year) after the big plunge starts, which could lose over 25% in a few months. The exceptions are investing in contra ETFs and selling short for aggressive investors.

    I estimate it will take a year from the start of the plunge to the bottom, so I will normally sell stocks early in the plunge and do not buy stocks that are in the sector (sometimes sectors) that cause the bubble for about two years after the plunge.

    At the bottom, the high-yield corporate bonds (i.e., junk bonds) would prosper when the interest rate is decreasing to stimulate the economy.

    From mid-2007 to mid-2008, bonds suffered as the investors thought the sky was falling down - it was to those who lost their jobs and/or their houses. After that, some bonds, especially the long-term bonds, could appreciate about 50% in the following year.

    The government lowered the interest rates and these bond prices with high interest rates surged. Correct timing in buying bonds could be very profitable.

    Long-term bonds have more impact by the interest rate: The lower the interest rate, the higher the bond prices of higher-yield bonds. The older bonds with higher interest rates are more valuable to the newer bonds with lower interest rates.

I define this period of the bottom from the start of the plunge to the start of Early Recovery.

- **Early Recovery**
  It usually starts after one year from the plunge; no one can pinpoint the exact time consistently. By this time preferably earlier, we should have closed out all positions in contra ETFs and shorts.

  Roughly speaking, October, 2007 (some use 2008) is the start of the market plunge. March, 2009 is the end of the bottom stage and the start of the early recovery stage of the 2007 cycle. However, every market cycle is different in where it starts and ends.

  The one-year gain from the bottom is most profitable. It usually gains over 25% in a year from the market bottom. I, a conservative investor, had huge gains using some leverage in my largest taxable account in 2009. From my memory, I had a similar return in 2003 but I had not saved the statement as in 2009.

  In this phase, value is a better parameter than growth in searching for stocks. If your investment subscription provides a composite value score and a composite timing score, the sort parameter of your screened stocks could be "Composite Value / Composite Timing" in descending order. Select the top stocks in this order. You still have to analyze the top-screened stocks.

  Forward (same as Expected) P/E is a good metric. However, most companies may be losing money at this stage. Those companies that can last for more than one year with its cash reserve are potential good buys. The best appreciated stocks are beaten companies that have precious technologies and good customer bases. They could be candidates to be acquired if they are small enough.

- **Up**
  Usually, the growth metrics such as PEG could be better than the value metrics such as expected P/E during this phase. Most stocks are winners except contra ETFs and shorting stocks. When the growth stocks are making headlines and the defensive stocks are being

dumped, this is the hint that we're well into the Up phase of the market cycle.

Locate stocks with growth metrics such as favorable PEG and high SMA-200 (from Finviz.com). Do not be scared of how much they have already appreciated. The strategy "Buy High and Sell Higher" works in this phase. Protect your profits with stops.

Ensure that they have value too. Skip the stocks with expected P/Es higher than 35 unless there are good reasons. Most stocks will gain due to the tide of the market. However, when they're overbought (RSI(14) over 65), be careful. When institutional investors sell these stocks, they will crash.

- **Peak**

    When everyone makes easy money and the interest rates are high, watch out. Stop loss and/or stop limit should be used to protect your investment. Check out whether there is any bubble that would burst like the internet in 2000 and finance (and housing) in 2007.

    The internet crisis is easy to spot, but not the financial crisis. In 2007 we had a cycle longer than the average which is about 5 years. The plunge is very fast and very steep – thanks to the institutional investors who drive the market down.

    Run the technical analysis chart described in the Chapter on Spotting Big Market Plunges at least monthly (weekly if you have time). Protect your investment. Do not fall in love with any stock (you can buy it back later at a deep discount). Making the last buck is a fool's game.

    Accumulate cash according to your risk tolerance. A retiree or a conservative investor would accumulate from 25% to 50% and should be ready to move to all cash when the plunge starts.

    We can lower the cash percent if we use enough stop loss protection. Be psychologically prepared because the stock market may still rise for a while. There is no perfect market timing.

The 2007 Cycle

The market plunged starting in 10-2007 and ending in 3-2009 (bottom), started to recover in 3-2009 (early recovery), and trended up from 2010 to 1-2013 (the up phase of the market cycle). As of 3/2016, it is the peak phase defined by me.

As of 1/2013, we have recovered all the market losses since 2007. However, as of 7/2014, the economy has not fully recovered compared to the economy before the plunge. The employment judging by the medium salary has not fully recovered and the economy is not expanding. It is uncommon that the economy does not follow the market. It is due to the excessive supply of money by the government and partly due to globalization to allow companies to hire overseas.

Although a W-shaped recession seldom happens, we have a chance today. We hope we do not have a depression and/or the similar lost decades that Japan has been experiencing. Some may conclude we are close to completing a market cycle from 2007 to 2016. As of 2016, the economy is recovering slowly and we're better than most other global economies.

Again, market timing is not an exact science as it involves irrational human beings and government interventions. The timing using the market cycle described here is a guideline as it is hard to time it exactly.

The average market cycle is about 5 years, but they fluctuate. If we consider 2007 as the plunge, we have about 8 years of this cycle as of 2015.

In a typical cycle (few are typical), we have about one year in each of the 4 phases I defined (plunge, early recovery, up and peak).

Events/Triggers

There are financial events and triggers that cause the transition of one phase of the market cycle to another. They usually do not change the sequence of the phases (say not from Peak to Early Recovery), but they may change the duration of the phase. Examples are:

- The government announcing change of the interest rate,
- Change of employment, and
- Change of GNP.

Sectors in a market cycle (my suggestion)

Market Phase	Favorable	Unfavorable
Early Recovery	Financial, Technology, Industrial	Energy, Telecom, Utilities
Up	Technology, Industrial, Housing	
Peak	Mineral, Health Care, Energy, Long-Term Bond, Consumer Discretionary	
Bottom	Consumer Staples, Utilities	Consumer Discretionary, Technology, Industrial, Long-Term & high-yield Bond

The sectors that cause the recession usually take a longer time to recover. In 2000, the technology sector was not favorable in the Early Recovery phase, contrary to the above table. In 2007, the financial sector was not favorable in the Early Recovery phase. These are the "offending" sectors that cause the plunges.

In a recession, we usually cannot cut down on consumer staples and utilities, but we can cut down on buying consumer gadgets. Companies usually postpone investing in equipment and systems during a recession and expand when the economy is humming. The government usually lowers the interest rates right after the plunge to stimulate the economy.

Conclusion

When the market is about to plunge or change from one stage to another, run the described chart more frequently and read more articles written by the experts.

Again, market timing is not an exact science but it is based on educated guesses. The better guesses should have more rights than wrongs in the long term. Our actions depend on our risk tolerance. Be careful of using any new strategy that has not been fully understood and proven. Since 2000, market timing is very important to your financial health with two market plunges with an average of about 45% loss.

Afterthoughts

- The Dow Theory has a lot of followers in detecting market directions. In a nutshell, the market heading upwards is confirmed by the

Industrial Index and the Transportation Index (less important in today's market especially with internet sales such as songs and movies), and vice versa. As of 4/2014, the two indexes are not in uniform.
http://finance.yahoo.com/blogs/talking-numbers/this-is-a-130-year-old-warning-sign-for-stocks-231901097.html

- The bear market has the following three phases.
1. The market is overvalued.
2. Corporations are not doing well with decreasing earnings and sales.
3. Investors are selling due to fears.

It is the reverse for a bull market: 1.The market is under-valued. 2. The market increases due to increasing corporate profits/sales and 3. Investors are buying due to greed.
- Investopedia has several articles on this topic.
http://www.investopedia.com/terms/b/businesscycle.asp
- The yield curve could predict the interest rates change and hence the economy. There are three main types of yield curve shapes: normal, flat and inverted.

A normal yield curve is one in which longer maturity bonds have a higher yield. Similarly, the long-term CD should have a higher interest rate than the short-term CD.

When the shorter-term yields are higher than the longer-term yields, it indicates an upcoming recession. A flat yield curve indicates the economy is transiting. Now, you've read the essence of a book on this topic costing about $50 to buy.

However, especially today, it does not mean anything as the government supplies too much money to stimulate the economy unsuccessfully. My simple chart described using SMA-350 (Simple Moving Average for 350 trading sessions) which depends on the stock price works better. Click here for "The dynamic yield curve" (http://stockcharts.com/freecharts/yieldcurve.php).

The interest rate plays a role too. The easy money encourages folks to borrow money to buy stocks and companies to acquire other companies.

- As of Feb., 2013, I believe we're in the Up stage of the market cycle. I checked the performances of my top screens from each stage (a.k.a. phase) of the market cycle for the last 60 days. The best performance as a group belongs to the screens for the Up stage. Controversial! Always use the screens (same as searches) that perform well recently.

  In addition, the market has recovered 120% of the loss of 2007-2008. Hence the duration for an average Up stage of the market is quite close.
- Total Market Cap / GNP ratio is hotly debated on the market value. Different from the traditional 100%, I would suggest that the boundary ratio should be 130%. If it is over 130%, the market is overvalued and vice versa.
  http://www.investopedia.com/terms/m/marketcapgdp.asp
  Market cycle: https://www.youtube.com/watch?v=ebWL2TrIssA
  Bull market: https://www.investopedia.com/terms/b/bullmarket.asp

Bull / Bear market

This is a summary of my views. In short, most investments appreciate in a bull market, and vice versa in a bear market. It is indicated by the described Golden Cross and Death Cross. In 2022's bear market, even the bonds did not fare well. It is partly due to raising the interest rates too fast to counter inflation. If inflation is under control, the Fed would not have another interest hike.

The market cycle is usually ahead of the economy cycle. When conditions such as low interest rates, companies make easy money and hence boost the general economy. When the economy is overheated, the Federal Reserve has to increase interest rates to cool down the economy and prevent the formation of a bubble. At that time, most companies suffer and lay off workers. At the end of this cycle, the Federal Reserve most likely lowers the interest rates to stimulate the economy and start the cycle again.

Investors should be very careful in investing during the bear market and avoid failing companies. In the beginning of the bull market, invest in companies that their stock prices have been beaten up but have a good chance to survive. Many S&P 500 companies were formed during the bear market. The lack of venture capital is offset by lower expenses and fewer competitions.

#Filler: Destruction of a country

Is the membership of NATO worth the destruction of a country? Definitely not. A good politician should get the membership before his announcement. Murdering citizens is a war crime to me.** Book 5: Sector Rotation

Sector rotation has been proven to make good profits with the least risk if it is properly implemented. However, sectors are risky, less diversified and more volatile than the market. In the long run, this book improves your odds in making profits rather than traditional schemes in sector rotation by:

- Market Timing. When the market is plunging, do not buy any stock including sector ETFs and sector funds. This book provides a simple chart to detect market plunges. The simplest (for beginners) is a sector rotation between SPY (an ETF that simulates the market) and cash (or an ETF of short-term bonds).
- The next rotation strategy involves four ETFs in a rising market. Optionally, advance investors can include a contra ETF to time the market further. Buy the best performer from the last month of these four selected ETFs.
- Some sectors perform better in different stages of a market cycle.
- Many free sites describe the best sector performers such as Seeking Alpha and CNNfn.
- Evaluate sectors using Technical Analysis (simple charts available free from the web and Fundamental Analysis.
- You should spend one or two hours a month to determine which sector to rotate to, or move your portfolio to cash when the market is risky. The "Buy and hold" strategy has not performed since 2000.
- Subscription services of which there are many. Even if you subscribe to these services, you should read this book to evaluate their services and use this book as a second opinion. When your portfolio is over $100,000, $100 for a yearly subscription should pay for itself in the long run.
- Market timing by calendar and presidential cycle.
- My recent experiences in sector trading. Be careful with many of the books on this topic that were written by professors who may never have made a buck in the stock market. When you see a lot of equations, run as fast as you can.
- Some "best" sellers were written more than 10 years ago that do not use today's basic tools such as technical analysis and the extensive

offers of so many sector ETFs. They bear little resemblance to today's market, which can be manipulated by institutional investors.
- Most large companies today are global companies. The importance with investing in foreign companies or diversifying is less important than in the past.
- When China expands, natural resource-rich countries would most likely benefit, and vice versa.
- Most likely for luck but with good reasons, I predicted correctly that a disaster would happen in China as reported in August, 2019 in my article "Disasters in 2020". The second prediction has not happened yet, but it has more impact to our economy.

The third prediction: China would not agree to pay for the damages of this pandemic and that would lead to the freezing of their debts to us (1.07T as of Dec., 2019). Eventually it could lead to cold war or even a military war. I hope it would never happen.

Besides industrial sectors, I include bonds, contra ETFs, sector mutual funds, countries, commodities, etc. Today, most sectors are covered by ETFs. For example, you do not need to buy gold coins to invest in that sector but the ETF GLD.

18 Ask AI (ChatGPT) for 2025 Outlook

Ask "The probability of a market crash" on 1/2025. Try it as the current market could indicate otherwise. However, most likely their data bases have **not been outdated.** As of 2/10/2025, DeepSeek has not been banned. Most factors have been described in this book. The following is displayed on with my comments.

The chance of a market crash depends on various factors, including economic indicators, geopolitical events, monetary policies, and investor sentiment. While predicting the exact timing of a crash is impossible, several signals can indicate heightened risks. Here's an overview of factors that can increase the likelihood of a market downturn:

Comment. Technical Analysis is more important than fundamental analysis in market timing. I prefer my version of Death Cross for no chart and SMA-350 (when SPY dips below the SMA-350 line)

Key Risk Indicators for a Market Crash
1. **Economic Slowdown or Recession**:
    - Declining GDP growth, rising unemployment, or reduced consumer spending are warning signs.
    - If inflation outpaces wages, consumer demand may decline, leading to a slowdown.
2. **High Valuations**:
    - When stock valuations (e.g., Price-to-Earnings ratios) are far above historical averages, it signals a potential bubble. For example, the tech sector in 2000 or housing in 2007.
3. **Rising Interest Rates**:
    - The Federal Reserve (or other central banks) raising interest rates to combat inflation can hurt growth, increase borrowing costs, and weigh on company profits.
    - This often results in capital flowing out of equities and into bonds.
4. **Excessive Market Leverage**:
    - High margin debt or leveraged bets often precede crashes, as forced selling can trigger rapid declines during corrections.
5. **Geopolitical Tensions**:

- Events like wars, trade conflicts, or major political instability (e.g., U.S.-China relations or the Ukraine war) can rattle markets.
6. **Corporate Earnings Decline**:
    - A sustained decline in corporate profitability reduces investor confidence, particularly in high-growth sectors.
7. **Overdependence on Stimulus**:
    - Post-COVID-19 market growth was partly driven by fiscal stimulus and low interest rates. A withdrawal of liquidity from the market ("quantitative tightening") could lead to corrections.
8. **Sectoral or Asset-Specific Bubbles**:
    - Overheated sectors, such as tech stocks (e.g., FAANG), cryptocurrencies, or real estate, could drag down broader indices if bubbles burst.
9. **Market Psychology**:
    - Fear-driven selling often exacerbates downturns. This can be triggered by events such as a high-profile corporate failure, surprising inflation reports, or aggressive Federal Reserve actions.

Likelihood of a Market Crash in 2025
Current trends (as of early 2025) influencing crash probabilities include:
- **Persistent Inflation or Deflation Risks**: If central banks tighten policy too aggressively or fail to manage inflation, growth could stall.
- **High Debt Levels**: Both government and corporate debt remain high, making markets more vulnerable to shocks.
- **AI and Tech Volatility**: Overvaluation in emerging technologies (like AI) may pose risks if optimism fades.

However, it's essential to note that:
- Most crashes are preceded by years of warning signals.
- Markets tend to rebound over time after downturns, which underscores the importance of long-term investing.

Comment. AI usually does not give you exact numbers. You can search them from many sources. Fidelity's Viewpoint (register required) usually have good insights.

How to Prepare for a Potential Crash
1. **Diversify Investments**:

- Spread your portfolio across sectors, regions, and asset classes (e.g., bonds, commodities, real estate).

  Comment. Gold (GLD for ETF) and silver (SLV for ETF).

2. **Focus on Quality Assets**:
   - Invest in companies with strong balance sheets, consistent earnings, and low debt.
3. **Consider Defensive Sectors**:
   - Healthcare, utilities, and consumer staples often perform better during downturns.
4. **Use Stop-Loss Orders**:
   - Set automatic sell orders to limit losses on individual stocks.
5. **Maintain Cash Reserves**:
   - Having liquidity lets you capitalize on opportunities during corrections.

   Comment. Aggressive investors can buy contra ETFs (betting the market going down further), and even shorting stocks (for taxable accounts).
6. **Monitor Indicators**:
   - Keep an eye on key metrics like the yield curve, corporate earnings, and market sentiment.
7. **Avoid Panic Selling**:
   - Market downturns are often temporary. History shows that markets recover, sometimes within a few years.

Comment. Return to equity when the market recovers. They are among my best years in investing.

As of Jan., 2025, the market is tough to predict. Several major investors including Buffett is accumulating cash, while many fund managers predict a bull market for the year. The market is making new heights in January.

I choose the middle ground. Usually I sell 2 stocks and buy one. At the end of January, I have about 10% in cash, CDs and some contra ETFs from my rough estimate. I watch technical indicators more frequently.

Book 5: Sector Rotation

1   Sector rotation in a nutshell

How to start

I have been rotating sectors in my annuity investments for quite a long time with a sum of more than my annual salary at the time. As of 1/2020, it had increased about four times. My mutual fund employer had a lot of restrictions for me trading stocks, so rotating sector funds in my annuity was the best investment tool for me.

For a starter, I recommend to paper trade your strategy first. Use Finviz.com, SeekingAlpha.com and/or Fidelity.com to select the best performing sector and/or use my quick analysis of ETFs. Switch it every month (or two) to the ETF corresponding to the best sector. Again, switch to cash when the market is risky. You may consider sector mutual funds which are managed, but most have restrictions such as holding periods and fees. Most if not all sector mutual funds do not have contra funds that expect the sector to go down in value. Sector mutual funds cannot be shorted.

After the basics, this book provides many features to further refine your strategy such as technical Analysis. Beginners should use Strategy 1 in Book 2. After that, start with the technical indicators such as SMA-50 and RSI(14) with a handful of sector ETFs to rotate (suggested sectors are technology, bank, health care, housing, consumer and material).

In addition, some sectors are more profitable in different phases of a market cycle. We will examine several industry sectors and country sectors in more detail. China is affecting the global economies including ours. When the interest rates are low, it would affect bonds and stocks yielding high dividends. Many books ignore market timing. It turns out to be the most important technique as the last market plunges have had an average loss of 45%!

The keys to profitable sector rotation

Sector rotation could be very profitable and less risky than most of us may expect. However, it is volatile and risky if not properly implemented. There are two ways to profit from the following:

1. Buy the sector when it is trending up and sell when the sector is trending down. It is the common approach to sector rotation.

2. Buy at the bottom or close to of a sector and sell at the peak or close to. It is hard to detect the bottom/peak.

Many investment subscriptions and free sites such as Finviz.com select favorable sectors every month. We assume the best-performing sector last month will perform better in the coming month or months. It does not always happen such as the tech sector in April, 2000 and the reversed direction of the drug sector in 2015. To protect your investments, use stops.

Alternatively, we can select them via simple charts as described in this book. Beginners should start with Single Moving Average (SMA-20 and SMA-50 for 20 sessions and 50 sessions respectively) provided by Finviz.com without charting.

Detecting the bottom of a sector
It is not easy and no one can detect the bottom or the peak of a sector consistently but easier with trends. Enter the ETF for a specific sector or the SPY for the market in Finviz. Use a short-term SMA such as SMA-20 and SMA-50 (expressed in percent), and check these two parameters every week. If both SMA-20 and SMA-50 are positive, most likely the market or a sector is trending up.

For market timing, the SMA-350 (Single Moving Average with 350 sessions) detects the market quite accurately for the last two market plunges. I have tested out the "days" with different numbers and 350 is the best fit for the last two market plunges. In recent days, 400 could be a better choice to reduce the number of false alarms.

Besides technical indicators, there are hints that indicate a sector is close to the bottom. Using the ETF for the sector and check out the fundamental metrics similar to evaluating a stock. To illustrate, enter XLE in Yahoo!Finance or Finviz.com to get the current price and other info about this sector. Sites specializing in ETFs such as ETFdb that will give you more information about ETFs.

The intangibles for stocks and ETFs should be considered too. For example in 2020, the potential decoupling with China would make a lot of U.S. chip companies less profitable.

Detecting the trend
Detecting the trend is easier than detecting the bottom/peak. To illustrate, bring up Finviz.com from your browser and enter XLE. For most sectors, I use the SMA-50 (single moving average for last 50 days), which is readily available as one of the metrics. When the stock price is 3% above this SMA, it is most likely a buy. When it is 3% below this SMA, sell. It is simple, and it has been proven many times. Currently Finviz.com provides SMA-20 and SMA-50 only for short-term averages. For other durations, you can construct charts.

You can adjust the 50-day and the 3% (some use 1% or 5%) on how long your average holding period of an ETF or a stock that also depends on how often you want to trade). If your holding period is longer, use higher number such as 90 days; use SMA-20 if it is shorter. If you want to trade more often use 2% instead of 3% (or use 5% if you want to trade less often).

Personally I use 60 days if I use charts (from Yahoo!Finance among one of the many free sites that provide charts). One of my sector fund accounts requires 60 days for a minimum holding period without incurring a fee.

To detect a market crash and when to reenter the market, I use 350 days (some use 300 or 400 days). The 'days' are actually trade sessions.

The RSI(14) indicates whether the sector is overbought or oversold. RSI oscillates between zero and 100. Traditionally, and according to Wilder, the creator, RSI is considered overbought with a value above 70 and oversold with a value below 30 as described in the article. This indicator is available from Finviz.com.

> (http://stockcharts.com/school/doku.php?id=chart_school:technical_indicators:relative_strength_index_rsi)
>
> A simple way is to buy last month's winner(s). Ensure your ETFs are not leveraged if you are conservative. Include contra ETFs when the market is risky for aggressive investors. Here are the links to the websites that keep track of top performers varying from 1 to 3 months.

Seeking Alpha's ETF Hub.
http://seekingalpha.com/insight/etf-hub/asset_class_performance/key_markets
Morning Star. Select the period (1 month for example).
http://news.morningstar.com/etf/Lists/ETFReturns.htm

What to buy
I prefer ETFs for specific sectors and the second choice is sector funds (check out the holding period to exit without penalties). With good analysts, most sector funds are better than ETFs in specific sectors such as banking, drug companies and mining. Compare their performances.

ETFs charge less for maintaining and they have all the advantages of a stock. However, mutual funds select the stocks within a sector selectively. Fidelity offers the most complete list of sector mutual funds. Again compare the 3- or 5-year performance between the ETF and the fund in this same sector.

The third option is a top-down approach. First, when the market is not plunging, select the most favorable sector and then the bet stocks within the sector. Many free sites provide a filter to find favorable sectors.

Here is a list of sector ETFs.
(http://www.bloomberg.com/markets/etfs/)

Here is a list of commission-free ETFs from Fidelity.
(https://www.fidelity.com/etfs/ishares)

Some funds automatically switch sectors for you. From my experience so far, they have not proved to be very profitable. You should check out their past performances.

Favorable sectors according to the market cycle
Refer to the chapter on Market Timing and Spotting a Market Plunge for specific strategies. Close and/or adjust your positions when the market is plunging.

Favorable sectors according to the interest rate
It is similar to the above. Retailing, auto and housing are usually hurt by high interest rates. An improving economy would do the opposite.

Favorable sectors according to geography
It is not an easy task. China and India had their best performing years. The trade war with the U.S. may favor India as of 2020. Japan had one of the best years in 2013 during the last two decades. For foreign countries, currency fluctuation should be considered. Most emerging countries have their ups and downs. Most ETFs and sector funds in emerging countries buy larger companies that are more trustworthy as noted with their financial statements.

Global economies have never been that tightly connected. When the U.S. economy is down, China is affected and so are the resource-rich countries that China depends on.

Favorable and unfavorable events
The EU crisis has taken more than three years as of 4/2016 and the EU stocks are still close to the bottom. I prefer to buy ETFs or mutual funds which specialize in EU stocks, when the trend is up.

When the head of our Treasury says the interest will be lower, the market and the long-term bond funds will move up, and vice versa. To me, the interest rates will move up slowly from the 1/2014 bottom.

Recent favorable and unfavorable sectors
There are many sources to check which sectors performed best recently. Finviz.com is one of them. From the top menu bar, select Group, and the best and worst sectors will be displayed. Skip one day or one week unless you have a special interest on these short durations. Select the duration depending on your purpose. Personally I would use one month (or two) for my monthly rotation strategy assuming the momentum would pass to the next month.

Technical analysis would help to spot the trend. Select the Simple Moving Average. It is similar to the TA used in the chapter spotting a market crash. Instead of using SPY or another ETF market index, use an ETF that represents the sector.

Sector rotation by fund managers

We cannot beat these institutional investors. We need to follow them, or be one step ahead of them. They rotate sectors when they find another sector that has better appreciation potential, or the current favorable sector has reached its peak.

When to rotate

Rotate for the following reasons:

1. When the market is plunging, rotate the sector ETFs and/or mutual funds to cash. Aggressive investors would rotate their equities to contra ETFs. The average loss of the last two market plunges had been about 45%. This chart will not determine the peak (or bottom) as it depends on the falling data. However, it will tell you when to exit to prevent a further loss and tell you when to reenter the market.
2. When the fundamentals of the current sector you owned are turning bad.
3. When there is another sector that has better appreciation potential. Finviz.com tells you the rankings of the sectors.
4. When the sector is overbought or peaking, and / or has met our objective.

Do not forget about market timing

Do NOT buy any stocks except the contra ETFs for an aggressive investor, when the market is plunging. Playing defense usually wins the game more often than playing offense. When the market is peaking, protect your profits by placing stop loss orders.

Positions and how often to switch

It depends on the size of your portfolio and how much time you can afford to monitor your portfolio. To me, it varies from 2 to 6 positions and 20 to 90 days to monitor these switches.

Statistics show that a portfolio with 5 positions rotating in 20 days give you slightly better performance and less drawback (maximum loss for the period). I recommend 4 (2 for a portfolio of less than $20,000) and 30 days (and 60 days for Fidelity sector funds). You determine according to your portfolio size and the time available to you for investing.

Conclusion

Sector rotation is described in very basic terms here. The links in Afterthoughts provide additional information.

As a reminder, **roughly half of a stock's price movement can be attributed to the sector** it is in.

Afterthoughts

- There are many articles on this topic. They are:

    Sector rotation strategies ETF investors must know. There are many useful links.
    http://www.bloomberg.com/markets/etfs/

    Sector rotation based on performance.
    http://stockcharts.com/school/doku.php?id=chart_school:trading_strategies:sector_rotation_roc
    Fidelity on Sectors.
    https://www.fidelity.com/sector-investing/overview
    Video instruction.
    http://www.YouTube.com/watch?v=j5yYoOoATRM

- No one can consistently predict the bottom or the peak of any sector. Sometimes we move in too early and lose another 25% or so, or we leave the sector too early to lose another 25% or so potential gain. It is quite normal. Learn why we move with in the wrong time frame, and a lot of times it may be just bad luck or other events that are beyond our control.

- A free (as of this writing) service on sector rotation.
    http://www.gosector.com/

#Filler: Ambition is good

That is what I heard from the web. The little girl wanted to be a president when she grew up. After attending a circus, she wanted to be a clown. Her smart father told her that she could be both.

When a kid wants to be a president, most likely the kid will be a good citizen.

2   Outline on how to start sector rotation

As with everything in life, there is no guarantee that this book will make you a lot of money. However, the chance of success will be substantially improved especially when you practice with most of the ideas presented in this book. Always start with paper trading first.

1. First determine your objectives. Retirees select safer strategies. Millionaires can afford to select riskier strategies for larger returns.

2. Determine your risk tolerance, how much time you have for investing, your knowledge of investing, and your desire to continue to learn about investing and your portfolio size.

   To illustrate, when the market is risky, do not buy any stock. However for investors who can tolerate higher risk, buy contra ETFs as a hedge against the market for larger returns. Retirees may be less risk tolerant unless they're rich.

   If your job is very demanding, you should spend less time in investing even if you're knowledgeable on investing and have a desire to learn about investing.

   Check your net worth (= what you own – what you owe) and cash flow (incomes – debt payments). Reserve your emergency cash equal to your expenses for at least 3 months.

   If the above is limited, SPY or any ETF simulating the market is your only sector and market timing is your primary tool (Book 2, Strategy 1, Chapter 2). You can stop here for now, and continue reading the rest of the book when the limitations change.

3. When the market is peaking, invest cautiously. Use trailing stops described in this book. The same for your sector ETFs / funds that have appreciated a lot.

4. When you have lost two trades in a row, take a break and return to paper trading until you're comfortable.

5. Test your strategies on paper. This book requires you to try out the various strategies, and select the one you are comfortable with. All theories may not always work for real trading.

6. When a strategy has been thoroughly tested out recently and the results are good, use real money slowly and gradually. Then monitor your performance.

7. When you have a new strategy or you need to test a strategy whether it works in the current market, read "Testing strategies" (Bonus).

Not all of predictions (mine or others) have materialized, and no strategy is evergreen. Always use stops to protect your portfolio. Learn from your arguments for the predictions, not merely the accuracy of the predictions. Predictions are based on educated guesses, and hence hopefully more of them will materialize in the long run. Consult your financial advisor before investing with real money.

The rest of this book describes the other aspects of sector rotation such as Top-Down Investing (in case you prefer to find the stocks in the favorable sector), country sectors, specific industry sectors… Many investing ideas described here are applicable to other investing strategies.

3   Sectors

The primary sectors are: Materials, Consumer Discretionary, Consumer Staples, Energy, Financial, Real Estate, Health Care, Industrial, Information Technology and Utilities. Click the above links from Fidelity, or search from Fidelity, Investopedia and/or Wikipedia for a description of these sectors.

We can subdivide a sector into sub sectors (a.k.a. industries). For example, Information Technology can be divided into Computer and Software. When the computer industry is good, it does not mean that the software industry is also good. Some industries such as banking software can belong to more than one sector (banking and software in this example).

Fidelity has its own definition and overview as described in this link: https://www.fidelity.com/sector-investing/overview

In the above links, Fidelity describe sectors pretty well. Many vendors including IBD provide industry rankings. You may want to select the best sector or industry first and then select the best stocks in that sector or industry.

GIGS (developed by MSCI and S&P 500) separates more than 29,000 stocks into 11 major sectors. It is very similar to Fidelity but GIGS's industry classification is more complicated to deploy. Most other sources do not follow GIGS's industry classification.

Here is my additional description to cover the basic sectors and some will be described in more detail in their appropriate strategies that follow.

Materials
Material should be separated into two categories: Basic (a.k.a. Industrial) Materials and Precious Metals. Basic materials such as copper and iron rise in prices when the economy is humming, and vice versa. Precious Metals such as gold and silver do not usually correlate with basic materials. Gold and silver usually rise due to high inflation, political unrest and/or falling USD.

Consumer Staples and Discretionary
Consumer Staples are food, beverages, household products and the products we buy as necessities. They are recession-proof. Our products have demonstrated high quality and safety. With the growing middle class

in developing countries such as China and India, we expect they should grow well outside the USA. In early 2020, it has not been the case due to the trade war.

Consumer Discretionary are just the opposite. For example, car sales would be down in a recession.

Energy

Energy has many sub sectors (a.k.a. industries) such as clean energy, exploring, distribution, refining and even all of the above (using the term 'integrate'). When the economy is growing, usually energy sectors rise in price. When the market and/or oil price falls, Saudi Arabia, the largest oil exporter, would dump more oil and hence it would make the oil price fall further.

Financial

The sub sectors are banks, mortgage companies, brokerages (tough industry with no commission trades today), insurance companies and many other financial institutions. This sector would plunge during a recession. In the period of 2007 and 2008, this sector had a tough time.

Real Estate

Besides housing construction, this sector is primarily made up of companies that own and/or build properties and REITs. This sector should not do well during a recession.

Health Care
It should be divided into many sub sectors: hospitals, research / development of medical equipment and drugs. In some sense, hospitals and generic drugs also belong to Consumer Staples that you need to use or buy regardless of the condition of the economy. Most likely, we do not need new equipment and new drugs in a depressed economy.

Industrial

This sector includes Boeing, construction equipment companies such as Caterpillar and defense companies. Most of GE's subsidiaries belong to this sector. With the global economies slowing down and the problems with Boeing in 2019, this sector has not been doing well in 2020.

Information technology
It is a very wide sector covering hardware companies and software companies. If Telecommunication is not a separate sector, it should be under this sector too. Microsoft, Facebook and Apple are under this sector. From 1/2010 to 1/2020, this sector is very profitable. With the decoupling with China, the profits will be reduced.

Utilities

It is a consumer staple sector. However, we use more electricity, fuels and water when the economy is humming.

Other sectors

Transportation, Services and Retail should be separate sectors but are not classified so by many institutions. Retail has had a tough time since the rise of Amazon, and now it is even worse during the pandemic of 2020.

Links

A list of sectors.
http://www.investorguide.com/sector-list.php
Check's sector analysis.
http://seekingalpha.com/article/2806655-the-stock-market-2015-a-sector-by-sector-valuation-perspective-part-1-an-overview

#Filler: My grandson

My six-year-old grandson called the library about the availability of the book Mine Craft. The lady told him that only "Mine Craft for Dummies" was available. He told her it was not for him as he was not a dummy.

#Filler: My daughter's wedding banquet

How do you have a wedding banquet that the entire town will talk about and at the least cost? It is at the Burger King where they treat you like a king. All the fries are super-sized and the drinks are bottomless. The king's crown and the most popular party favor, are included. Of course, my daughter flatly refused.

4   Subsectors (i.e. Industries) and sector funds

Sectors are further divided into subsectors (same as industries). For example, Oil Energy is a sector while Oil Exploration and Oil Service are industries. Industries cover a very specialized segment of the sector, so they consist of fewer companies and sometimes smaller companies; they are more volatile and hence riskier. To illustrate, the ETF for an industry (say Oil Exploration) has less companies than the entire sector Oil Energy. Some industry ETFs such as Uranium are very small with a handful of stocks; they are highly volatile with high risk.

Sector mutual funds are managed by fund managers who select stocks instead of including most stocks in the sector. The disadvantages over ETFs are fees, restrictions of holding periods (the usual 1 to 2 months) without a penalty, offering fewer industries and you cannot short a fund.

SeekingAlpha.com has a good performance summary for each sectors including many countries and industries. Select the best ETF from the last month, use stop loss to protect momentum reversal and switch when there is a better sector or industry to buy. Aggressive investors can also short an ETF, or buy contra ETFs for the worst performed sectors or industries.

5 Selecting ETFs

Judging by the popularity, ETFs are a better way to rotate within sectors compared to sector mutual funds. Select ETFs from my ETF tables (Book 2, Strategy 3, Chapter 1). You rotate an ETF(s) from your selection of ETFs. I will explain my selection here starting from a few to about 25. It is less time-consuming to limit your selection to 4 to analyze and keep track of their performances. A larger selection gives you more choices and hence supposedly improves your performance.

The selected ETFs must have assets over 100 million. If there are two similar ETFs, check out their expense ratios. As of today, Fidelity offers commission-free for most ETFs. Check your broker for similar offerings. The corresponding sector fund is also provided in my tables; you cannot rotate ETFs within Fidelity's Annuities.

Beginners should skip subsectors (a.k.a. industries), which are riskier as they are too specialized. Skip the leveraged ETFs unless you can bear the risk.

Some sectors especially the subsectors are more volatile than others and they would be on the top and bottom performers more frequently. From Finviz.com or other sources, check out the RSI(14) to ensure the sector is not overbought (i.e. the value is greater than 65). I prefer to select the one of the top ETFs with a lower volatility and an RSI(14) between 30 and 60. From my testing using ETFReplay, it is better to use 2 months rather than 20 trade days for selecting the best-performing ETFs.

Starting with ETFs

To start, I recommend the following ETFs: SPY and GLD (in the risky 2020). Add a money market fund, or a bond ETF with a short duration when the market is risky. Beginners should NOT use SH (a contra ETF to SPY) for monthly rotation and only aggressive investors should buy SH when the market is plunging.

Add the following ETFs to broaden your selection on market cap: DIA, QQQ, SPYG, SPYV, NOBL, IWM, IWC and BOND. The market may favor very large companies (DOW), tech (QQQ), growth (SPYG), value (SPYV), NOBL (dividend), mid cap (MDY), small cap (IWM) and microcap (IWC; risky). Add a total bond (BOND) if desirable. Optionally I add buy back (PKW) and momentum (MTUM).

It is better not to include bond funds in monthly rotation. Long term bond funds rise opposite of the interest rate.

Skip foreign countries if you do not want to take the foreign exchange risk. Otherwise, I would include some foreign exposure: small cap (SCZ), Europe (VGK), China (FXI), Latin America (ILF), EFA(EAFE), global (KXI) and VWO (Emerging; risky).

If you're into specific foreign countries, add Australia (EWA), Brazil (EWZ), Canada (EWC), India (INDY), Indonesia (EIDO), Hong Kong (EWH), Japan (EWJ), Singapore (EWS), Taiwan (EWT), United Kingdom (EWU) and Vietnam (VNM; profitable if decoupling with China).

The last selection could be the only selection for some investors specialized in industry sectors (a.k.a. sub sectors). They are the industry sectors: bank (KBE), Bio (XBI), consumer discretionary (XLY), consumer staple (XLP), finance (IYF), energy (XLE), health care (IYH), house builders (ITB), industrial (IYJ), material (XME), oil (USO), oil service (OIH), oil exploration (XOP), gas (UNG), real estate (VNQ), retail (RTH), regional banking (KRE), semiconductor (SMH), software (XSW) and technology (XLK).

My summaries from testing (mainly from using ETFReplay):

- Slightly better results using relative strength of 1 month than 2 months. 1 month means 20 trade sessions (30 days - 10 weekends / holidays). Relative strength means picking the best performing ETF from your selected group of ETFs.

- There were better results not using contra ETFs (could be due to our long bull market from 2009), so I skipped them especially for beginners.

- The same for interest-sensitive ETFs, so I actually skipped them.

- Do not include the offending sectors that caused the market to crash – these sectors take longer to recover. They are internet ETF (not available then) in 2000 and banks / house construction in 2008.

6   An example: Rotating Apple

Contrarian

I have been contrarian several times and most times I made good money. We need to have good arguments to be contrary. Otherwise, we're committing financial suicide.

Many investors commit the same error: Invest in a company because they love the company's products. We need to check out the fundamentals of the company and its prospect. I have nothing against Apple. Actually I recommended Apple before based on its great fundamentals when many institutional investors were dumping it.

Scoring Apple

When I was writing the book Scoring Stocks, first I used IBM but its low score would not be a good example. Then I switched to Apple (AAPL). It scored almost the highest. I recommended AAPL at $55.72 (split adjusted) on April 19, 2013, the date the book mentioned was published. It is another example that fundamentals work. However, when we're swimming against the tide, we need to be patient. At that time, the media and institutional investors ignored fundamentals. The best argument of not buying Apple was "Apple has turned from a growth stock to a value stock". They think they cannot get fired by thinking the same as the herd. Just garbage talk from the smartest folks!

Fundamental analysis as of 02/23/2015

	Passing grade	AAPL	Industry
Score System #1	>=15	16	
Score System #2	>=2	2	
Pow EY	>=5	6%	
Expected Earning Yield	>5 & <35	7%	5%
Debt / Equity	<.5	.30	.29
Analyst Rating	>7	9	
EB/EBIT	>5	13	
F-Score	>7	6	
ROE	>=15%	37%	27%
SMA-200	>0%	29%	
RSI(14)	<60	78	
Price		$132.06	

Explanation
- The first scoring system incorporates many vendors' grades. The second scoring system is from my book Scoring Stocks using metrics available free from many websites.
- Pow EY – Earning Yield (E/P) takes cash and debt into consideration.
- Expected EY, Debt/Equity, ROE, SMA-200 and RSI(14) are obtained from Finviz.com.
- Analyst Rating (now it is Equity Summary Score) is from Fidelity. Alternatively, use Recommendation from Finviz.com.
- EB/EBIT and F-Score are from GuruFocus.com.

How Apple scores

It scores fine but not spectacular. The score from my book in April, 2013 is 5 and as of this writing it is 2. Fundamentally it is not as good as before.

P/B and P/S are usually not useful for high tech companies. However, Apple's P/B at 6 is exceedingly expensive as compared to Google's 3. When most analysts like the stock, usually it will rise in the short-term. RSI(14) shows it is overbought. To conclude, its fundamental score passes but not in flying colors.

The brief Fundamental Analysis should be followed by the following:

Qualitative Analysis includes articles for Apple. First, search articles on Apple from Finviz.com and Seeking Alpha. Large companies like Apple are hard to manipulate, so most articles are not 'pump and dump'.

Technical Analysis detects the trend and overbought condition. Many investors do not buy a stock that is in its downward trend. SMA-200 is a good long-term trend indicator. Its price should be above the SMA-200 (same as SMA-200 is positive in Finviz.com).

Intangible Analysis
Apple has lost a visionary leader Steve Jobs. I hope he was not replaced by similar managers at Microsoft, who are responsible for Microsoft's lost decade with few innovative products. Apple has a lot of cash to finance new projects. High tech business is tough as they need to build a better mouse trap continuously. When the mouse trap becomes a commodity,

the profit margin would be reduced. This is the major reason that Buffett does not invest in Apple. If he read my book in May, 2013, he would buy Apple instead of IBM saving his company millions minus $10 for my book. LOL.

There are bright and bad spots for Apple:

1. Apple Textbook. Imagine all students carry iPads instead of textbooks. Several educational apps have been created for iPads. The competition is laptops and Chrome Book.

2. Apple TV.
   It is a loser so far with a lot of risk and potential competitors. However, the potential is great. It could give all cable companies a run for the money. Wider internet channels would make it more feasible. Will the cable companies provide these speeds to allow Apple TV and similar products to step into their turfs?

3. While the iPad and iPhone are peaking in the hardware, iTunes, software and contents for these devices to access have no limit. We have witnessed how iPad helps the folks with autism and iPhones for the blind. I can envision many other similar applications.

4. Will Apple move into Kindle's market?

5. All the mobile phone technology is originated by the first generation (if not counting Motorola) that Apple has a lot of patents. Its lawyers will milk money from Samsung. It also prevents cheap mobile phones from coming to the USA. U.S. helps Apple by not letting Huawei's phones in.

6. Apple Pay.
   Apple has a proven history of picking up some failed products and turning them into gold. This product could be the next innovative and most profitable for Apple. Apple Pay will not make a splash in the bottom line initially.

7. Apple Watch.
   There will be cheap Chinese products flooded in our market. However, the selling point is the prestige of Apple and its integration to other Apple products. The major problem of Apple Watch is the short battery

life. With the reduced urge of upgrade and competition on Apple phones, Apple Watch is a bright product for Apple.

8. The major worry is whether they can maintain the urge of upgrade. If the new enhancements would not give me reason to upgrade, I would not be the one waiting in long line in bitter cold weather to upgrade my iPhone just to satisfy my dumb ego. It accounts the majority of Apple's profit.

9. Apple has a lot of cash. Dividends usually boost the stock price and the option values granted to the management. However, it is important to plow back to development and acquiring technologies.

10. U.S. stops Huawei and Xiaomi from coming to the U.S. Apple is not the state-of-the-art phones.

#Filler: iGeneration

Almost everyone has an iPhone. Folks including myself in the lower class of the society carry imitators and/or those 'outdated' iPhones that are several months old.

My grandchild of just over one year old had a good time in playing with the iPad and it usually kept her busy for hours. Before she could say Mom, she said "I" for iPad. During my family gatherings, my cousins communicate with each other via their smartphones even when they sit next to each other. When they do not text messages, they play games with their smartphones.

Even with one pair of eyes and one pair of ears, they can play iPad, listen to iPod and text using iPhone at the same time. Thanks Apple for demonstrating what multi-tasking really is. I prefer to do one task correctly than several tasks incorrectly. Chinese and Indian students are leaving us further behind by spending more time in study. Do you believe those children spending extra 2 hours every day in games would accomplish the same later in life?

Some parents have a hard time to explain to their children that their existence was due to the blackout of the iPad and iPhone caused by the hurricanes.

7   Profit from bull, bear and sideways market

We can profit from bull, bear and sideways markets with minimal effort and no knowledge in investing. This can be determined by my version of Death Cross /Golden Cross, or using 350-SMA (Simple Moving Average). When the average line and the price line cross each other frequently, it should be a sideways market.

Bull Markets. Emphasizes momentum trading, breakout strategies, and growth investing. Advocate for trend-following techniques and the use of leveraged instruments cautiously Protect your portfolio by using stops and trailing stops.

Bear Markets. Focuses on staple stocks, CDs, short-selling, contra ETFs, and defensive assets such as gold and silver. Highlights risk management, including stop-loss orders and position sizing. Accumulate cash and move back to stocks when the market returns.

Sideways Markets: Explores range-bound strategies, such as trading support/resistance levels, options strategies (e.g., straddles/strangles), and mean-reversion approaches. Sell risky stocks when the market moves to a bear market.

8   Daily events

Recently, we could have profited from many events/news. The following are examples for illustration. The buy dates are estimates and today is 1/24/2025. No one can time the market tops. Most likely, the AI databases are **not up-to-date** (could be more than three months old). **Disclaimer**: It does not always work.

Event/Stock	Buy date	Return	Annualized	Average Ann.	RSP Ann.
Israel war	11/1/2023				
GLD		39%	32%		
SLV		33%	27%		
				29%	27%
Artificial Intelligence	7/3/2023				
NVDA		236%	151%		
SMCI		34%	21%		
VST		633%	404%		
MSFT		31%	20%		
				149%	14%
CA fire	1/8/2025				
XHB		6%	147%	147%	83%

RSP is the ETF of the unweigh S&P500 index.
I traded most of the stocks mentioned above.

Aggressive investors should consider buying the contra ETFs and/or shorting insurance companies in CA fire. Other factors affecting house prices are interest rate, lumber tariffs on Canada and the economy.

Eli Eilly and Moderna (both drug companies) had their short peaks when their new drugs / vaccines were announced.

I had at least six day to sell AI stocks such as NVDA when DeepSeek (an AI product from China) was reviewed. I did nothing, and I should have read my book and acted accordingly. However, NVDA recovered nicely after the 17% drop in one day.

When a major event occurs, you can ask AI (ChatGPT or Deepseek) which stocks and/or ETFs to buy in a specific event.

9   Black swans

This article on **Black Swan** events provides a retrospective and forward-looking analysis of significant, unpredictable events that have had or could have a major impact on the economy, markets, and society. I reflect on past events and offers predictions for potential future disruptions. Here's a review of the key points:

1. Historical Black Swan Events:
- **2000 Dot-com Bubble:** I highlight the poor quality of Super Bowl ads and the small size of internet companies as indicators of the bubble. I personally shifted investments from tech mutual funds to traditional funds or cash, avoiding significant losses.
- **9/11/2001:** The market plunged by 14%, and my stop-loss orders were executed, leading to losses. However, the economy recovered relatively quickly, and the event did not cause long-term economic harm.
- **2008 Lehman Brothers Collapse:** The collapse of Lehman Brothers led to a 21% market drop. China's intervention helped stabilize the global economy. The event underscored the importance of diversification.
- **2024 China Housing Market Bubble Burst:** I predicted the bursting of China's housing bubble far earlier than 2024, drawing parallels to the 2000 internet bubble.
- **January 2025 Tech Stock Plunge:** I speculated that DeepSeek (possibly an AI or tech-related event) caused a plunge in tech stocks, particularly affecting companies like NVDA. Despite the drop, I still believe NVDA's products will remain essential for AI.

1. **Future Black Swan Predictions (as of February 2025):**

I outline several potential future black swan events, emphasizing the need for preparedness:

1. **National Debt Crisis:** If the U.S. cannot service its national debt, it could lead to a depression. I mention Musk's efforts to cut expenses as potential contributing factors.
2. **Military Conflict:** The possibility of Trump starting another war or using military force to capture foreign land is raised, though I hope this will not happen.

3. **Cybersecurity Threats:** i warn that cyberattacks could cripple national infrastructure, emphasizing that this is a real and present danger.
4. **Economic Downturn:** Inflation (partly due to tariffs) and unemployment (due to AI, robots, and layoffs) could bring down the economy.
5. **Social Unrest:** High unemployment could lead to widespread social unrest.
6. **Bitcoin Collapse:** I question whether Bitcoin is peaking and suggests that quantum computing or new NVDA chips could disrupt cryptocurrency mining. Outlawing Bitcoin by countries could also trigger a collapse.
7. **Decoupling from China:** A total economic decoupling from China could have severe consequences, given the reliance on China for rare earth elements and consumer products.
8. **Corruption:** I suggest that corruption within government agencies is a significant issue, with former government employees often getting jobs from companies they previously favored. Insider trading among politicians is also highlighted as a concern.

3. Themes and Takeaways:

- **Unpredictability:** This article emphasizes the unpredictable nature of black swan events and the importance of being prepared for the unexpected.
- **Diversification:** I repeatedly stress the need for diversification to mitigate the impact of such events.
- **Historical Parallels:** I draw parallels between past events (e.g., the dot-com bubble, 9/11, Lehman Brothers) and potential future crises (e.g., China's housing bubble, tech stock plunges).
- **Speculative Nature:** Many of the predictions are speculative, and the author acknowledges that they may not come to pass. However, the exercise of considering these possibilities is valuable for risk management.

Conclusion

This article provides a compelling overview of past black swan events and offers a series of speculative predictions for future disruptions. My emphasis on diversification and preparedness is sound advice, though the speculative nature of the predictions should be taken with caution. This article serves as a useful reminder of the importance of being vigilant and adaptable in the face of uncertainty.

I agree with many of Trump's policies except the tariffs in 2025, and believe Musk has done a great job despite the many objections from citizens affected by their actions. Due to the high deficits even without including the obligations to our aging population, the mild recession should have occurred two or three years ago. I did prepared for it in those years, and failed miserably – no government wanted to bite the bullet. In 2025, our government finally cuts deficits (by increasing incomes and decreasing expenses), as we cannot let the national debts piled up with no control. Unfortunately, the poor would suffer most.

#Filler: My no ghost theory

If there are ghosts, the Chinese ghost and the ghost from the West should be the same. However, Chinese ghosts jump only and stick their tongues. In addition, Chinese never see the tunnel. Hope someone would prove my theory, and possibly get a Nobel prize. It is better than Obamas's for doing nothing.

Book 6: Simple Techniques for Beginners

Summary
The book provides a comprehensive guide to investing, focusing on simple techniques, risk management, asset allocation, and market timing, particularly **for beginners**. It covers both beginner-friendly strategies (such as investing in ETFs and CDs) and advanced trading methods using technical indicators and market timing. The book also highlights the importance of avoiding scams, using secure brokerage accounts, and staying disciplined in investment decisions.

Key Themes & Takeaways:
1. **Protecting Your Investments & Avoiding Scams**
    - Use **two-factor authentication** for brokerage accounts.
    - Avoid financial scams promising unrealistic returns.
    - Be cautious with personal financial information.
2. **Beginner's Guide to Investing**
    - Start with low-cost ETFs like SPY, VOO (S&P 500 ETFs) before moving into individual stocks.
    - CDs and money market funds are suitable for conservative investors looking for stability.
    - The book discourages using hedge funds due to their high fees and underperformance compared to index funds/ETFs.
3. **Portfolio Construction & Asset Allocation**
    - Asset allocation should be based on age and risk tolerance (e.g., 70% stocks, 30% bonds for a 30-year-old).
    - Sample portfolios for normal markets, downturns, and crashes are provided, emphasizing ETFs.
    - Gold (GLD) and cash holdings can serve as inflation hedges and defensive assets.
4. **Technical & Fundamental Analysis**
    - Use **moving averages (SMA-50, SMA-200)** to identify stock trends.
    - Fundamental metrics such as P/E ratio, ROE, and debt/equity ratio help evaluate stocks.
    - The book provides step-by-step ETF and stock screening methods using tools like Finviz, Yahoo Finance, and Fidelity.
5. **Market Timing & Trend Following**

- Market timing strategies use Simple Moving Averages (SMA-50 & SMA-200) to signal when to enter or exit markets.
 - **My version of Death Cross (Bearish) and Golden Cross (Bullish)** indicators help investors make informed decisions.
 - Investors should hold cash or invest in contra ETFs (e.g., SH, PSQ) during downturns.
6. **Simplified Trading Strategies**
 - Avoid high-risk trades such as penny stocks, leveraged ETFs, and shorting stocks.
 - Use stop-loss orders to protect profits and minimize losses.
 - Follow a disciplined, unemotional approach to investing rather than reacting to market noise.
7. **Investment Strategies for 'Lazy' Investors**
 - A set-it-and-forget-it strategy using a mix of broad market ETFs (SPY, QQQ, VTI, VUG) can outperform actively managed funds.
 - Market timing can be applied to ETFs to enhance returns and reduce risk.
8. **Common Mistakes & Don'ts for Beginners**
 - Avoid excessive trading, market speculation, and following financial media hype.
 - Do not blindly follow stock tips or investment gurus without verifying research.
 - Avoid hedge funds, overpriced investment seminars, and high-fee mutual funds.

Conclusion

The book emphasizes simplicity, risk management, and disciplined investing over speculation. By using ETFs, market timing, and fundamental analysis, investors can maximize returns while minimizing risk. The strategies outlined require minimal effort yet have historically beaten actively managed funds.

Investing safely: Security and smart strategies

Prioritizing Security in Investing

Before diving into investing, it is essential to **protect your financial accounts**. Secure your **brokerage and bank accounts** by enabling **two-factor authentication (2FA)**, which is widely available at most financial institutions. For instance, after logging in, your broker will send a verification code to your phone, adding an extra layer of security. Additionally, using a **dedicated device**, such as a Chromebook or a separate PC for financial transactions, can further safeguard your investments.

Avoiding Scams and Financial Pitfalls
Protect yourself from fraud by following these fundamental rules:
- **Be discreet with your wealth** – Avoid drawing unnecessary attention to your financial activities.
- **Stay cautious online** – Do not click on unfamiliar links or share sensitive information with unverified vendors.
- **Steer clear of unrealistic promises** – If an investment offers **returns significantly above market rates** (e.g., 12% when the best CDs offer 5%), it is likely a scam.
- **Keep personal data private** – Avoid sharing your **email, bank details, and credit card information**, as it can lead to spam, phishing attempts, or financial loss.

Beginner Investing: ETFs as a Strong Start
For those new to investing, **Exchange-Traded Funds (ETFs)** provide an excellent entry point. Investing in ETFs mentioned in this book can often **outperform hedge funds**—especially when considering the high fees hedge funds charge. Once you have a grasp of the basics, you can explore **more advanced trading techniques** outlined in later chapters.

One of the best starting points is investing in **broad-market ETFs**, such as:
- **VOO (Vanguard S&P 500 ETF)** – Expense ratio: **0.03%**
- **SPY (SPDR S&P 500 ETF)** – Expense ratio: **0.09%**

Historically, these ETFs have outperformed the majority of actively managed funds. There is little justification for paying hedge fund fees when these ETFs consistently **deliver strong, long-term returns**.

Market Timing Made Simple
Timing the market does not require advanced skills or constant monitoring. With just a few minutes each month, you can follow a simple strategy:
- **During market downturns** – Sell your ETFs to preserve capital.
- **When the market recovers** – Reinvest to capitalize on growth.

Many investors miss **key profit opportunities** because they react emotionally to downturns. Following a disciplined approach based on market signals can significantly improve investment outcomes.

Additional Tips for Smart Investing
- **For portfolios under $50,000**, focus on ETFs for simplicity and diversification.
- **Educate yourself** by reading investment articles from reputable sources such as **Fidelity, Morningstar, and Investopedia**.
- **Consider premium research services** like **AAII, Value Line, GuruFocus, Zacks, or IBD** once your portfolio surpasses **$50,000**.
- **Test strategies through paper trading** before investing real money in individual stocks.

Historical Portfolio Performance Insight
According to data from **Portfolio Visualizer**, a diversified portfolio consisting of **25% SPY, 25% RSP, and 50% MDY** yielded an annualized return (**CAGR**) of **10%** from **2000 to November 2022**, despite a maximum drawdown of **51%**.

Useful Investing Resources
Explore these free educational resources (paperback readers can type the links) to enhance your investing knowledge:
- **Morningstar Classroom:** Morningstar
  http://morningstar.com/cover/classroom.html
- **Vanguard Investor Education:** Vanguard
  https://investor.vanguard.com/investing/investor-education
- **Investopedia Tutorials:** Investopedia
  http://www.investopedia.com/university/
- **Yahoo Finance Education:** Yahoo Finance
  http://finance.yahoo.com/education/begin_investing
- **Fidelity Investing Basics:** Fidelity
  https://www.fidelity.com/investment-guidance/investing-basics

Conclusion
By following **secure investing practices**, avoiding scams, and focusing on **proven investment vehicles** like ETFs, investors can build a **solid foundation** for long-term success. Whether you are a beginner or an experienced trader, **staying disciplined and well-informed** is key to achieving financial growth. As you progress, consider advanced strategies detailed later in this book to further enhance your investing journey.

#Filler: The Ten Commandments of Investing

http://www.investopedia.com/articles/basics/07/10commandments.asp

* Set goals. * Personal finances in order. * Ask questions. * Do not follow the herd. * Due diligence. * Be humble. * Be patient. * Be moderate. * No unnecessary churning. * Be safe. * Do not follow blindly.

My additions: * Diversify. * Study market timing. * Protect your losses and profits. * Monitor your screens and your metrics. * Be emotionally detached from investments.* Learn from mistakes. * Stay away from bubbles. * Be socially responsible.

1 Money Market, CDs & Bonds

Overview

CDs are suitable for conservative investors or for temporarily parking money during market downturns. While they offer lower returns compared to stocks or ETFs, they provide stability in uncertain times.

Key Points about CDs

1. Rates and Returns:
    - One-year CD rates have varied from 1.5% in 2020 to 4% in 2024.
    - After accounting for inflation and taxes, returns may be negative. CDs serve better as a defensive investment rather than for growth.
2. Laddering Strategy:
   To ensure liquidity while maximizing returns:
    - Split your investment across CDs with staggered maturity dates (e.g., 3 months, 12 months).
    - Renew maturing CDs for shorter terms to adjust for changing interest rates.
3. FDIC Insurance:
    - FDIC insures up to $250,000 per bank, not per account.
    - Some foreign bank CDs are also FDIC-insured and may offer higher rates.
4. Tax Considerations:
    - CDs from local banks may receive favorable tax treatment in some states.
    - However, brokered CDs often offer better rates and convenience.
5. Avoid Callable CDs:

- Callable CDs allow banks to terminate the agreement early, typically when rates drop.
    - Be careful on non-callable CDs unless the offered rates are significantly higher.

Alternatives to CDs

- Money Market Funds:
  Brokers like Fidelity offer competitive money market funds (e.g., SPAXX). These provide liquidity and variable yields but are more sensitive to interest rate changes.
- Bond Funds and ETFs:
  Bond funds like HYG or JNK provide higher yields but come with added risk. Remember, bond prices generally fall when interest rates rise. The following is my illustration.

Their annualized returns are compounded. SPY is the benchmark I use. Check out their past performances. In 2008, the market crashed. It was a bad year for both bond funds and ETFs, but the bond funds lose less than SPY.

	2007	2008	2009
HYG	3%	-18%	29%
JNK	Not avail.	-25%	38%
SPY	5%	-37%	26%

Link: Government bond default? https://www.youtube.com/watch?v=wMxj6iB92ZA
- Broker CDs (Recommended):
  https://www.youtube.com/watch?v=zhEiyW2N7KE
- More on CD: https://www.youtube.com/watch?v=FRWMsGJ2-NE
- Money market fund: https://www.youtube.com/watch?v=N53wZ_80abU
- Its risk: https://www.youtube.com/watch?v=k3wGqD_9SzY
- Better than cash: https://www.youtube.com/watch?v=SrQTOhafE4A

2   Sample investment portfolio: A strategic guide

Building a Personalized Portfolio
Investing is not one-size-fits-all. Your portfolio should reflect your personal risk tolerance, financial goals, and investment horizon. As a rule of thumb, a **balanced stock-to-bond allocation** can be estimated using the formula:

Stock Percentage = 100 – Your Age
For example, a 30-year-old investor should allocate approximately 70% to stocks and 30% to bonds, gold, CDs, and cash.

Three Investment Approaches Based on Market Conditions
1. Regular Market Conditions (Steady Growth)
- SPY (S&P 500 ETF) – 40%
- QQQ (Tech-heavy NASDAQ ETF) – 10%
- VTIAX (International Stocks ETF) – 20%
- LQD (Investment-Grade Bond ETF) – 15%
- GLD (Gold ETF) – 5%
- CDs (Certificates of Deposit) – 5%
- Cash Reserve – 5%

2. Current Market (As of 2021, Increased Volatility)
- SPY – 30%
- QQQ – 10%
- VTIAX – 5%
- LQD – 20%
- GLD – 15%
- Cash Reserve – 20%

3. Market Crash Scenario (Defensive Positioning)
- LQD – 5%
- GLD – 15%
- Cash Reserve – 60%
- SH (Inverse S&P 500 ETF) – 5%
- PSQ (Inverse NASDAQ ETF) – 15%

Key Considerations
- **Rebalance** your portfolio **twice a year** or as market conditions change.
- **Stay diversified** – sector performance varies over time.
- **Avoid relying on hedge funds** – index ETFs often outperform them due to high fees.
- **Ignore financial media hype** – news often benefits institutional investors at the expense of retail investors.
- **Consider inflation protection** – Increase exposure to **GLD** (gold ETF) if inflation rises.

Additional Resources:
- Best Vanguard ETFs
  https://www.youtube.com/watch?v=mSEyghlZchQ
- VTI vs. VOO Comparison

https://www.youtube.com/watch?v=v7staXdVE8c

#Filler "How to make a 50% return"

https://www.youtube.com/watch?v=eEto5nEkf1Y

#Filler Buffett, the person.
https://www.youtube.com/watch?v=w-eX4sZi-Zs

3 Anatomy of a trade: From selection to exit

For Beginners:
- Start with **ETFs like VOO** for broad market exposure.
- Use **CDs** with varying maturity dates for stability.
- Avoid individual stock selection until you are comfortable with investing fundamentals.

For Experienced Investors:
1. **Stock Screening** – Use tools like **Finviz** to find stocks with strong fundamentals and positive insider activity.
2. **Portfolio Diversification** – Hold **no more than 10 stocks** and limit **each sector to three stocks max**.
3. **Risk Management** – Use **stop-loss orders** (5-10% below purchase price) to minimize losses.
4. **Profit-taking Strategy** – Utilize **trailing stops** to lock in gains when prices rise.
5. **Capital Gains Awareness** – Holding stocks for over **one year** reduces tax liabilities.

Pro Tip: Never add money to losing stocks. Instead, increase investments in winning stocks if trends remain favorable.

4 Investing for 'lazy' folks

f you lack time or expertise, **low-cost ETFs** offer a simple yet effective investment strategy. Below is a portfolio optimized for passive investors:

Most returns started on July 1 and ended on July 1 the following year; this article is written on July 20, 2021. All are annualized returns for easy comparison. Fees, commissions and dividends have not been included.

Symbol	Name	YTD[1] Return	1 Year[2]	5 Years[3]	Bear[4]
IWF	Russel1000Grow	30%	34%	40%	-33%
QQQ	QQQ	30%	46%	42%	-31%
VTI	Vang. Viper Tot	34%	22%	42%	-35%
VUG	Vang. Growth	37%	33%	41%	-32%
Avg.		31%	34%	41%	-33%
SPY[5]		34%	21%	39%	-35%
Beat[6]		**-9%**	**60%**	**6%**	**7%**

[1] The start date is 1/4/2021 and the end date is 7/1/2021.
[2] The start date is 7/1/2020 and the end date is 7/1/2021.
[3] The start date is 7/1/2016 and the end date is 7/1/2021.
[4] The start date is 1/2/2008 and the end date is 4/1/2009. My estimates.
[5] SPY is the ETF for the S&P 500 index. It is used as a yardstick.
[6] = (Avg. – SPY) / SPY. Again, it does not include fees, commissions and dividends.

Market Timing Strategy for Passive Investors
- **Exit ETFs** when major market indicators suggest a downturn.
- **Re-enter when conditions stabilize** – usually following the **Golden Cross pattern**.
- **For risk-averse investors**, contra ETFs (e.g., **PSQ, SH**) can be used instead of holding cash.

Annual Review: Evaluate your portfolio once per year or as needed using **ETFdb.com** for updates.

Final Takeaways
- **Market timing techniques** can **enhance returns** and minimize losses.
- **ETFs offer diversification and lower fees** compared to hedge funds.
- **Invest with discipline** – avoid emotional trading and market noise.
- **Regularly rebalance** based on market conditions.

By following these strategies, even the busiest investors can achieve steady portfolio growth with minimal effort.

#Filler: Silence is golden. I am glad I did not give advice to a friend who had to decide whether to take a lump sum payment or an annuity. The correction in March, 2020 would wipe out a lot of his portfolio if he took the lump sum payment. No one would share his profits when the predictions are correct, but the blame if it does not materialize.

It is the same in investing that nothing is certain. With educated guesses, we should have more rights than wrongs especially in the long run.

5   Simplest guide to analyzing ETFs

Evaluating an ETF

ETFs (Exchange-Traded Funds) consist of a basket of stocks based on a specific market, sector, country, or investment theme.
To assess an ETF's valuation:

- Previously, Yahoo! Finance provided ETF P/E ratios. Now, check ETFdb.com by entering the ETF symbol (e.g., XLU) and selecting "Valuation."
- A P/E ratio below 15 but above zero could indicate a value ETF.
- If the ETF's price is lower than its NAV, it is trading at a discount (or vice versa, a premium).
- Compare its Year-to-Date (YTD) return with that of SPY.

Alternatively, check http://www.multpl.com/ for additional valuation metrics such as:
- Shiller P/E
- Price/Sales ratio
- Price/Book ratio

For technical analysis, use Finviz.com:

- Enter the ETF symbol.
- If the SMA-20, SMA-50, and SMA-200 are positive, the ETF is likely in an uptrend.
    - SMA-200 represents the Simple Moving Average over the last 200 trading days.
    - If the stock price is below the SMA, it is in a downtrend.
- If your holding period is around 50 days, focus on SMA-50.
- Use RSI (14) to gauge oversold/overbought conditions:
    - RSI > 65: Likely overbought
    - RSI < 30: Likely oversold

Additionally, ensure:
- Average trading volume exceeds 10,000 shares.
- Market cap is over $300 million.
- Low expense ratios.
- Beginners should avoid leveraged ETFs.

Identifying Sector Recovery
To identify if a sector has recovered:
- If SMA-20, SMA-50, and SMA-200 are positive, the ETF may be in an uptrend or has recovered.
- Always use stop-loss orders to protect investments.

Resources:
- Fidelity ETF Overview: YouTube https://www.youtube.com/watch?v=tUsFTN7iDcQ
- Vanguard offers numerous low-cost ETFs.

Example: Evaluating ETFs
1. Assess market risk—beginners should avoid risky markets.
2. Limit sector ETFs to those in an uptrend or showing a potential bottom.
3. Compare ETFs:
    - SPY (Large-cap market ETF)
    - XLP (Consumer Staples)
    - XLY (Consumer Discretionary)

Sample Analysis (as of 2/5/2016)

Metric	SPY	XLP	XLY
Price	190	50	71
NAV	192	50	73
Technical Indicators			
SMA-50	-4%	0%	-7%
SMA-200	-6%	2%	-7%
RSI (14)	44	50	36
Fundamentals			
P/E	17	20	19
Yield	2.1%	2.5%	1.5%
YTD Return	-5%	0.5%	-5%
Net Assets	$174B	$9B	$10B

Interpretation
- XLY had the best discount, likely due to recession fears.
- XLP performed better in downturns (consumer staples are necessities).
- SPY had the best value based on P/E.
- XLY had the lowest dividend yield, likely due to higher tech exposure.
- All three ETFs had net assets above $500M (specialized ETFs require at least $200M).

Additional metrics like Debt/Equity are often unavailable but can be estimated by averaging top ETF holdings.

#Filler: Illogical logic
If we do not test for the pandemic, we would have zero increase in this pandemic. Some silly folks buy this argument. What happens to the once-great country?

Filler: The problems of the U.S.
1. Our political system. We waste time arguing between the two parties. There is no long-term planning, as the other party could claim the credit. Same as corporations' CEOs who care about their yearly bonuses.
2. The politicians have to satisfy their voters. Today give them free cash by jacking up the printing press. And ignore the long-term consequences.
3. We have to protect our workers, our environment... Hence, we cannot compete with many countries.
4. We have spent too much on the military and ignore our crumbling infrastructure.
5. Historically no country can rule the world forever.
6. We blame China, but ignore how hard-working Chinese are.

Example: Evaluating RING (gold miner ETF)

Data from July 6, 2020

Key Details from ETFdb.com:
- **Sector:** Gold Miners
- **Asset Size:** Large-Cap
- **Issuer:** iShares
- **Inception Date:** Jan. 31, 2012
- **Expense Ratio:** 0.39%
- **Tax Form:** 1099 (preferred for non-taxable accounts)

Valuation and Trends:
- **P/E Ratio:** 17.39 (reasonable for this sector)
- **Dividend Yield:** 0.52% (ETFdb) / 0.70% (Finviz)
- **Short-Term Trend:** Up (SMA-20 = 8%, SMA-50 = 7%)
- **Long-Term Trend:** Strong uptrend (SMA-200 = 26%)
- **RSI (14):** 64% (near overbought at 65%)
- **Price Movement:** -4% from 52-week high
- **Performance:** Strong across multiple timeframes

Holdings Analysis:
RING holds **39 stocks**, providing decent diversification. Top holdings:
- **Newmont (NEM) – 19%**
- **Barrick Gold (ABX) – 18%**

These stocks can be analyzed separately for deeper insights:

Stock	Forward P/E	Debt/Share	ROE	Sales Q/Q	EPS Q/Q	SMA-50	RSI (14)	Insider Trans	Equity Score
NEM	20	0.31	17%	43%	389%	2%	59%	-13%	6.1
ABX	25	0.24	22%	30%	254%	4%	60%	N/A	6.8

Conclusion
By leveraging tools like **ETFdb.com, Finviz.com, and Multpl.com**, investors can analyze ETFs using:
- Valuation metrics (P/E, P/S, P/B)
- Technical indicators (SMA, RSI)
- Performance trends (YTD return, discount/premium to NAV)

A disciplined approach helps identify the best investment opportunities while mitigating risk.

6   Simplest ways to evaluate stocks

Who is this for?

This section is for intermediate investors ready to move beyond ETFs and into individual stock trading. Beginners are advised to focus on ETFs due to their diversification and lower risk.

Step-by-Step Stock Evaluation

1. Use free web sites
- Fidelity: Offers Equity Summary Scores for comprehensive ratings and many metrics.
- Finviz: Provides detailed financial metrics and screening tools.
- Yahoo! Finance: Useful for key financial ratios like EV/EBITDA.

2. Focus on Key Metrics

Metric	Preferred Range	Purpose
Forward P/E	5 to 20 (up to 25 for tech)	Measures expected profitability.
EV/EBITDA	Below industry averages	Evaluates valuation, including debt and cash.
Debt/Equity Ratio	Below 0.5 (higher for utilities)	Indicates financial stability.
ROE (Return on Equity)	Greater than 5%	Assesses efficiency in using shareholder capital.
Insider Transactions	Positive or minimal selling	Tracks confidence from company insiders.
Momentum Metrics	Positive SMA-50 and SMA-200	Confirms the stock is trending upward.

3. Compare to Sector and Historical Averages
- **Sector Comparison**: Compare the stock's metrics (e.g., P/E) to others in the same industry.
- **Historical Comparison**: Look at the stock's 5-year averages for key metrics.

4. Assess the Market Environment

- **Risky Market**: Avoid buying when SMA-50 and SMA-200 of major indices (e.g., SPY) are negative.
- **Sector Trends**: Use Finviz to evaluate the ETF representing the stock's sector. Only buy when the sector is trending upward.

5. Additional Considerations
- **Volatility**: Prefer stocks with a beta under 1 if you are risk-averse.
- **Event News**: Check recent developments like lawsuits, earnings surprises, or management changes.
- **Cap and Volume**: Ensure the stock's market cap is above $800M and daily trading volume exceeds 10,000 shares for stability.

Example: Scoring a Stock
Use a scoring system to assess potential investments. Assign points to each metric and sum them to evaluate overall viability.

Metric	Good	Bad	Score
Forward P/E	5–20: +2 points	Over 50 or < 0: -1 point	
P/FCF (Price/Free Cash Flow)	<12: +1 point	Over 30 or < 0: -1 point	
Sales Q/Q Growth	>15%: +1 point	Negative: -1 point	
EPS Q/Q Growth	>20%: +1 point	Negative: -1 point	

Passing Grade: Total score of **3 or higher**. Stocks scoring 2 may warrant further analysis.

Very Basic Advice for Beginners
1. Stick to U.S. stocks with market caps over $800M.
2. Avoid highly leveraged companies (Debt/Equity > 0.25, except for utilities).
3. Diversify: No more than 20% in one stock and 30% in one sector.
4. Practice paper trading or use simulators like Investopedia Simulator.

Link: Buy stocks/ETFs: https://www.youtube.com/watch?v=4vjkeC_4EmU
https://www.youtube.com/watch?v=wMxj6iB92ZA

7   Simplest market timing

Why Market Timing Matters

Before the 2000s, market timing was often dismissed. However, with major market plunges (e.g., 2000 and 2008) averaging losses of 45%, timing has become a practical tool to minimize losses and improve overall returns.

The goal of market timing is not to predict exact peaks and bottoms but to reduce exposure during downturns and re-enter during recoveries. Using Finviz, no charting is used.

Most gurus do not believe in market timing. The following simple techniques have been proven profitable in 2000 and 2008 market plunges. Accumulate cash when the market plunges and re-enter the market when the indicator tells you so. My most profitable years are the early recovery stage of the market for both 2000 and 2008.

When the SPY (or RSP) price dips below SMA-350 (Simple Moving Average for 350 days), it indicates the market is crashing, and vice versa. The following does not require charting.

My key Indicators for Market Timing

1. **Death Cross (my version):**
   - Occurs when the 50-day Simple Moving Average (SMA-50) crosses below the 200-day Simple Moving Average (SMA-200. Note: I use 200 as it is readily available from Finviz).
   - Signals a potential market plunge.
2. **Golden Cross (my version):**
   - Occurs when SMA-50 crosses above SMA-200.
   - Indicates market recovery and signals it's time to re-enter.

How to Detect a Market Plunge

- **Use a site like Finviz:**
    1. Search for SPY or RSP (representing the S&P 500). Check the SMA metrics:
        - SMA-200: Positive values suggest no immediate downturn.

- SMA-50 vs. SMA-200: If SMA-50 is more negative than SMA-200, it signals a market plunge.
2. Look for a negative trend in the Buy/Sell ratio (B/S) week over week.

Action Steps During a Plunge:

- **Conservative Approach:**
    - Sell riskier stocks (e.g., those with negative earnings or high P/E ratios).
    - Hold cash or low-risk assets like CDs or money market funds.
- **Aggressive Approach:**
    - Sell all stocks.
    - Consider buying contra ETFs like PSQ (shorts the NASDAQ) or SH (shorts the S&P 500).

How to Detect Market Recovery

- **Reverse the process used for detecting a plunge:**
    1. SMA-200 turns positive.
    2. SMA-50 crosses above SMA-200 (Golden Cross).
    3. Look for a positive week-over-week trend in the Buy/Sell ratio.

Action Steps During Recovery:

- Sell contra ETFs and close short positions.
- Reinvest cash in broad-market ETFs like SPY or VOO.

Tips for Monitoring Indicators

- Frequency: Check indicators monthly. Increase to weekly if prices approach SMA thresholds.
- Advanced Method: For fewer false signals, use SMA-350 (or SMA-400) instead of SMA-200.

Limitations of Market Timing

- Does not capture exact market peaks or bottoms due to reliance on past data.
- False signals may lead to minor losses (e.g., selling early and re-entering).
- Requires discipline to follow the strategy despite market noise or volatility.

Example Application
As of February 12, 2022:

ETF	SMA-200	SMA-50	Death Cross?
SPY	-0.8%	-4.2%	Yes
RSP	-0.5%	-1.9%	Yes

This data indicated a confirmed market downturn, suggesting a shift to defensive assets.

Another Simple chart example.
Bring up StockCharts.com and enter SPY. It indicates Death Cross occurred on around March 20, 2022.

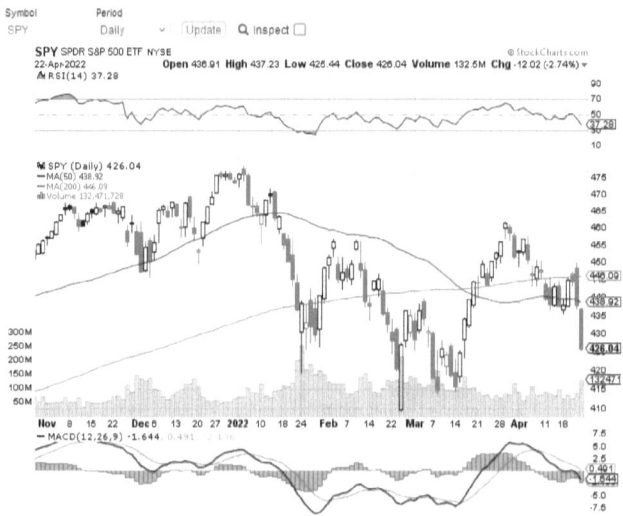

#Filler: A joke
Why do the majority of my friends find more beautiful ladies when they grow old. Most likely they use their spouses as the yardstick. I am the minority. Do not tell my wife please.

8 Rotate four ETFs for better returns

We can outperform the market by rotating one ETF that represents the market such as SPY and cash via market timing. Aggressive investors can add SH or PSQ (contra ETFs) to the four to have better returns during market plunges.

During a market uptrend, rotating the following four ETFs could be more profitable than staying with SPY (or any ETF that simulates the market). Be warned that a short-term capital gain in taxable accounts is not treated as favorably as the long-term capital gain; check current tax laws.

The allocation percentages depend on your individual risk tolerance. You can use indexed mutual funds. Compare their expenses and restrictions. Some mutual funds charge you if you withdraw within a specific time period.

Select the best performer of last month (from Seeking Alpha, cnnFn, or one of many ETF/mutual fund sites). Add a contra ETF such as SH to take advantage of a falling market for more aggressive investors. Add sector ETFs to the described four ETFs such as XLY, XLP, XLE, XLF, XLU, IYW, XHB, IYM, OIL and XLU to expand your selection.

ETFs	Money Market	U.S.	International	Bond
Fidelity		Spartan Total Market	Spartan Global Market	Spartan US Bond
Vanguard		Total Stock Market	Total International Market	Total Bond Market
My choice	Fidelity	SPY	Vanguard	Fidelity
Suggest %				
During Market plunge	90%	0%	0%	10%
After plunge	10%	60%	20%	10%

Explanation

- The above are suggestions only. If your broker offers similar ETFs, consider using them.
- Check out any restrictions of the ETFs and commissions.

- 4 ETFs (one actually is a money market fund) are enough for most starters. They are diversified, low-cost and you do not need rebalancing except during a market plunge.
- The percentages are suggestions only. If you are less risk tolerant, allocate more to a money market fund, CD and/or bond ETF.
- Have at least 10% allocated to the money market fund for safety.
- When the market is risky, reduce stock equities (i.e., increase money market and bond allocations).
- The symbols for Fidelity ETFs are FSTMX, FSGDX and FBIDX.
- The symbols for Vanguard ETFs are VTSMX, VGTSX and VBMFX.
- If you are more advanced, use additional sector ETFs to rotate. Also buy long-term bond funds (such as 30-year Treasury) when the interest rate is 10% or more.

#Filler: Glad to be an investor

After watching the following YouTube video, I am glad my parents did not push me to play piano and also glad I do not have any musical gene. How can I compete with this kid?

https://www.youtube.com/watch?v=yf0B4rVoq44

Also, glad not into some life-threatening professions such as surgical doctors, soldiers, fire fighters, etc. I can make mistakes in investing from time to time without suffering from the consequences. With the uptrend market for most of the last 50 years, most investors should make good money. Thank God.

#Filler: Where common sense is not common sense

Excessive printing of money is not a long-term solution. Servicing the huge debt weakens our competitiveness. The politicians just want to buy votes today and finance their campaigns. Our next generations have to pay for these huge debts.

#Filler: Cayman Island
Most global corporations are making fun of our tax system. Moving the "headquarter" to low-tax countries such as Cayman Island with a mailbox, a bank account and/or an office that has never been used is a norm. The profitable Boeing has negative tax liability. What a shame!

9 Simplified technical analysis

Simplified Technical Analysis
- Stocks, their sectors, and the overall market should all be above their **SMA-N** averages before buying.
- **Caution**: If the SMA-200 is over 5% and/or RSI(14) is over 65%, the stock might be overbought.
- Stop losses should be set to manage risk.

The Best Strategy
- **Weighted ETFs**: SPY holds all S&P 500 stocks but gives higher weight to larger companies.
- **Market Timing**: Reduce exposure when the SMA-350 method indicates risk.
- **Minimal Effort**: This strategy requires only a few minutes per month and significantly reduces long-term risks.

Common Mistakes Beginners Should Avoid
1. Avoid leveraged investments (options, margin, leveraged ETFs).
2. Do not short stocks.
3. Buy **value stocks** and hold for at least a year to maximize tax benefits.
4. Use stop-loss orders to protect investments.
5. Avoid penny stocks (market cap < $200M or price < $1).
6. Do not day trade; most beginners lose money.
7. Be wary of investing seminars promising guaranteed profits.
8. Avoid hedge funds with excessive fees.
9. Don't blindly follow expert recommendations—always do your research.
10. Never add more capital to losing positions.

Final Summary
1. Before investing, check SPY's **SMA-50 and SMA-200** on **Finviz**. If both are negative, avoid investing.
2. Gather stock recommendations from free sources and evaluate key metrics.
3. Use simple, proven market timing strategies to minimize losses and maximize returns.
4. Stick to well-researched ETFs or stocks with strong fundamentals and positive momentum.

By following these principles, investors can improve their odds of success while maintaining a disciplined approach to investing.

10 The best strategy

- **Weighted ETFs**: SPY holds all S&P 500 stocks but gives higher weight to larger companies.
- **Market Timing**: Reduce exposure when the SMA-350 method indicates risk.
- **Minimal Effort**: This strategy requires only a few minutes per month and significantly reduces long-term risks.

11 Common mistakes beginners should avoid

1. Avoid leveraged investments (options, margin, leveraged ETFs).
2. Do not short stocks.
3. Buy **value stocks** and hold for at least a year to maximize tax benefits.
4. Use stop-loss orders to protect investments.
5. Avoid penny stocks (market cap < $200M or price < $1).
6. Do not day trade; most beginners lose money.
7. Be wary of investing seminars promising guaranteed profits.
8. Avoid hedge funds with excessive fees.
9. Don't blindly follow expert recommendations—always do your research.
10. Never add more capital to losing positions.

Link
Common mistakes: https://www.youtube.com/watch?v=zkNueyFs8zQ

12 Final Summary

1. Before investing, check SPY's **SMA-50 and SMA-200** on **Finviz**. If both are negative, avoid investing.
2. Gather stock recommendations from free sources and evaluate key metrics.
3. Use simple, proven market timing strategies to minimize losses and maximize returns.
4. Stick to well-researched ETFs or stocks with strong fundamentals and positive momentum.

By following these principles, investors can improve their odds of success while maintaining a disciplined approach to investing.

*** Bonus

1   Trading plan

You should have a trading plan and it should include the following basics:

1. Your overall objective.
2. When to buy, what stocks and how many.
3. When and what stocks to sell.
4. When and how to monitor your trading strategies.

The follow are my suggestions. Adjust them according to your personal requirements.

Be disciplined

Being disciplined will provide better results in the long run and save you time. Following the trading plan will not allow your emotions to take over.

To illustrate, you have a specific day (Monday or the first day of the month) to check the value of your portfolio. By checking it several times a day, it becomes a waste of time and energy. It could cause harm to your emotions.

Set your objective(s)

Set up your objective and requirements first. Your objective could be seeking the highest profit, profit at the least risk, protecting principal, generating income or a combination. Beating the market should not be your primary objective.

For example, a better objective is making more than 5% per year in the next 10 years with the least risk. Why 5%? I estimate that we have a 3% inflation rate and 2% taxes. The higher risk you can take, the higher the return it would be.

You can be conservative and aggressive at the same time by setting up two accounts, one for each objective. In addition, you may want to define the maximum investment amount for each account.

I have three objectives and they usually fall into different accounts and different holding periods.

- Non-taxable account. Profit at the least risk. Buy value stocks. Review purchased stocks every 6 months.
- Roth account. Buy momentum stocks seeking for the maximum short-term (1 month) profits.
- Conservative investing in all accounts. Define a larger safety net. Conserve my cash. Move all to stocks only when the market is the most favorable.

Contrary to the above, most investors' or traders' tend to have an objective in beating the market by a specific percent. It is fine also to measure how you perform against the market. For ultra conservative investors, not losing money may be your primary objective. In any case, consider safety.

If you made 10% and the market was up by 20%, you under-performed the market. However, do not blame yourself if your primary objective is conserving wealth. Most likely you may have had a high percent of your portfolio in cash and/or safer investments which do not appreciate a lot but they conserve your wealth.

Be flexible
Every one's trading plan is different. You should start with a simple one and add features that would be useful for you. Keep it simple as you will not likely follow a complicated one.

Other features are: how to screen stocks, your average holding period, tax consequences, performance monitoring, etc. This chapter shows you the very basics of a trading plan and you should start one if you do not have one.

You can refer to any chapter of this book in your trading plan. To illustrate, refer to the chapters when to sell a stock and spotting market plunges.

You can change your objective. When the market is risky, you may want to be more conservative for example.

Disciplined but adaptive
Stick with your plan consistently unless you have a good reason. When your previous strategy that has worked but it does not work now, you should

still stick to it. It is a common mistake for traders switching different technical indicator when the current one does not work. It explains why most of the beginner traders lose money.

It should be adaptive. When the current market favors growth, stick with a growth strategy.

A sample trading plan

You can review what stocks to buy and sell once a week or once a month depending on how active you are in the market. List the criteria you buy stocks. Define your average holding period for a specific objective. Also define when and why you want to sell a stock.

Personally I prefer to have two sections: Common Tasks and Specific Tasks. Common Tasks include 4 categories: **Weekly Tasks, Monthly Tasks, Quarterly Tasks and Yearly Tasks**. Evaluate stocks to buy on Tuesday on every week for example. Update the portfolio and check out the chart on marketing timing on the first week of every month. Review the performance of your portfolio quarterly (or half a year). Perform year-end tasks.

Specific Tasks include tasks we have to do on specific dates such as filling tax return, transferring stocks to my children and renewing investing subscriptions.

Weekly Tasks:

Mon	Covered calls
	IBD-50 review.
Tue	Finding momentum stocks.
Wed	Sell Momentum stocks held over 2 weeks.

Monthly Tasks:

Mon	House keep all stock transactions.
	Review market timing and any corrections.
Tue	Find stocks using selected strategies.
	Find stocks using screens.
Wed	Evaluate stocks
Thur.	Buy stocks
	Review sector rotation.
Fri	Evaluate any stocks to sell.
Any	Monitor momentum performance.

Quarterly Tasks:

1	Monthly tasks.
2	Monitor performance.

Year-end Tasks:

1	Tax adjustments for taxable accounts including selling losers in non-retirement accounts.
2	EOY purchases.
3	Fully invested on Dec. 15-Jan. 15 esp. on 2nd year of the presidential cycle.
4	Monitor performance of screens.
5	Review Dogs of the DOW.
6	Optional. Gift appreciated stocks to your heirs.

Review your performance and your trading plan

If you do not know what you did, how will you know where you're going? Review every trade transaction and monitor their performances.

Learn from your losses. Did you stick to the trading plan? If you lose too many times and/or take too much risk (evidenced by many losses and/or big losses), you may have to modify your trading plan. However, the trading plan may not be good in the current market (for example trading growth stocks in the bottom of the market cycle).

If you have to let the winners get away too often, review what went wrong. Sometimes, a lesson is not a lesson but just bad luck.

Learn about yourself

Learn about your risk tolerance, how mentally prepared are you for big losses and big wins. If you have more money than you can use for the rest of your life, conserving wealth should be your primary objective.

To illustrate with a portfolio of one million dollars, your average stock position is $100,000 if you only have time to follow 10 stocks.

To many, a portfolio with 10 stocks is quite risky. You may consider having 10 stocks of $50,000 each and invest the rest ($500,000) in ETFs, mutual funds and/or bonds. Ensure that no more than three stocks (some prefer 2) are in the same sector.

Prepare for some losses. Reduce the average loss to only small amounts. I prefer to use 25% maximum loss for volatile stocks and 20% for other stocks. Some prefer using stop loss orders of 10% to 15% loss. Today's market is too volatile to stop losses less than 15%. My opinion. You should have some big winners but you may let some get away by selling them too early. One way is to use stop orders (10% less than the market price) and adjust the stops periodically (say a month) for the appreciating stocks.

Summary

Write down your objective and what tasks you do every week, month and year in the inside back cover of this book (hard copy only). If you don't do it now, you never will.

Trade journal

Keep a journal of your trades along with your ideas. Review it from time to time and look at why you bought a specific stock. It is far better than trying to recall the experiences from memory.

Your journal should be part of a trading plan. You use it to monitor the performance of your trade and how the current market conditions affect your performance. When you use a screen that is for short term, you want to exit the trade accordingly. When the screen does not perform, it may mean the market is not favorable to this screen and you should skip using it with actual money. Here is a screenshot of mine. I group the trades under different screens.

	A	B	C	D	E	F	G	H	I	J	K	L	M	N	O	P
1	Performance			Price		$					Date			Return		Status
2	Stock	QTY	Account	B.P	S.P	Buy $	Se $	Profit	Curr P	% better	Buy Date	Se Date	Days		Ann. Ret	
3	LAKE	2,000	401k	10.93	13.99	21,860	27,975	6,115	9.45	48%	07/15/15	11/24/15	132	28%	77%	S
4	ABT	1,500	ROTH	16.60	18.50	24,900	27,750	2,850			07/16/15	09/10/16	422	11%	10%	B
5	ELMD	5,000	401k	4.01	4.22	20,054	21,095	1,041	4.81	-12%	03/17/16	04/07/16	21	5%	90%	S

When using an excel spreadsheet, the formulae is:

B.P. (Buy Price) =IF(B3="","",IF(D3="","",D3*B3))
% better =IF(I3="","",(E3-I3)/I3)
Days =IF(K3="","",L3-K3)
Return =IF(D3="","",(E3-D3)/D3)
Ann. Ret =IF(N3="","",N3*365/M3)
Add any columns you want such as Account.

2 Order prices

Market orders
It is simply trading the stock at the prevailing market price. Place market orders only when it is necessary as stocks price can easily be manipulated especially on stocks with low trading volumes. To avoid manipulations, do not place market orders after hours.

However, in a rising market, many fast-rising stocks can only be bought via market orders. Many winners never take a breather on their way up. In this case, you can only buy the stock via market orders.

Consider bid and ask. A 'bid' is the price a potential buyer would like to buy while the 'ask' is a potential seller would like to sell. Your market price is usually the worst price in either case, but it is a guarantee that you would trade the stock. A large spread would mean that it would take a longer time to use a limit order and/or the trade volume of the stock is small.

In my momentum portfolio on 11/2013, I placed a sell price for GERN far higher than the market price. Surprisingly I sold it for this price making an annualized return of 1,176% for holding it for 21 days. When there are few or no other sellers for the stock, the market price would be the price you set. If I cannot sell it in the next 9 days (30 days is my holding period for momentum stocks), I would set it lower. Update: One year later, GERN lost 29%.

Sensible discounts
I prefer to buy the stock at the price closest to the last trade price (to most it is the market price) via a limit order. I seldom lose buying these orders. Sometimes I use the day's lowest price to buy (or the highest to sell) plus a penny (or minus a penny for sell prices to sell).

My other purchase strategy is using 0.15% or 0.25% less than the current prices for stocks I really want. For some promising stocks, I buy them at almost the market price and then place another order on the same stock at 0.5% less than the last traded price (and sometimes 2% depending on the current market trend).

We all want to buy less and sell at higher prices. However, if the trade price is too far away from the current market price (such as 5% from the market price), these trades may never be executed. I have had a long list of buy orders that were not executed and turned out to be big gainers. Learn from my bad experiences.

Use a good discount (such as 10% from the market price) if you believe the market, the sector or the stock will dip by 10%. After you bought the stock, you place a sell order 10% more than the price you paid for it hoping the stock will return to the original price and you pocket 10%. Wishful thinking! However, it has happened to me several times primarily due to temporary market dips.

It works when there is a correction and/or the stock is very volatile. It is usually within the 5% range to take advantage of these situations, not the 10% as described. For a 10% plunge, it usually is due to some serious problem of the company surfacing. One common reason is not meeting its earnings expectation and in this case it usually continues its downward trend.

Larger discounts on a falling market
During a falling market (or a mild correction), 3% less than the current prices for buy orders may be fine for some stocks (use 5% for volatile stocks). To illustrate, I placed about 10 of these orders over the last two months during a market dip. Most of the orders were filled. When the market is plunging, do not buy any stock.

Caterpillar and Cisco were some of my buys at these discounts. They were in my watch list to buy. Initially these shares often fall even lower as the trend was downward. As of 12/18/12, CAT earned me from 3% and 14% (bought in 6/12 and 7/12) and CSCO bought in 7/14/12 returned about 34%. My original objective: Buy deeply-valued stocks, wait and sell them when the economy returns.

When you predict the market will dip by 5%, set your buy orders accordingly. Again, predictions are just educated guesses. From my experience, they work most of the time but not all of the time.

On the day of the earnings announcement, the fluctuation of the stock is usually high. Check any change in the earnings estimate before the announcement and act accordingly. Zacks is supposed to be a useful tool to predict earnings estimates. Do not leave orders during the earnings announcement dates, which can be found in Finviz. When the earning turns out to be good, the stock price surges and your order will not be executed.

When the earnings are bad, the stock price will plunge usually and you most likely overpaid.

Option expiration dates usually cause more volatility. Retail investors do not have to be concerned except you may use wider stops. In theory, dividend days have little effect on the stock price as it will be lowered by the dividend amount.

High volume of a stock could mean opportunity

High volume usually increases the stock price volatility. If the volatility of a stock increases substantially (such as doubling its average daily volume), there could be important news on the company, recommendation changes from a major analyst or trading by the institutional investors. It usually takes the institutional investors a week to trade a stock with their sizable positions.

Many times it is started by the insiders who know about the breaking news of a stock before it is publicized. Some investment services / sites specialize in identifying the increasing volumes on these stocks.

Because day traders do not want to leave any open positions overnight, higher volatility occurs at the end of the day. It is the same on the day (usually on Friday) when the options are expiring.

Monitor your trade prices
You cannot tell whether you are paying a fair price without keeping a record. To illustrate, you're paying 1% less than the market prices in buying stocks. You may have missed buying some winners. If the 1% you saved is smaller than the appreciation of the stocks you would have bought at market prices, then you should adjust the buy prices to 0.5% less than the market price and monitor again.

Market trend makes a difference too. When the market is trending up, buying any stock would most likely be profitable and usually the purchase orders with higher discounts will not be executed.

Follow the same logic on sell orders. Need to have at least 25 stock purchases (and potential purchases) to make the conclusion meaningful. If you do not trade a lot, you will not have enough data to verify. As described, I prefer not to place an order during the earnings announcement dates which can be found in Finviz.com. If you cannot buy the stock, consider to use market order the next day. With most brokers offer no commission trades, the "All or none" option is not valid.

Good prospects
When you find gems especially those stocks that are followed by analysts, buy them at market prices and consider doubling the bet if you are really sure you have a winner. From my super stock screens, I spotted NHTC. I placed several bets and one market order. All of them were NOT executed except with the market order. At the end of the day NHTC is up 18% and my executed order is up 14%. I did not have the best buy but made a good profit. NHTC was on its way to a huge appreciation and I sold it too early. I have earned not to sell a winner and protect the profit with a stop.

Lower the buy for risky stocks (if the beta from Finviz is greater than 1 for example) even if they have good fundamentals.

Quality over quantity
If your time is limited, spend all the time on researching one stock one at a time. However, you need to own at least 3 stocks (more stocks for a large portfolio) for your diversification purposes.

Double your normal purchase position on stocks that look great after the research. For risky stocks that look good, you may want to halve your normal purchase position to cut down on the risk. If you are less risk tolerant, do not buy risky stocks at all. My results are not conclusive on risky stocks but I do get a good sleep.

A recent example
Recently I sold EA with $1 more than my order price but $2 less than the current price of the day, which was the earnings announcement day. I do recommend not placing orders right before the earnings announcement day for the stock. If the earnings are good, you do not get all the profit as in this real example; my broker did get me $1 more. If the earnings are bad, you will not sell it any way. It is the same for buying stocks.

Afterthoughts
- Besides luck, the smart investor never sells at the peak but usually within 10% of the peak. No one can predict the peaks consistently.

- I made mistakes like most of you. One time my buy price was higher than the last price executed. Luckily my broker adjusted it to the right price but I may not be that lucky next time. Several times I switched the buy price and sell price by mistake. One time it was due to my boss coming by that forced me to enter my order hastily. Try to avoid the first hour of a trade session.
- Some experts do not suggest their clients to buy stocks on the way down. With respect, I offer opposing arguments.

    - It is fine to buy them on the way down, if you have the conviction that the company or the economy will recover.
    - No one knows where the bottom is, but averaging down could be beneficial if the company or the economy can recover. Check why its stock price is falling and whether the company can fix its problems. Some major problems are only temporary or easy to fix.
    - Most of my big profits are made by buying close to the bottom prices on stocks that have a good potential to recover.
    - Many value stocks are on sale when the market dips. The most favorable time is in the Early Recovery, a phase in the market cycle defined by me.
    - Most experts agree that: The best time to buy is when there is blood in the street. It is demonstrated by the year 2003 and 2009.
    - Contrarians never follow the herd, but you need to have a good reason to be contrary. I recommended Apple in 2013 when every institutional investor was dumping Apple.
    - Stocks are manipulated via selling shorts. When the shares of a stock to short (like over 30% of shorts) are running out, there is a good chance for a short squeeze. Ensure the company being shorted heavily is not heading into bankruptcy.
- Make good money when you are right only 45% of the time by: 1. Limit your losses via stops and 2. Place higher stakes on stocks with higher appreciation potential.

Links
Selling short:
http://en.wikipedia.org/wiki/Short_%28finance%29
Short squeeze:
http://en.wikipedia.org/wiki/Short_squeeze
Fidelity Video: Stop Loss.
https://www.fidelity.com/learning-center/trading/trailing-stops-video

3   Trading in retirement accounts

There are some restrictions in trading in retirement accounts. Since the tax rules change once in a while, use the following as hints and consult your tax lawyers and /or tax accountants to confirm. I write down what I know as of this writing and the links could be obsolete.

Advantages

Defer taxes on dividends and capital gains. Most have lower tax brackets during retirement.

Restrictions

According to IRS rules, you cannot borrow from an IRA account. This restriction blocks short selling, leverage using margin, and the sale of naked put or call options.

However, you can trade inverse (a.k.a. contra) ETFs and ETNs such as SH and volatility funds such as VXX, SVXY and ZIV. Some trades may require extra reporting and qualification.

You need to be careful not to use the money before the settlement that is termed as two-day settlement rule violation. You can have stop loss orders after the two days for the settlement rule.

Your broker may have extra restrictions.

Links

Trading in an IRA link.
https://sixfigureinvesting.com/2012/11/top-15-questions-about-trading-in-an-ira/

Seeking Alpha 1
https://seekingalpha.com/article/907431-simple-rules-for-using-options-in-an-ira

4 Stop loss & flash crash

You can limit your stock loss with stops. There are some incidents where you do not always want to use a stop loss.

- <u>Flash crash</u> (May 6, 2010 also August 2015).
  It would turn your stops into market orders that could be substantially lower than your stop prices. Some brokers offer stop limits, but they do not guarantee the orders will be executed.

  The better way is a "mental stop" (my term). You do not place a stop order but place a market order to sell when your stock falls below a pre-defined price. During flash crashes, you do not want to place the market orders to sell but place orders to buy from your watch list.

  I bought some stocks at more than 10% discount during the flash crash (actually I could buy them even at better discounts) and within a week most had returned to the prices as before the flash crash.

  Placing buy orders with huge discounts to the market prices works better for volatile stocks. You should cancel the unexecuted trades before the weekends / holidays and reenter them afterwards to avoid unexpected events that may affect the stock prices.

  Avoid trading drug and bio tech companies with huge differences to the market prices. High tech is a good sector for this purpose and fluctuating 10% in this sector is more of a norm than an exception. Buying an ETF at 5% discount is a better bet than buying specific stocks from my experience.

- My experience with 911.
  I sold many stocks due to stop orders during 911. The market came back in the next three days and I missed the recovery from the stocks that were sold and did not buy back them in time.

- If your stocks are rising, you need to adjust the stop loss prices accordingly. To illustrate- in maintaining a 10% stop loss, your stop is at 90 when the current price is 100. When the stock price rises to 200, it should be adjusted to $180 (10% less than the current price). It is also called a trailing stop. Need to review these rising stocks, and change the stop price periodically (one week to one month depending on how volatile is the stock)).

Most brokers allow you to enter most trades "Good till Cancelled". Even for that there is an expiration date such as 6 months for Fidelity. Fidelity's trades for Short Sell expire by the end of the trade session. Check your broker's current policy.

- Risky markets.
  When the market is risky, you may want to use a stop loss. To prevent another flash crash, you may want to use a 'mental' market order. It is not perfect, as it requires constant watching of the market.

  There are many investing services and sites that give you the 'right' prices for a stop loss. Basically it depends on how volatile are the specific stocks. The chartists will tell you under normal conditions stocks are trading between the resistance line and the support line. Use the stop loss just below the resistance line to avoid the stop order from being executed due to the volatility of the stock.

  For simplicity as I have too many stocks in my portfolio, I use a percent. In the old days, it was recommended 8% or so below the prices you paid. In today's volatile market, I recommend 12%.

- Risky stocks.
  A stop loss is the only way that you can limit your loss for big drop (such as 25%). Affimax lost 85% of its stock value in one day with the news that three of its patients died.

- Low-volume stocks.
  The market order could drive the prices right down as there are few buyers in low-volume stocks. If there is only one buyer, he will buy with the best price for him (or the worst price to the seller).

  Unless I have good reasons, I would skip the low-volume stocks. I define low-volume: If my buy amount is higher than 1% of the average daily amount (= average daily volume * stock price).

- Beta.
  Stocks may be more volatile than the market. Beta is used to measure its volatility. The market can be measured by the S&P 500 index. If the

beta of a stock is 1, its volatility is the same as the market. If it is 1.2, it is 20% more volatile.

Set a lower stop loss for volatile stocks to prevent stocks from selling due to regular fluctuations.

Afterthoughts

Let me show you my bitter experience. The following are 5 stocks I wanted to buy and the average return was quite good.

Stocks	Return
URI	63%
GMCR	572%
MTW	186%
PII	-74%
TSCO	-127%
Avg.	124%

I placed buy orders at 5% less than the market prices as most 'bargain' investors do. I bought both of the two losers but no winners. The winners never took a breather on its way up, but the losers went down. I did buy GMCR via a market order in my momentum strategy in a separate account.

5   Short selling

You sell a stock and buy it back later betting the stock would go down. You borrow the stock from your broker (you need a margin account with enough collateral). The broker charges you interest for borrowing the stock.

The following describes the advantages, disadvantages and how to avoid the pitfalls in selling short. Next, we describe the procedures.

Advantages
You consider short selling (same as shorting) when you believe the stock and / or the market is going down. It is easier to make money by selling short than buying stocks, especially in a plunging market. Many mutual funds cannot short stocks, and consequently they spend less time searching for poor companies. The other factor is psychology: Most retail investors do not want to sell losers.

You should start paper trading. Commit a small amount of money gradually when you have proved to yourself your strategy (i.e., what and when to short sell, and exit) is profitable. Consult your financial advisor first and read my Disclaimer under Introduction.

Beginners should try to short the sectors by buying contra ETFs. The major advantages are: 1. Less volatile, 2. Can trade in retirement accounts (some brokers have some restrictions), 3. Do not lose more than your initial trade position, and 4. Fees and dividends are handled for you. Short selling stocks is riskier but more profitable than groups of stocks in ETFs.

Disadvantages and some suggestions
- Short stocks when the market is plunging and limit your shorting positions when the market is rising. The market rises more than falls, and hence be careful. However, when the market plunges, it is fast and steep.
- Could lose more than 100% of the investment.
  Actually, in theory, there is no limit. If the price of the shorted stock rises by 10 times, the loss is well over 10 times the money of the short position. The 2015 example was Weight Watchers. The price boosted up by more than 170% when Oprah took out a position on them. Fundamentally this stock was not sound and it should be shorted. No stock pickers without insider information (that is illegal) can predict

that. Use stops to protect your trade (i.e., cover your short when you lose a percent specified by you).

- Need to pay dividends and interest for the shorted stock.
  The higher the dividend rate for the stock, the more you have to pay. Investors should avoid high-dividend stocks when shorting unless the expected shorting period is only brief.

  In addition, you need to pay interest for 'borrowing' the stocks to sell. Brokers charge interest rates differently and it could be a huge saving to shop around if you short stocks a lot.
- The above disadvantages of shorting could be fixed by buying contra ETFs, which are usually based on a sector, a country or a stock index such as S&P 500 and they can be traded in retirement accounts.
- Beside contra ETFs, you can buy put options.
- Need both fundamental and technical analyses.
  From my experience, technical analysis is more important than fundamentals in shorting especially for short holding periods.
- If shorting a stock is successful and closed within a year, the gain is usually subjected to the short-term capital gains taxes which are typically higher than the long-term capital gains taxes. Check the current tax laws and consult your tax lawyer.
- Not all of the stocks can be shorted. Your broker may not have the stock you want to short. It is also possible that your broker can close out your short positions for various reasons; they need to protect their 'loans' to you. Check the margin status with your broker.
- Selling short is not allowed in retirement accounts as of 2020. However, you can buy contra ETFs for a group of stocks to bet against the market or a specific sector, but not on a specific stock in retirement accounts.
- The following sectors are riskier: the drug, mine, bank (unless you know the quality of their mortgages) and insurance sectors. An approval of a drug could drive the stock price up by more than 25% in one day. The same for earnings announcements. It could drive the stock more than 10% in either direction.
- Your screens may find many stocks in biotech companies. These companies especially with a market cap of less than 1B may have the worst fundamentals. However, when they have a new discovery, the stock prices could rocket. Do not short them when insiders are buying (Insider Transaction in Finviz.com) and high SMA-20 or SMA-50 (from Finviz.com).

- There is no perfect timing. Some stocks fluctuate a lot with no rational reasons, or the prices are driven by institutional investors. Some stocks could be manipulated. The shorted stocks could move up for a long time until they finally crash. Hence, do not short against a rising stock, a sector or a market. When the market is rising, shorting a rising stock in a rising sector is dangerous, and the opposite could be profitable for shorting.
- The best time to short is when the market is plunging. At that time, the best sectors to short are those sectors that are plunging. Hence, find the worst stocks in a worst sector in a plunging market.
- A bad company could be acquired by another company due to a good buy; it could boost its stock price. It is the same when the major problem of a company has been fixed.
- Use mental stops (i.e., set a price you can afford to lose and when it reaches the specific price, place a market trade to exit the shorted shares. You do not want to make 5% several times and lose 50% in one trade.
- You may not want to short companies that are fundamentally unsound but with a good momentum (i.e., trending up). They may have good prospects such as improved profit, being turned around, settling a lawsuit and/ or new products are being legalized and/or approved. If you do, then use mental stops to protect your trades.
- Never short sell the stocks that are rising even if they are not fundamentally sound such as FAANG in 2015 to 2020. Tesla has gained many times and you have to pay the gains, not limited to your short position.
- I have turned some short selling candidates into buying due to the high insiders' buying and/or high short squeeze potential.
- Watch out for short squeezes when the short percentage approaches over 25%. In a nutshell, the stock is running out of shares to be shorted. As a result, it would rise in price especially on any good news. As of 8/2015, I expect short squeeze for PPC and SAFM (CALM in 12/2015) for the following reasons:

  1 The shorting has no bases. It is most likely from one or two hedge funds.
  2 Fundamentally sound.
  3 Beef will be replaced by a lot of healthier and cheaper chicken if not already, esp. during the drought in California.
  4 In Hong Kong for example, they did not allow live chickens imported from China during the bird flu breakout, but they did

allow frozen chicken from the USA if there was no political game going on.

What to buy & how

Refer to the chapter on screening short candidates. If Fidelity's Equity Summary Score for the stock is below 4, it is a short candidate.

The following are my suggestions on shorting stocks that have the potential to go down. Basically, these stocks are both fundamentally unsound and technically unsound. Many sites (some require paid subscriptions) provide a composite grade for fundamentals and technical. Finviz.com. a free financial site, does provide most of these metrics and many of them are discussed here. If you do not hold the shorts for a long period, technical (the trend) parameters are more important. Parameters for short candidates are:

- Fundamentals
  - The price is more than four times the book value.
  - EY (= 1 / (P/E) is negative. Negative PEG is another consideration.
  - High debts (Debt/Equity > .5) except for industries that require high debts such as utilities.
  - Insiders are unloading their company's stocks. They do this for many reasons. But, when they are buying, do not short the stock as they may know some positive events that we do not know.
  - Bad intangibles such as losing market share and/or a major lawsuit(s) is pending.
  Read articles on the company from Finviz, Fidelity, Seeking Alpha, etc.
  - Do not short stocks that are on their uptrend. It includes the current marijuana stocks that most have no fundamental values and/or historical data.
  - Do not short small stocks with a small market cap or float. I usually short stocks with a market cap or float > 200M (100M for riskier investors). Use higher values for conservative investors.

    The stocks with small floats may be controlled by the owners; if they do not sell, the stocks available to trade will be limited. Another indicator is the Avg. Daily Vol. Personally it should be 100 times higher than my bet.
- Technical metrics:

- Be careful of stocks that have plunged more than 15% recently (Finviz's last quarter performance gives us some hint). It could mean the bottom has been reached.
- Overbought (RSI(14) > 65). There may be a reason, so it is only a secondary consideration. Most stocks to be shorted may have RSI(14) less than 30.
- The momentum metrics such as SMA-20 and SMA-50 are important too. SMA-20 and SMA-50 from Finviz.com should be negative (i.e., trending downwards).
- Some sites, especially the paid sites, may give you a momentum grade. Select the stocks with a bad momentum grade (a.k.a. timing grade). However, if it is the lowest grade, be careful, as it has nowhere to go but up.

Trading considerations
- Do not trade in the first hour (first half hour for me) as there may be new developments overnight.
- I use subscription services. I do not trade on Monday or the day after a holiday, as the data is at least one day late.
- Your broker may limit your short trade (limited order) to be valid for the day; check this with your broker.
- Your broker may need to approve whether you can short stocks based on your experiences.
- When you sell short and are using limit orders, enter a sell price higher than the last trade price just like selling a stock.
- Close the short position when your trade loses a predefined percentage which depends on your personal tolerance.
- Put Option is similar to shorting a company. It is not for beginners.

Margin
Margin should not be used extensively. It is expensive and most brokers try every trick they can to squeeze profits from all transactions to subsidize their low-commission incomes. Usually, you can borrow up to 40% of your current position and the rules and the margin rates vary among brokers.

Many investors had losses during the last two market plunges. However, many including myself had made a killing in 2003 and 2009 using margin. I use it for the following reasons.

- For convenience in placing buy orders that exceed my cash position in my taxable accounts.

- I can pay back my outstanding margin loans from my home equity loan (check the current tax laws) as it is far, far lower than my broker's margin interest rates. However, I do not recommend this for conservative investors.

Random cases

- As of 7/2013, shorting Amazon, Netflix and Tesla as a group was not beneficial. It is best to stay away from shorting, except during the plunging (from peak to bottom) in the market cycle.
- Did you watch 60 minutes on Lumber Liquidators in 2015? That's how you do shorting. Find out why the company boosts its profit and stock price in such a short period. If it has been proven to be fishy, place a short position. However, when the news becomes public, it could be too late for us to act.
- As of 1/15/2015, GME had a short squeeze. The stock was up by 10% with a decent earnings announcement. I am surprised that the short % was over 45% for a decent stock with a decent P/E. It had low debts and decent cash reserves. The shorters (same as short sellers) must be losing their shirts. Even for the fundamentally sound Netflix and Tesla, the shorters (one by a famous hedge fund manager) would lose a fortune; Tesla was at one time 11 times its lowest price.
- I found out the hard way in not using stops to protect my trade.

Links & Articles

Introduction https://www.youtube.com/watch?v=oMnmTV5HF5Y
https://www.youtube.com/watch?v=2VQp6-alQMg

Tilson
Put Options. http://en.wikipedia.org/wiki/Put_option
https://www.youtube.com/watch?v=TyZsemV_0YA
Fidelity Video: Options.https://www.fidelity.com/learning-center/options/finding-options-strategies/options-analysis-tool-video
Fidelity Video: Selling short.https://www.fidelity.com/learning-center/trading/selling-short-video
Option: https://www.youtube.com/watch?v=EfmTWu2yn5Q

6 Follow the trend

Many sectors are affected by the aging population such as health insurance, drug companies, health care delivery... I had a great year in drug companies in 2014 but not that great in 2015.

Common sense is the best way to look at specific sectors and follow with a thorough analysis. As of 09/24/2015, the following were my holdings including sold stocks in my taxable account in 2015.

Health insurance stocks:

Stock	Buy Date	Sold Date	Return	Annualized
AET	10/15/14	N/A	59%	63%
CI	10/15/14	N/A	63%	67%

Video game stocks:

The video game industry is thriving too as we spend a lot of our time in playing video games. It is very expensive to produce a franchise video game, so it will be limited to a few companies. The franchise video games have their product cycle. GLUU produces games for the mobile devices. They have a deal with a Chinese company to dip into that huge market. Game Stop may not be a good one long-term as most games will be delivered on-line by-passing the retail stores.

Stock	Buy Date	Sold Date	Return	Annualized
EA	03/26/15	N/A	23%	45%
EA	03/26/15	N/A	23%	45%
GLUU	01/28/15	N/A	32%	48%
TTWO	10/08/13	01/05/15	59%	47%
TTWO	10/07/13	01/05/15	63%	50%
TTWO	09/11/13	01/05/15	64%	48%

## 7	Rocket stocks

There are stocks making yearly highs and continue to do so for a while. They defy fundamental rules. Among many examples, Tesla appreciated about 400% from 4/2013 to 10/2013. However, when they reverse direction, they may lose more than they have gained. BBRY lost 95% of its value in 4 years after gaining about 30 times in 5 years. Some are manipulated by institutional investors. Most have new products that could change the world. When they have unfixable problems such as competing products and/or major pending lawsuits, they will tend to plunge. I call them rocket stocks and they may plunge at the speed they surge.

From my tests on these stocks, they share common metrics. Most of these stocks are hitting 52-week highs or close to them, and they can be found in your stock section of the newspaper and many investing sites. Usually their SMA-50 is higher than their SMA-200, which are both available from Finviz.com.

The other metrics are stock prices greater than $10 and the market cap is between 3 billion and 8 billion. I would also include 100M to 500M stocks for a larger appreciation potential although they are riskier. They should be listed in the major 3 exchanges. These are the stocks institutional investors would evaluate (greater than 4B); institutional investors drive the market. The volume should be at least double the average volume; it is a confirmation. Their rating grade on timing from many investing sites (some are free) are high.

You can alter the above criteria especially on many small drug companies and small high-tech companies. Insider purchases are another good criterion to search for rocket stocks. Avoid bankrupting stocks no matter how high they surge.

Do not be greedy as some will return to the original prices and even go to zero. When the institutional investors switch to the next rocket stock or sector, these rocket stocks will plunge in their prices. As recommended on how to sell rising stocks, use mental (a.k.a. trailing) stops such as 10%. When it falls to 10% of the last time you set the stop, sell it and **do not look back**. The average holding period of 3 months is the best in my limited testing. However, some rocket stocks do not obey the law of gravity. No one can time the peaks and bottoms consistently. Never buy a growth stock in a downward trend.

Link: 52-week high:
https://www.barchart.com/stocks/highs-lows/highs?timeFrame=1y

8   FAANG stocks

To many investors, FAANG stocks define the market. To me, as a conservative investor, it is not. For market-cap ETFs such as SPY, FAANG has more weight than other stocks. As a group, FAANG has been very profitable for the last year. To me they seem to be risky today. The following tables summarize these stocks, and I'll check them again in a year and/or after September (usually the worst month) to confirm my findings. It is also a case of momentum vs. value.

All the info is available free on websites such as Finviz.com. All data is from 8/5/2017. These are for info only and I'm not liable for any errors. Returns are annualized and dividends are not included.

Stocks	Current Price 8/5/17	From 8/5/16 to 8/7/17	From 8/7/17 to 8/7/18	From 8/7/18 to 10/7/18	From 01/03/22 to 1/03/23
FB (Meta)	169.62	37%	7%	-84%	-63%
AMZN	173.85	29%	88%	2%	-50%
AAPL	156.39	48%	30%	48%	-31%
NFLX	180.27	48%	94%	-4%	-51%
GOOGL	945.79	17%	33%	-47%	-39%
Avg.[1]	247.41	44%	50%	-17%	-47%
Beat SPY by		214%[2]	233%	-440%	-130%
SPY		14%	15%	5%	-20%

[1] All averages in this article are estimates. Fees and dividends are not included.
[2] Beat = (44% - 14%) /14=214%. Similar to other calculations for "Beat".

From the above and assuming using the recommended trailing stops, you should have exited your positions of FAANG before 2022 and saved the loss of about 50% in 2022.

Fundamentals as of 8/5/2017 (recommend to do the same analysis whether they good buys now.

Stocks	P/E	P/E FWD	P/S	P/B	Debt/ Eq.	Sales Q/Q	EPS Q/Q	ROE
FB	37	26	15	7	0.00	45	69	23
AMZN	16	14	6	4	1.11	2	18	27
AAPL	18	15	4	6	0.73	5	10	35
NFLX	221	90	8	25	1.55	32	58	13
GOOGL	34	24	7	4	0.03	21	-28	14

Avg.	65	34	8	9	0.68	21	25	22
Beat SPY [1]	164%		277%	186%				
SPY[2]	25		2	3				

[1] Very rough estimates.
[2] Most fundamental metrics are from other sources than Finviz.com, so there may be small discrepancies.

Technical as of 8/5/2017

Stocks	SMA50%	SMA200%	RSI(14)	52-week height	Short%	Insider Trans.
FB	8%	23%	67	-3%	1%	-86%
AMZN[1]	35%	8%	51	-6%	1%	0%
AAPL	5%	17%	63	-2%	1%	-31%
NFLX	10%	26%	59	-6%	6%	-69%
GOOGL[2]	-2%	8%	41	-6%	0%	0%
Avg.	11%	16%	56	-5%	2%	-37%
Beat [3] SPY by	1020%	173%	-9%			

[1] Recent double top. Bearish.
[2] Multiple tops.
[3] Very rough estimates.

The two SMA (Simple Moving Averages) technical metrics are positive.

Summary

As a group, FAANG is fundamentally unsound but technically sound compared to SPY. I said the same about the market. As suggested, use trailing stops if you own any of these stocks. When they turn to be technically unsound, this is the time to exit. They could stay in the current valuations for a long time. However, when the institutional investors are dumping them, they will fall very fast and steep. SMA-20 would be a good indicator for an exit. NFLX is the most fundamentally unsound stock.

The rosy pictures of these stocks have been priced in. I recommend that you sell the stocks with a P/E over 35 unless you have a good reason not to. It is insurance to protect your profits. Even if they still rocket higher, you still will have a good sleep. When any bad news occurs, they may rocket back to earth. Newton's Law of Gravity? If you are one of the lucky owners of these stocks, use trailing stops (i.e., stops from the current prices instead of your buy prices) to protect your profits. As 1/2020, most of these stocks are still not fundamentally sound but technically sound.

9 Politics and investing

You may ask why politics is discussed in this investing book. Politics have been proven to affect the market. For example, the market had reacted to the different stages of Quantitative Easing whose dates had been pre-set. The following is a more recent example.

As of September, 2015, I predicted 2015 and 2019 would be profitable years even during the fierce correction in August. Why was I so sure? Very **seldom is the market down in a year before an election** including 2007. The last occurrence was 1939, the year when WW2 started. Investing is a multi-disciplined venture including statistics and politics. It may not always happen, but the probability is high for these years.

How to profit

2015 was a sideways market. The market reacted to good news and bad news. The strategy for a sideways market is: Buy at a temporary down and sell at a temporary peak. Define 'temporary' according to your risk tolerance.

For the 'temporary market down', personally I used 5% down from the last market peak. To me the 'temporary market peak' is 10% up from the last market down. The percentages can apply to the percentage changes in the stocks within your watch list. In other words, I buy the stock when the market is 5% down from the last peak and sell it when it gains 10%, or the market gains 10%. Be reminded that this strategy is opposite from market plunges, where you should exit the market totally - again depending on your risk tolerance.

The following are my purchases on 08/26/2015. I should have bought more stocks one day earlier if I were not blinded by fears (human nature) during this correction. Below you will see my actual purchase orders. The four stocks were described as value stocks in an SA article and I did a simple evaluation. As of 12/31/2015, I sold all of the four stocks except Gilead Sciences. The annualized returns are more impressive such as GNW's 10% gain in one day.

Stocks	Buy Price	Buy Date	Return	Sold date
AAPL	107.20	08/26/15	12%	10/19/15
GILD	105.94	08/26/15	-4%	
GM	27.69	08/26/15	12%	09/17/15
GNW	4.54	08/26/15	10%	08/27/15

There were similar examples in 2013 and 2014.

2016: Politics and the market

No one including all the Federal Reserve chairmen / chairwomen and all the Nobel-Prize winners in economics can predict market plunges. One chairman predicted a smooth market and a few months later the housing market crashed! Many correctly predicted market crashes by pure luck. One even received a Nobel Prize and became famous. However, you would have been glad to ignore his later market predictions.

There were at least two best sellers asking us to exit the market in 2009. If you followed them, you would have missed all the big gains from 2009 to 2014. They did have a point though. However, you cannot fight the Fed. The market had been saved by the excessive printing of money and hence created a non-correlation between the market and the economy. I bet these authors (famous economists and gurus) may have not made a buck in the stock market except selling their books or teaching where their students should request refunds. It is a classic case of the blind leading the blind, or diversion of theory and reality.

From their articles, they do not know the basic technical indicators. You only want to react to the market when the market is plunging and not too early. That's why most fund managers cannot beat the market as most are not allowed to time the market. Buffett had mediocre returns in the last five years – I had warned my readers three years ago in my blogs/books. To me, the 'buy-and-hold' strategy has been dead since 2000. The average loss from the peak for the last two market plunges is about 45%. Most charts depend on falling prices, so you will not save 45% and a 25% loss is my objective.

Fundamentally speaking
The market in 2016 is risky due to the proposed interest rates hikes (as of 4/2015 the Fed indicated only .5% so it would not be a factor), our record-high margin, strong U.S. dollar (as of 4/15, it was weaker) and the high expenses of the wars. Each reason could be a good-size article. Personally, I try to maintain 50% in cash and would flee the market if my technical indicator tells me to.

Politically (and statistically) speaking
The election year is the second best for the market, but it may not be this year. We **seldom** have three terms from the same political party. For that, I predict a win by the Republicans. Republicans are usually pro-business, but ironically the democratic presidency has a better track record for a better market performance.

The market has more than recovered since the day when Obama took office. The S&P 500 performance under Republicans vs. Democrats since 1926 to 2014 is approximately:

Annualized return under Democratic presidencies: 13%
Annualized return under Republican presidencies: 6%

The market is riskier based on the above statistics. In addition, there is a good chance that we will have either a non-politician president, or a lady president for the first time (more materialized in 4/16). The market usually would not favor this kind of change. Statistics do not mean it will happen but history repeats itself more often than not in investing.

Critical political issue for 2016

On our way back at about 4 pm on a Saturday, the bus was full of Spanish-speaking workers. I bet most are illegal workers working in my suburb such as our malls, the hospital and many restaurants. Why illegals? I bet most legal folks would get welfare instead of working on that shift. If they work, the state would take away the freebies such as healthcare in many states. The illegals do not have this option. I do not think the politicians understand this. There is no need to build a border wall but rather punish the employers who hire illegals. Before we do this, we need folks willing to take the jobs that are taken by the illegals today.

What will happen if the politicians allow all the illegals to be legal? There will be nobody doing these low-level jobs I predict. No one in his right mind wants these jobs when it is far easier to collect welfare. Why would politicians make this stupid decision? They want to buy Hispanic votes as evidenced in the last two elections.

In addition, most politicians side with the welfare recipients. Since 40% of the population does not pay Federal taxes, the politicians have to satisfy their needs in order to buy votes.

We should encourage folks to work. Representation without taxation is worse than taxation without representation.

Our high taxes, increasing minimum wage, regulations and strong US dollar dampen our competitive edge.

Some political decisions/regulations that affect the stocks
Beside the presidency and the interest rates hikes, there are many political decisions and regulations that affect the stocks. Just to name a few here:

- The never-ending wars postpone our secular bull market beyond 2020.
- Solar City (SCTY) and this sector depends on a government energy credit.
- My Chinese solar panel stock evaporated when the US banned them from importing them to the US.
- Any gun control measure will affect gun stocks (initially positive).
- When Hillary spoke against biotech stocks or the coal mines, that sector sank.
- Restrictions on cigarettes if China and Russia follow our bans.
- Our immigration policy and great colleges attract the best from all over the world to come to the U.S. At the same time, we need to limit economical refugees from burdening our entitlement systems.
- France imposes extra taxes on foreign investors.
- Government bailouts on 'too big to fall' companies.
- High corporate taxes boost the exodus of corporate headquarters to tax havens outside the US.
- Infrastructure projects.

- Taking out the ban on exporting oil would increase the profits for oil companies.
- After the annexation of Crimea, the Congress restricted the use of Russia's rocket engines and gave some new opportunities to the US companies in this area. Besides political consideration, Chinese rockets are the most cost effective and more reliable.
- China's suppression of corruption affected Macau's casinos. Actually, every major change in Chinese policy affects the world and global investors.
- Currently the policy of forcing Chinese banks to take stocks in failing companies makes me stay away from investing in all Chinese banks.
- As of 7/2017, the market has gained a lot since Trump's election, especially those sectors fulfilling his election promises. Freddie Mac and Fannie Mac tripled after the election.

Summary
Politics affects the market. I predict a risky market beyond 2018. It is better to use market timing (based on stock movements instead of fundamentals) to determine when to exit the market, and use trailing stops to protect your winners. The riskiest stocks and ETFs are rocket stocks with high P/Es.

Economy and religion also affect the market. Statistically speaking, the market is ahead of the economy by about 6 months. However, the current market is an exception due to the excessive money supply. The correlation will return to normal.

Religions in the Middle East have caused wars. These huge expenses are consumption-related, not investing. It will not be good for most sectors of the economy, especially in the long run.

If you feel bad on seeking profits from others' miseries such as wars, donate your 'loots' to the related charity organization.

10 Testing strategies

You can use the free screener in many sites including your broker's website and Finviz.com. However, most do not provide a historical database for back testing. Some include historical data for technical indicators such as SMA (Simple Moving Average) and/or P/E.

Here are some services that have historical data for back testing: VectorVest, Zacks and Portfolio 123 at low prices. This article outlines some of the hints for evaluating their services. You should list your requirements. They are expensive and time-consuming to learn. However, they should give you valuable tools if they are properly used.

- Price. Most would charge $500 and up for a yearly subscription. If you cannot afford it, use Finviz.com which is free. It does not have a historical database for fundamental data and you need to save the test results.
- Most sites do not compensate for survivorship bias by taking out the unlisted companies. There are more bankrupt companies than merged or acquired companies hence making your strategy looking better than it actually is. If you take out Enron and/or Lehman Brothers, your test would look better.
  Since more small companies go bankrupt than large companies, try to include companies with a market cap greater than 500 million (100 million for strategies for small companies) to reduce this bias.
- I prefer the historical database which starts from the year 2000 so we have two full market cycles from 2000 to 2019.
- I prefer dividing the test periods into phases of the market cycle. Some screens perform better in the down market than the up market for example.
- Most have a comparison to the S&P 500 index or SPY for simplicity. In the last few years (as of 2019) SPY has been doing great because SPY is weighted by market cap with a lot of high-flyers. If these high-flyers fall, this index and SPY would fall accordingly. Use related ETF for comparison. For example, if you are testing a strategy on dividend stocks, your yardstick should be one related to dividend stocks and most likely you need to add dividends to your results and the ETF. Personally, I would buy SPY for the money left over, and hence SPY is a logical choice for me. Do not use DOW index: 1. It has only 30 stocks, and 2. It is price weighted and that is not practical.
- I prefer to enter the filter parameters via 'click-and-select'.
- It is easier to understand annualized return; a 1% return per month is equivalent to 12% in a year, especially for short-term trades. However, if the period is less than 15 days, the annualized return would be amplified too much.

- Most do not include dividends and it is fine when you do not include the same in your benchmark such as the SPY. For screens specialized on dividends, add the extra dividends to the performance.
- Many vendors group several parameters such as P/E and Debt/Equity into a value score. The other popular score is momentum score with the simple moving average for example. The combining of these two scores is a summary score. There are many other scores such as a safety score using beta.
- Determine that whether the search is for value stocks or momentum stocks. You need to hold value stocks longer (one year for me) and momentum stocks shorter (1 month for me). Then do the same for testing.

  To illustrate, SMA-20, Sales Q-to-Q and Earnings Q-to-Q are momentum parameters while P/E, Debt/Equity and P/B are value parameters. If you test a value strategy, the holding period should be more than 6 months.
- Some screens find more volatile stocks than others. It is measured by the maximum drawback, which is defined as the loss from the recent peak. For stocks from volatile screens, use a higher stop loss otherwise they would be stopped out during stock price fluctuations.
- Read the evaluations of the service you are interested in by googling it. It could save you a lot of money by learning from others' experiences.
- A screen has many criteria such as P/E. My basic parameters are: in one of the 3 major exchanges, U.S. stocks, Market Cap within a specified range, Earnings Yield > 5% and Stock Price > 1. Vary it for your requirements for the specific screen.
- Sorting. You may want to sort Earnings Yield (E/P) in descending order.
- Testing. You may want to test the top 5 stocks according to your sort specified.
- Testing period. For value screens, you may want to hold the stocks for 6 months or a year.

  The following uses the Year-End screen as an example. You have the following start date: 11/1, 11/15, 12/1, 12/15, 1/15 and 1/30 and hold the screened stocks for 1, 2, 4 and 6 months.

  The number of simulations from 2007 to 2017: 10 years * 6 start dates * 4 (1, 2, 4 and 6 months holding) = 240 simulations. For each sort variation, you double the number of simulations to 480.

  Adding every variation to the screen such as Market Cap > 1000 would again double the number of simulations to 960.

  It is a time-consuming process. Some sites may have strategies simulating what gurus such as Buffett would buy.
- In reality, after you have found a handful of stocks, be sure to start further research using Debt/Equity, Q-Q sales / earnings, short % and Insider Transaction from Finviz.com; also use Fidelity.com's Equity Summary Score and average 5-year P/E and Yahoo!Finance.com's EV/EBITDA.

- If you have found too many stocks, restrict your criteria and vice versa for too few stocks.
- Ensure the calculations are correct. When you compare the returns to SPY, the negative values could give you wrong interpretations.
- Define your tests according to the phases of the market cycle. Market Peak (a phase defined by me) should have different strategies rather than Early Recovery.
- The last 5 years is better than the last 10 years as it is more similar to the current market.
- A spreadsheet is the tool to summarize all your test results.
- Short-term strategies should use a holding period of one to three months, while long-term strategies should use 1 year (6 months when appropriate) or annualized.
- A strategy with more losses than wins could be profitable depending on the positions (such as higher position for stocks with better scores) and/or stops (such as 50% for gains and 15% for losses).
- There has been no evergreen strategy, which is defined as a strategy that works well in all market conditions. High Insider Purchases is close to one. Recently, the following were the actual averages for my six strategies. I interpret that the period "2007 to 2014" does not favor stock pickers.

	Beat SPY by
From 2000 – 2006	490%
From 2007 – 2014	-96%
From 2000 – 2014	180%

Fidelity Video:
Trading strategies
https://www.fidelity.com/learning-center/trading/types-of-trading-strategies/overview
Top swing pattern: https://www.youtube.com/watch?v=wH8GnsjoFb0

11   ChatGPT (and other AI models)

Besides Finviz and Fidelity as the major sources for gathering information, today we have ChatGPT and other similar AI systems. You can ask ChatGPT or Deepseek "What are the best sectors today", and ask Google "the ETF or stocks in that sector(s)". However, most likely their data bases **have not been outdated**. As of 2/10/2025, DeepSeek has not been banned.

Screening stocks. You can create a free account. I asked "best stocks for now", and it gave me 10 stocks. It gave me FB instead of the new name META and made me suspicious of the accuracy of the rest of its database. Currently, the database of ChatGPT is updated to 2021 as this writing, and hence it is not good to use it to evaluate stocks. Most are high-tech and all are large companies. It could lead to many asking the same questions and it would result in these stocks rising consequently. Watch out for the flood of selling these stocks, when they are no longer recommended.

You need to be careful how current is the database the AI model reads. Recently, DeepSeek's data was about 6 **months old,** and hence the recommendation was outdated. In Jan., 2025, both ChatGPT and DeepSeek recommended NVDA that was down by 17% on the day AI stocks crashed. We should still use it for a second opinion at best.

Analyzing stocks with MSFT as an example.
Enter "Microsoft MSFT stock". It would give you general information about the stock.
Enter "Fundamental analysis". It would give you the most fundamental data on MSFT, which are appropriate for long-term holding.
Enter "Technical analysis". It would give you the most common technical data on MSFT, which are appropriate for short-term holding.

Most sites provide duplicate data. The following lists some unique data or data that can be easily accessible from the following sites.

Use Fidelity's equity summary score and at least one report for further evaluation. Comparing its P/E to the industry's P/E is helpful." Comparing to the average 5-year P/E" and "its industry" have been moved to "More" under the tab "Statistics" .

Finviz provides most data. Insider Transaction, SMAs, Shorting % … are quite easily accessible. Yahoo!Finance provides EV/EBITDA under Statistics.

ChatGPT recommendation

You can create a free account. I asked "best stocks for now", and it gave me the following stocks. It gave me FB instead of the new name META and made me suspicious of the accuracy of the rest of its database. The current database was updated to 2021. Most of the recommended stocks are high-tech and all are large companies. It could lead to many asking the same questions and it would result in these stocks rising consequently. Use AI (ChatGPT and DeepSeek for example).)". However, most likely their data bases **have not been outdated**. As of 2/10/2025, DeepSeek has not been banned

ChatGPT's recommendation is based on 01/03/2022. My estimate on the performance.

Stock	6 Months	12 Months	18 months
AAPL	-22%	-31%	6%
AMZN	-33%	-50%	-23%
GOOGL	-22%	-39%	-17%
JPM	-30%	-16%	-9%
META	-50%	-63%	-16%
MSFT	-21%	-28%	1%
NVDA	-50%	-52%	41%
TSLA	-42%	-72%	-30%
XOM	33%	68%	69%
Avg	-26%	-32%	2%
SPY	-21%	-20%	-7%

Only XOM passed my proprietary score, and the above proves my scoring system works at least this time. Oil prices affecting XOM would be reduced in demand when electric vehicles replace combustion cars. JPM would suffer from the reduced number of IPOs in the current market conditions. The recent rise of NVDA and MSFT is due to ChatGPT. GOOG would benefit using AI in their products.

More info from ChatGPT

Use MSFT for illustration. Type "Microsoft MSFT stock", then "Fundamental Analysis", "Technical Analysis" and lastly "Buy or sell". Even if the database is not updated, you still get some good information.

12 ChatGPT recommendation

You can create a free account. I asked "best stocks for now", and it gave me the following stocks. It gave me FB instead of the new name META and made me suspicious of the accuracy of the rest of its database. The current database was updated to 2021. Most of the recommended stocks are high-tech and all are large companies. It could lead to many asking the same questions and it would result in these stocks rising consequently.

ChatGPT's recommendation is based on 01/03/2022. My estimate on the performance. Remind that most AI databases are not up-to-date.

Stock	6 Months	12 Months	18 months
AAPL	-22%	-31%	6%
AMZN	-33%	-50%	-23%
GOOGL	-22%	-39%	-17%
JPM	-30%	-16%	-9%
META	-50%	-63%	-16%
MSFT	-21%	-28%	1%
NVDA	-50%	-52%	41%
TSLA	-42%	-72%	-30%
XOM	33%	68%	69%
Avg	-26%	-32%	2%
SPY	-21%	-20%	-7%

Only XOM passed my proprietary score, and the above proves my scoring system works at least this time. Oil prices affecting XOM would be reduced in demand when electric vehicles replace combustion cars. JPM would suffer from the reduced number of IPOs in the current market conditions. The recent rise of NVDA and MSFT is due to ChatGPT. GOOG would benefit using AI in their products.

More info from ChatGPT

Use MSFT for illustration. Type "Microsoft MSFT stock", then "Fundamental Analysis", "Technical Analysis" and lastly "Buy or sell".

13 The 5G revolution

During the pandemic, it is easy to find the importance of 5G to enable us to work and study at home and also the inequality of the poor. That is the primary reason for the U.S. trying to suppress Huawei as they are passing us in 5G technology.

Many potentially profitable companies on 5G are in the Far East including China, Taiwan, South Korea and Japan. Some companies in Taiwan and some acquired candidates have seen their stocks doubled; they are very risky though. I hope the following ETFs would contain some of these companies: FIVG, NXTG and SNSR; use ETFdb.com for more info.

This article concentrates on U.S. companies. They can be classified in the following categories:

Network provider: Verizon (VZ) and all others. VZ started earlier.

Network builder: Huawei (a private-owned Chinese company), Ericsson (ERIC) and Nokia (NOK). As of 2021, Ericsson is not doing well because China is cutting down their sales there.

Equipment/Infrastructure: Corning (GLW), Ciena (CIEN) and American Tower (AMT), which is a REIT.

Chips: Qualcomm (QCOM), Skyworks Solutions (SWKS), NVIDIA (NVDA) and Xilinx (XLNX). Some of these stocks may suffer due to the export restrictions to China in early September, 2020.

Most of the info are from this link. Search for other articles from the web.
https://www.fool.com/investing/stock-market/market-sectors/communication/5g-stocks/

The following is my simple evaluation of selected stocks on 8/1/2020. Before you invest, do your own research and consult your financial advisor. I am not responsible for any errors.

The list

Symbol	Fidelity's Score[1]	Cheaper By[2]	True EY[3]	Debt/ Equity[4]	Insider Trans.[4]	Short %[4]
VZ	8.8	1%	12%	1.96	0%	1%
GLW	2.8	-876%	6%	0.79	-20%	3%
CIEN	9.9	44%	6%	0.34	-13%	3%
AMT	9.6	-3%	3%	6.76	-2%	1%
QCOM	9.1	-102%	5%	5.24	-18%	2%
SWKS	6.3	-78%	6%	0.00	-9%	2%
XLNX	4.8	-43%	3%	0.54	-8%	3%
NVDA	9.4	-110%	2%	0.00	-23%	1%
Symbol	Fidelity's ESS	Cheaper by	True EY	Debt/ Equity	Insider Trans.	Short %

[1] Equity Summary Score. This and "Cheaper by" can be obtained from Fidelity's website requiring free registration.

[2] Cheaper by % based on the current P/E (PE) for the last twelve months and compared to its 5-year average (PE5). If it is negative, it means it is more expensive. Cheaper % = -(PE – PE5) /PE5.

[3] True EY is the earnings yield considering debts and cash. Compare it to one-year Treasuries and CDs which are basically risk free. It is the reciprocal of "EV/EBITDA". It is obtained from Yahoo!Finance (under Statistics). Most use P/E and not Forward P/E (guessing the future earnings). Even if Forward P/E is used, it may not be upgraded during this fast-changing period.

[4] From Finviz.com.

From the above, I do not want to buy stocks whose Insider Trans is more than 10%. Most likely, the insiders think these stocks have approached the peaks. I would ignore the stocks that are "Cheaper by" more than -30% - another sign of over-value.

VZ is the only stock that has good value even. I may want to wait for the market crash and reevaluate them again.

14   Computer chips

As of 4/2023 (today), the U.S. chip industry is not doing well. It is primarily due to the recovery of the pandemic. During the pandemic, more people worked at home and hence the demand for laptops and related hardware was high. The increased investment on new factories give to today's over supply of chips. The recovery would materialize hopefully by 2024, and our policy and China's is a factor.

The other reason is our sanctions on China, and China was their primary customer to many of our chip companies. We do not allow China to buy advanced products based on our technology including ASML's chip-making machines. I estimate China will have DUV (a lithography, 28 nm machine) in 2024 or 2025 that would satisfy 70% of China's chip fabrication. Based on several breakthroughs in China, I also PREDICT 14 nm chips available in 2027, and EUV that can produce 7 nm chips in 2028. Our chip companies have been suffering a lot from importing chips to China. Even more so, when China fixes these problems, the world would be flooded with cheap chips from China. Our politicians look for short-term gains.

The only positive development is the demand of high-end GPUs due to Artificial Intelligence (AI). Nvidia is the most promising stock since the introduction of Microsoft's ChatGPT during the last quarter of 2022. The new product H100 is about 4 times as fast as the current A100. Nvidia is working on reduced versions for China to overcome the sanctions. Many companies have implemented or are going to implement AI. Nvidia, many other AI chip companies, Microsoft and Google would profit.

Afterthought
My friend told me about ChatGPT and in a month Microsoft's stock appreciated by 15%; he did not buy the stock. My friend figures it wrongly that Google would be too late to dinner. Lessons follow. We need to check the impact of revolutionary products if we do not understand it (opposite to what many investors including Buffett preach). If the stock is rising, your order prices should not be too far from the current prices.

Links
China's EVU: https://www.youtube.com/watch?v=nWU6x-XHw9k
China's GPU: https://www.tomshardware.com/news/ai-and-tech-sovereignity-drive-number-of-gpu-developers-in-china
Losers: https://www.youtube.com/watch?v=3TxsVw5XWDs
Chip materials: https://www.youtube.com/watch?v=tjLEFXEbUws
AI stocks: https://www.youtube.com/watch?v=PWbEkenszec.

#Filler: Cooperation vs confrontation
Can music unite the world? I wish it could if we and the Chinese do not let our and their dumb nationalism cover our eyes. https://www.youtube.com/watch?v=gf6v59c5yuY

The song is "Hotel California", one of our best songs, being played by a Chinese girl named Moyun using a traditional Chinese instrument and is being enjoyed by the world audience.

15 Money Market, CDs & Bonds

CDs are used for parking money to avoid market crashes. As of 2022, the market was still making new highs. From my own **predictions**, today may be similar to 2007, the peaking phase of the last market cycle (termed as melt up).

Many of my one-year CDs paid about 1.5% in 2020 (around 4% in 2023). After inflation and taxes, it is a loss, but it is far better than virtually nothing from the money market funds. Our financial system punishes us for not taking risks. However, at the market peaks, we need to play defensively with conservative investments such as CDs.

The holding periods of my CDs depend on when I need the cash to buy contra ETFs such as SH during a predicted market plunge or when I expect the market returns. As of 2020, I don't predict the market will crash in 3 months. Even if it would, I should have enough cash then within a short period of time.

Another consideration is the interest rate hikes. I predict that there will be a 0.5% increase in 6 months. Hence, all the new CDs in 6 months will have a 0.5% increase in interest in my theory. [Update. In 2022, there are several rate hikes and many analysts expect rate hikes would be done by the end of 2022.]

We can "ladder" the CDs letting them mature in different months. For example, we can have one CD maturing in 3 months and another one in 12 months. When the first CD matures, we renew it for another 3 months. In this method, we always have cash in 3 months and one CD has a higher interest rate. The more the CDs you have, the better the distribution will be.

Ensure that the FDIC limit of $250,000 is per bank, NOT per account. Some CDs from foreign banks which are also insured by the FDIC offer higher interest rates such as the Bank of China as of this writing. Most brokers sell CDs in units and one unit represents $1,000.

Some states offer special favorable treatment for taxing interest for CDs from local banks. Being a Mass. resident, I prefer local banks. However, the CDs from my brokers make it easy to trade and select the better rates. In one case, my bank offered a special CD deal of 1.55% for 14 months in 2020. It saved me about $200 but it requires me to go to the bank two times (vs. doing it on-line).

Do not select CDs that are callable. It means the banks have the right to cancel the deal for their advantage. It is no longer a popular feature – you can cheat folks sometimes, but not all the time. Try to select the CDs having the settlement date closest to today's date. Otherwise, you do not get interest on the extra days. Avoid "automatic renew" unless you do not have time to renew them. Usually there are better rates than the renewal rates.

For the last 5 years from 2020, SPY is returning 15% and beats the 1.3% CDs by a good margin. Today buying CDs is an insurance bet. When the market crashes, it usually is fast and deep.

Other safe investment besides CDs
As of 7/2023, your broker's core money market fund could be your best deal for holding cash and you do not have to do anything. At Fidelity, I prefer SPAXX. The yield of most money market funds changes fast. Hence, the one-year (or longer) CDs have advantage when the interest rate drops.
https://www.youtube.com/watch?v=KU6HYRHj3jg

You may also consider bond funds and/or bond ETFs. They have higher dividends but most likely they are riskier. As of 2020 (2022 too) I do not consider long-term bonds. Their performances are inversely proportional to the interest rate. I predict there will be interest hikes. Short-term (less than two years for me) bonds are fine.

Compare the performance of the bond funds. Most make a mistake by comparing the current performance. You should compare their performances during market peaks such as in 2007 and 1999.

In 2023, the short-term interest rates are better than the long-term rates. The money market funds are about the short-term interest rates and you can withdraw them anytime. The risk is minimal. If you believe there are future rate hikes such as in 2022, you can buy a treasury ETF betting rate hikes.

The two ETFs I consider are HYG and JNK. Their annualized returns are compounded. SPY is the benchmark I use. Check out their past performances. In 2008, the market crashed. It was a bad year for bond funds and ETFs. Based on this, I would sell them when the market crashes. However, in 2009 both recovered from the previous losses quite nicely.

	2007	2008	2009
HYG	3%	-18%	29%
JNK	Not avail.	-25%	38%
SPY	5%	-37%	26%

Link: Government bond default? https://www.youtube.com/watch?v=wMxj6iB92ZA
Broker CDs (Recommended): https://www.youtube.com/watch?v=zhEiyW2N7KE
More on CD: https://www.youtube.com/watch?v=FRWMsGJ2-NE
Money market fund: https://www.youtube.com/watch?v=N53wZ_80abU
Its risk: https://www.youtube.com/watch?v=k3wGqD_9SzY
Better than cash: https://www.youtube.com/watch?v=SrQTOhafE4A

16 Overview of Fidelity.com

The following is written by DeepSeek (AI). It has a lot in common with my article on Fidelity.

Fidelity.com is a robust platform offering a wide range of tools and resources for investors, from beginners to seasoned professionals. Known for its depth of research and user-friendly interface, it is an essential tool for building and managing an investment portfolio.

Key Features
1. **Stock Research Tools**:
   - Access detailed stock profiles, including fundamental metrics, technical indicators, and analyst ratings.
   - Use the *Equity Summary Score* (powered by third-party analysts) to gauge overall market sentiment for a specific stock.
2. **Portfolio Management**:
   - Track portfolio performance and compare it against benchmarks like the S&P 500.
   - Use tools to analyze asset allocation and identify diversification opportunities.
3. **Investment Education**:
   - Browse *Learning Center* content, including articles, webinars, and interactive courses on topics such as market timing, risk management, and retirement planning.
   - Access video tutorials that explain fundamental investment concepts like "P/E Ratios" or "Dollar-Cost Averaging."
4. **Screeners for Stocks, ETFs, and Mutual Funds**:
   - The *Screener* tool allows you to filter investments based on key parameters like P/E ratio, dividend yield, and market cap.
   - Save custom screens for future use and refine criteria as market conditions change.
5. **Advanced Trading Tools**:

- Active Trader Pro, Fidelity's downloadable platform, provides advanced charting and real-time data for active traders.
- Use options analytics, back testing, and strategy planning tools to optimize trades.

How to Use Fidelity.com Effectively

1. **For Beginners**:
   - Start with the *Learning Center* to build foundational knowledge about investing.
   - Use pre-defined stock or ETF screeners to identify high-potential investments without needing extensive technical expertise.
2. **For Intermediate Investors**:
   - Explore the *Equity Summary Score* to complement your own research.
   - Use the *Portfolio Analysis Tool* to identify gaps or overlaps in your investments.
3. **For Advanced Investors**:
   - Download Active Trader Pro for in-depth charting and technical analysis.
   - Leverage advanced screeners to customize your searches based on specific metrics like ROE (Return on Equity) or insider transactions.

Advantages

- **Extensive Free Resources**: Many features are available at no cost; opening an account provides full access.
- **Integrated Education**: Tutorials, webinars, and articles make it easy to improve your investing skills.
- **All-in-One Platform**: Combines portfolio management, stock screening, and research in one place.

Limitations

- **Complexity for Beginners**: The sheer volume of tools and data may overwhelm new investors.
- **Limited Access Without an Account**: Some features, such as portfolio tracking and advanced screeners, require account registration.

Example: Screening for Dividend Stocks

1. Navigate to Fidelity's *Stock Screener*.

2. Set the following parameters:
    - **Dividend Yield**: Greater than 3%.
    - **P/E Ratio**: Below 20.
    - **Debt/Equity Ratio**: Less than 0.5.
3. Save the screen and review the results for companies with consistent dividend growth.

How to Get Started
1. Visit Fidelity.com.
2. Create an account or log in if you already have one.
3. Explore the available products and services based on your financial goals.
4. Use the tools and resources to manage your investments, plan for retirement, or seek financial advice.

Conclusion
Fidelity.com is a one-stop destination for individuals and institutions looking to manage their finances, invest wisely, and plan for the future. Whether you're a beginner or an experienced investor, Fidelity offers the tools and support to help you achieve your financial objectives.

17 Overview of insider trading

This article is written by ChatGPT (AI)

What is Insider Trading?
Insider trading refers to the buying or selling of stocks based on material, non-public information about a company. While some forms of insider trading are illegal, corporate executives, directors, and employees are allowed to trade shares of their own companies as long as they follow disclosure requirements set by regulatory bodies like the SEC.

Legal vs. Illegal Insider Trading
- **Legal Insider Trading:** Company insiders must report their trades through filings such as Form 4 with the SEC. These reports provide transparency and allow investors to track executives' trading activity.
- **Illegal Insider Trading:** This occurs when individuals trade securities based on confidential information that is not publicly available, violating laws designed to ensure a level playing field.

Using Insider Trading Data for Investments
Investors can monitor legally disclosed insider trades to gauge confidence in a company's future performance. Key considerations include:
- **Buying Trends:** Large purchases by multiple executives may indicate strong future growth.
- **Selling Trends:** Insider selling does not always signal trouble, as executives sell for various personal reasons, but significant selling could indicate concerns.
- **Timing and Size:** Large, concentrated purchases near earnings reports or major company developments can be a bullish signal.

Tools for Tracking Insider Trading
Investors can use public databases and financial news platforms to track insider trades, including:
- SEC's EDGAR database
- Websites like OpenInsider and Finviz
- Financial news services reporting insider activity

Risks and Limitations
- **Misinterpretation:** Insiders may buy or sell for reasons unrelated to company performance.

- **Regulatory Changes:** New laws may alter how insider trades impact stock performance.
- **Market Reactions:** Not all insider trades lead to significant stock movement.

Conclusion

While monitoring insider trades can provide valuable insights, it should be used alongside other fundamental and technical analysis strategies. Successful investing requires a diversified approach rather than relying solely on insider activity.

18 Screen the Insiders' purchase.

Bring up OpenInsider.com (http://www.openinsider.com/)

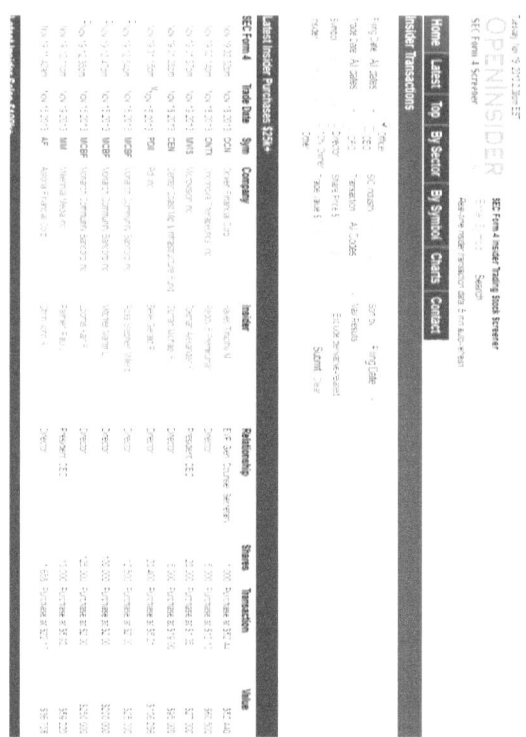

Source: OpenInsider
The following is for illustration purposes only. This screen is displayed on 11/19/2013.

If your screen is too small, open your PC's browser and type:
http://ebmyth.blogspot.com/2013/12/insider-screen-for-profit-from-insider.html

Here is an illustration looking for candidates.

- Select the Officers only. Including the Director is the second choice.
- Ignore the transactions that have values less than $100,000. We only have PDII and MCBF. You should not have the same stocks on a different date. Select the stocks that have purchase values more than $100,000.
- Next bring up Finviz.com in your browser. Enter PDII and scroll all the way down to find the net purchase (= purchase amount – sold amount). For example, if the insiders bought $100,000 worth of stock and they sold $100,000 of your stock, it would not be considered as a purchase. There was no insider sell for PDII, so it is fine.
- Was the stock purchased close to the market price? From Finviz.com again, the purchase price was $5.25 and the current price is $5.29. So, it looks good.

Summary of selected criteria

The displayed screen does not have all the selection criteria as below.

- Select Officer only.
- Filing Date and Trade Date within the last 7 days.
- Transactions: Purchase only.
- Sorted by Value. Omit transactions less than $100,000 (adjust to the value you're comfortable with).

Skip stocks that meet any of the following (adjust them to your own requirements).

- The purchase price is not close to the market price.
- Penny stocks (less than $2) or market cap less than 50 million. It is too risky to me, but it is your call.
- Stock daily volume less than 8,000 shares (I prefer 10,000).
- Poor fundamentals. If you do not have time to do a thorough analysis, use Fidelity's Equity Summary Score. GuruFocus.com (fee) has a nice evaluation with warning signs.
- If they are not listed in one of the three major exchanges.

My steps

Be flexible and use the tools you have.

1. Select the stocks with heavy insider trading. OpenInsider.com provides many features. Select Officers, Purchase Only, and Last 7 Trade Days and Last 7 File Days. Sorted by Trade Value.

   As an alternative, Finviz's screener using Insider Trans is easy to find these stocks.

2. Use Finviz.com. Understand the company and their fundamentals.

   If the stock cannot be found, most likely it is not traded here. Skip these companies and also the companies with small market caps and average daily volumes.

   Check the insider trade prices. If the trade prices are too low from the market prices, skip these stocks.

   Understand the company such as the country, the sector and general financial shape. I would skip most foreign countries especially from emerging countries and small companies as I do not trust their financial information.

   For safety, I usually examine the fundamentals of the screened stocks.

   Skip companies with more than 5% appreciation in the last five market sessions. We may have missed this opportunity, but there are many others.

3. Use OpenInsider.com again to list the 90 days transactions (all) for the stock. If the CEO sells 1,000 shares and buys back 1,000 shares, there is no insider purchase.

#Filler: My daughter's wedding

How to have a wedding banquet that the entire town will talk about and at the least cost? It is at the Burger King where they treat you like a king. All the fries are super-sized and the drinks are bottomless. The king's crown and the most popular party favor are included. For the reasons I do not understand, my daughter flatly refused.

Epilogue

I've received a lot of good responses and thanks. The 3ⁿᵈ Edition incorporates a lot of your feedbacks and my recent updates. Some complaints are not valid though and some could be from my competitors.

- The primary objective of this book is helping you make money, not improving your English skill. How many writers whose first language is not Chinese have written books in Chinese?
- As described in Introduction, charts and tables can be displayed in the full size of your reader by selecting it. I also provide links to the more important charts so you can display them on the large screen of your PC.
- I have my annuity increased by 4 folds using the techniques described in the book over the years.

Reviews

There are many reasons you should write a review (use any name if you're shy) on this book:
https://www.amazon.com/dp/B075WCR65L

- As of this writing (01/2018), I do not know any reviewers on all of my books. Some reviews were obviously written by friends and family members.
- How can a 50-page book have far more and better reviews than my books that are more than 300 pages?
- I bet some reviews were written by my competitors or ones with strong bias against me being an Asian. I beg you to write an honest review.
- A best seller tells us to exit the market in 2009 when my book told you until recently using simple charts for similar period. They had so many excellent reviews from celebrities. If you followed this author, you would have lost a lot of money
- I can take bad reviews, so I can improve. This book is about the size of three books. I bet you have got your money worth. It is organized as a reference book than a novel.

Summary why sector rotation fails
- Not using stop orders. For simplicity, use 5% for most stocks and 8% for volatile stocks. I prefer stops less than the support line to reduce the chance of stopping out due to normal stock price fluctuation. Recommend trailing stops (based on current price) for winning stocks.
- Not timing the market. Include SH or any contra ETFs but not as good as timing the market.
- Not considering different phases of the market cycle. Some sectors are more favorable than others in different stages of the market cycle.
- Not disciplined. If you stick with a proven strategy, it will work in the long term.
- When a sector is in full value, it will be switch to another one with less value. Beware, the market is driven by institutional investors.
- The market is not always rational and it can be manipulated. Hence, do not bet the entire arm.

Parting words
There are 12 strategies in Sector Rotation and several strategies in Momentum Trading described in this book. Try out the first three strategies first. Paper trade your strategies before you commit with real money. If your bet is high, subscribe a newsletter on this subject. There are many to choose from. A current event such as interest hike, a new president…would change the sector performance.

Andrew McElroy, writing articles on this topic in Seeking Alpha, said,
"Great stuff, Tony. It's great to meet experienced traders such as yourself.
I had a browse through the book and think your method is a little more refined than mine." On the next day, he said,
"Your strategy is very rules based and solid. I sometimes envy people who have developed something like this.

That said, if I tried to copy it I would make a dog's dinner of it. There's no way I can undo the way I see the market now. It allows me to make incredible trades, but is also open to errors. No trade is quite the same and I couldn't write down my exact system and rules."

http://seekingalpha.com/article/4029288-sector-rotations-december-update
A link is provided for future updates and announcements.
https://ebmyth.blogspot.com/2020/01/updates.html
My blog:
https://tonyp4idea.blogspot.com/

Afterthoughts
Thanks to Amazon for making self publishing easy and at no cost. Promoting books is a different story, especially with no budget in advertising. Every time I mentioned my books in public, most likely it would be deleted. I received more unfavorable remarks than encouragement when I mentioned it to my friends or in mail lists of old friends and classmates. English is not my native language. Imagine how hard it is to write a book in Chinese when your native tongue is English. However, I enjoy writing books and hopefully some readers would benefit. I could be happier writing notes for myself instead of publishing it. Your positive comments is my driving force to write books.

Recommend the next books.
"Investing Lessons and Plunders", which Includes my and gurus' experiences and many articles not included in this book. For example, the reader of "Art of Investing" would learn more about "Sector Rotation", "Shorting", "Economy", "Investing Strategies" and "Investing advices / News".
https://www.amazon.com/dp/B09L8NVJNH
Market Crash 2022: https://www.amazon.com/dp/B0BJ7PVKZL

"Best stocks" series. A new book may be published on Dec. 15 every year (not a promise). Best Stocks for 2023 is available.
https://www.amazon.com/dp/B0BQCLCZP9

Performances (not indicative of future performances) of the primary lists of my last five books in this series:

Book	Stocks	Return	Ann.	Beat RSP by[1]
Best stocks to buy for 2022	10[6]	4%	4%	153%[7]
Best Stocks to buy as of July, 2021[4]	8	5%	13%	487%
Best Stocks for 2021 2nd Edition	10	42%[3]	52%[3]	220%
Best Stocks for 2021	4	29%	44%	118%
Best Stocks to Buy from Aug, 2020	14	45%	45%	3%[5]
Avg.	9	25%	32%	196%[2]

Detail: https://tonyp4idea.blogspot.com/2022/12/best-stocks-series.html

Appendix 1 – All my books

Book	No. of Pages	Link	ebook
Art of investing 5th Edition	570	Click here	link
Sector Rotation: 21 strategies 5th Edition	525	Click here	Link
Be a stock expert in 5 minutes. Expanded Edition.	203	Click here	Link
Using Finviz 5th Edition	570	Click here	Link
Using Fidelity 5th Edition	570	Click here	Link
Momentum Investing 3rd Edition	285	Click here	Link
Using profitable investing sites	500	Click here	link
Investing successes and plunders	415	Click here	Link
Best stocks to buy for 2025	375	Click here	Link

If you already have my book that is over 300 pages, most likely you do not need to buy the above books except "Investing successes and plunders" and the "Best Stock" series, which may be available every December – not a promise.

For paper-bag readers, access the links via the following link.
https://www.blogger.com/blog/post/edit/7608574268453692676/1786802320953936467

Most books have paperbacks. Links and offers are subject to change without notice.

Best stocks to buy for 2025

The current book is "Best stocks for 2025" in this series.
https://www.amazon.com/dp/B0D2459JDT

If the sales of my books in this series were based on past performances, I should have sold many books, but obviously not.

Book	Stocks	Return[3]	Ann.	Beat RSP by[1]
Best stocks to buy for 2024	8	46%	48%	132%
Best stocks to buy for 2023	8	36%	36%	290%
Best stocks to buy for 2022	10[6]	4%	4%	153%[7]
Best Stocks to buy as of July, 2021[4]	8	5%	13%	487%
Best Stocks for 2021 2nd Edition	10	42%[4]	52%	220%
Best Stocks for 2021	4	29%	44%	118%
Best Stocks to Buy from Aug, 2020	14	45%	45%	3%[5]
Avg.	9	34%	40%	208%[2]

Here is the detail:
https://tonyp4idea.blogspot.com/2024/12/best-stocks-to-buy-for-2025.html

---

Sector Rotation: 21 Strategies 5th Edition

- On 5/26/2020, I searched for "Sector Rotation" under Amazon's Book. They are listed in the same order except my book Sector Rotation: 21 Strategies.

Book	Date	Size[1]	Kindle $[1]	Hard $
Sector Rotation: 21 Strategies	**05/2020**	**425**	**$9.95**	**$24.95**
Super Sectors	09/2010	289	$26.39	$49.95
Dual Momentum Investing	11/2014	240	$40.40	$42.20
Sector Investing	05/1996	260		$29.94
Sector Trading Strategies	08/2007	164	$26.39	$16.66
The Sector Strategist	03/2012	225	$26.39	$44.96
ETF Rotation	10/2012	125	**$9.95**	**$14.99**
Optimal... Sector Rotation	07/2015	80		$44.07

[1] From Amazon on size and prices as of 5/25/2020.

My book won in all categories except the price for hard copy in one. However, my book won as the lowest cost per page by a wide margin. In addition, as of 5/2020 I bet that no author besides me made over 4 times using sector rotation starting the amount more than his yearly salary then.

- I have **21** strategies in sector rotation while most books have only one. It ranges from simple rotation of a stock ETF and cash for beginners to many advanced strategies for experts. Most other books have one or two strategies.
- Andrew, a contributor on Sector Rotation article at Seeking Alpha, said, "Great stuff, Tony. It's great to meet experienced traders such as yourself. I had a browse through the book and think your method is a little more refined than mine."
- "You have written the book in a way that makes good and logical sense." Bill.
- Do not be fooled by past performances. Just check the recent performance of the top 50 stocks selected by IBD in the last five years. The mediocre result (hopefully it will change) could be due to too many followers and/or there is no evergreen strategy. I seldom heard the fantastic results from the followers of O'Neil, our greatest chartist. The adaptive strategy of this book shows you how to select the most profitable strategy for the current market.
- I switched most (if not all) my sector funds in April, 2000 from technology sectors to traditional sectors (better to money market fund). We can reduce losses by spotting market plunges and the sector trend.

Shorting Stocks and ETFs

Recent performances.

Stocks	Short Date	Close date	Duration	Return	Annualized
ACVA	06/10/21	09/29/21	111	22%	72%
CCL	07/14/21	09/29/21	77	-8%	-36%
CENX	09/17/21	09/29/21	12	3%	105%
CLOV	09/16/21	09/29/21	13	10%	291%
CSPR	09/16/21	09/29/21	13	33%	917%
EOSE	09/15/21	09/29/21	14	10%	261%
MILE	07/22/21	09/29/21	69	53%	279%
NCLH	07/27/21	09/29/21	64	-5%	-27%
REAL	06/04/21	09/29/21	117	22%	68%
UAVS	06/04/21	09/29/21	117	41%	127%
Average	07/30/21	09/29/21	61	18%	206%
RSP	S&P 500			0%	

It is for education purposes and I am not responsible for any errors. As in most parts of this book, commissions, dividends and fees (interest for shorts) are not included, and hence the returns are less than specified. They are real and all trades for the period.

Stocks	Short Date	Close date	Duration	Return	Annualized
BBIG[1]	09/30/21	11/19/21[1]	50	35%	258%
BFLY	09/30/21	11/18/21	49	14%	107%
EOLS	11/10/21	11/17/21	7	10%	523%
FLDM	10/13/21	11/18/21	36	14%	147%
MKFG	10/27/21	11/18/21	22	-9%	-149%
PAVM[1]	10/20/21	11/19/21[1]	30	34%	413%
TSP	10/05/21	11/18/21	44	-11%	-91%
VRM	10/13/21	11/17/21	35	13%	135%
Average	10/14/21	11/18/21	34	13%	168%
RSP	S&P 500			4%	

Appendix 2 – Art of Investing

Art of Investing 5th Edition consisting of 15 books in 1. Besides saving money and your digital shelve space, it gives you quick reference and concentration on the topic you're currently interested in. It covers most investing topics in investing excluding speculative investing such as currency trading and day trading. It has over 550 pages (6*9), about the size of two investing books of average size.

The 15 books

Book No.	Amazon.com
1	Simple techniques
2	Finding Stocks
3	Evaluating Stocks
4	Scoring Stocks
5	Trading Stocks
6	Market Timing
7	Strategies
8	Sector Rotation
9	Insider Trading
10	Penny Stocks & Micro Cap
11	Momentum Investing
12	Dividend Investing
13	Technical Analysis
14	Investing Ideas
15	Buffettology

The book links are subject to change without notice.

"How to be a billionaire" is for beginners and couch potatoes, who can use the advanced features of this book in the simplest and less time-consuming techniques. Most advance users can skip this section unless they want to use some of the short cuts described.

We start with the basic books Finding Stocks, Evaluate Stocks, Trading Stocks and Market Timing. You can select and start with one of the many styles and strategies in investing such as swing trading and top-down strategy. Many tools are described in other books such as ETFs, technical analysis, covered calls and trading plan.

Many books start with "Why" to lure you to read more and are followed by "How" and then the theory behind the book.

If the book you're reading is beneficial to you, imagine how it would with 850 pages.

\# Most readers' comments are on "Debunk the Myths in Investing", which this book is originally based on. As of 2018, I did not know any of the commentators on my books.

"I skipped ahead to his chapter book 14 (of "Complete the Art of Investing"), Investment Advice just to get a feel of his writing style. His research is phenomenal and doesn't overwhelm with big words or catchy "sales-like" tactics.

I truly believe this ordinary man, Mr. Tony Pow, has a gift of explaining his experience as an investor without the bull crap of trying to make you buy his stuff. He seemingly just wants to share his knowledge, tips, and clarity of definitions for the kind of folks like me who want to understand something FIRST before jumping in with emotions of trying to make a boat load of money. I like the technical analysis side he brings.

Mr. Tony Pow talks about hidden gems in his book; well....quite frankly, he is a hidden gem. Thank you and I will also post my comments about this author to my Facebook page!" – JB on this book.

"Excellent book, recommend to all investors... great knowledge. It has fine-tuned my investing strategies... Your book is hard to set aside, as I read it all the time learning good techniques and analysis of stocks, ETF... Since I purchased your book in March, I have underlined, highlighted and placed tabs on top of pages for quick reference." – Aileron on this book.

"Tony, I just finished reading your 2nd edition. It's my pleasure to report that I found it most interesting. You're welcome to use this blurb if you like:

Debunk the Myths in Investing is an all-encompassing look at not only the most salient factors influencing markets and investors, but also a from-the-trenches look at many of the misconceptions and mistakes too many investors make. Reading this book may save not only time and aggravation but money as well!"

Joseph Shaefer, CEO, Stanford Wealth Management LLC.

"Tony, Great work!" from James and Chris, who are portfolio managers.

"'Debunk the Myths in Investing' is a comprehensive book on investing that deals with many aspects of this tense profession in which with a lot of knowledge and a bit of luck (or vice versa) one can greatly benefit…

Therefore 'Debunk the Myths in Investing' is an interesting book that on its 500 pages offer a lot of knowledge related to investing world and many practical advice, so I can recommend its reading if you're interested in this topic."
- Denis Vukosav, Top 500 Reviewers at Amazon.com.

"490 pages (Debunk) of a genius's ranting and hypothesis with various theories throughout, written light-heartedly with ample doses of humor…Yes, the myth of not being able to profitably time the market is BUSTED…

One might ask… Why is he giving away the results of his hard-earned research for only $20? He states that his children are not interested in investing and wants to share his efforts with the world." - Abe Agoda.

"Excellent book, recommend to all investors… great knowledge. It has fine-tuned my investing strategies… Your book is hard to set aside, as I read it all the time learning good techniques and analysis of stocks, ETF… Since I purchased your book in March, I have underlined, highlighted and placed tabs on top of pages for quick reference." - Aileron on this book.

"Great stuff, Tony. It's great to meet experienced traders such as yourself. I had a browse through the book and think your method is a little more refined than mine."
"Your strategy is very rules based and solid. I sometimes envy people who have developed something like this."

Making 50% in one month
I claim to have the best one-month performance ever for recommending 8 or more stocks without using options and leverage. My following return is 57% in a month or 621% annualized. They are slightly different as I calculated the average from the averages of three different accounts. The average buy date is 12/26/18 and the "current date" is 01/28/19.

The performance may not be repeated. I will use the same screen for the coming years and even the expected 10% (or 120% annualized) is very good.

I used the same screen for searching stock candidates. I spent a total of about 20 hours from Dec. 15, 2018 to Jan. 5, 2019.

Stock	Buy Price	Sold or Current Price	Buy date	Sold or Current date	Profit %	Profit % Ann.	Status
CHK	2.13	2.99	01/03/09	01/18/19	40%	982%	Sold
MNK	16.41	21.45	01/03/19	01/25/19	31%	510%	Sold
MNK	16.43	21.45	01/03/19	01/25/19	31%	507%	Sold
NNBR	5.68	8.58	12/26/18	01/28/19	51%	565%	
NNBR	5.72	8.58	12/26/18	01/28/19	66%	727%	
ESTE	4.35	6.45	12/26/18	01/18/19	48%	766%	Sold
LCI	4.61	8.29	12/21/18	01/28/19	80%	767%	
MDR	8.01	9.13	01/08/19	01/28/19	14%	255%	
YRCW	3.29	5.78	12/21/18	01/28/19	76%	727%	
YRCW	3.26	5.78	12/21/18	01/28/19	77%	742%	
ASRT	3.56	4.18	12/26/18	01/28/19	17%	193%	
UTCC	7.13	11.00	12/26/18	01/28/19	54%	600%	
YRCW	2.92	5.78	12/26/18	01/28/19	98%	1083%	

Best one-year return

I claim to have the best-performed article in Seeking Alpha history, an investing site, for recommending 15 or more stocks in one year after the publish date without using options and leverage.

https://seekingalpha.com/article/1095671-amazing-returns-velti-alcatel-lucent-alpha-natural-resources

Appendix 3 - Links

The following may be repeated from the articles and it is for your convenience. To illustrate, Under YouTube (or Investopedia), search "Finviz". Some links have permanent values such as most articles from Wikipedia and Investopedia. Others reflect current events such as the current market. Learn from them and act when the current events have similar descriptions. For the printed versions and updatedlinks, enter the following in your browser: https://tonyp4idea.blogspot.com/2023/02/links-in-my-books.html

Beginners

Common mistakes: https://www.youtube.com/watch?v=zkNueyFs8zQ

Best Vanguard ETFs https://www.youtube.com/watch?v=mSEyghlZchQ

Buy stocks/ETFs: https://www.youtube.com/watch?v=4vjkeC_4EmU

Screener

Finviz https://www.youtube.com/watch?v=cHNUMPgEYGY

Recommended YouTube: https://www.youtube.com/watch?v=CJoN7wLfWNo
PEG: http://en.wikipedia.org/wiki/PEG_ratio
Short %: http://www.investopedia.com/university/shortselling/shortselling1.asp#axzz2LNDvpemo
Openinsider: http://www.openinsider.com/
Finviz: http://Finviz.com/
terms: http://www.Finviz.com/help/screener.ashx
Insider Cow: http://www.insidercow.com/
Current Ratio: http://en.wikipedia.org/wiki/Current_ratio
Cash Flow: https://www.youtube.com/watch?v=1v8hRZ36--c
Balance sheet: https://www.youtube.com/watch?v=DZjU0CHKyV4
How to find quality stocks.
http://seekingalpha.com/article/2381395-how-to-identify-quality-stocks-and-is-there-really-alpha-to-be-had

Investing strategies

Inflation: https://www.youtube.com/watch?v=Zpthvpy3UKg\

Swing: https://www.youtube.com/watch?v=C9EQkA7uVU8
       https://www.youtube.com/watch?v=a_wpfSXRSjo
https://www.youtube.com/watch?v=M8sNMhPJIN

Momentum: https://www.youtube.com/watch?v=PpUlOyZrl9
Penny stocks: https://www.youtube.com/watch?v=u7xZ3kF62u4

Scanning https://www.youtube.com/watch?v=7iZpWmwBhel

Peter lynch 2023: https://www.youtube.com/watch?v=CK1AkVVVXu8

Charlie: https://www.youtube.com/watch?v=8g2B6QJ2FEc
Dividend ETFs: https://www.youtube.com/watch?v=64NEiyoNBIM

- <u>Innovative sectors:</u> https://www.youtube.com/watch?v=LI1hMX8qtHg

Trading stocks
Beginners: https://www.youtube.com/watch?v=aod3cyUEu4k
Covered <u>call</u> https://www.youtube.com/watch?v=dzMOnI4Eh04

Tax Avoidance: http://en.wikipedia.org/wiki/Tax_avoidance
Tax Law: http://en.wikipedia.org/wiki/Income_tax_%28U.S.%29
Without paying (gift tax):
http://en.wikipedia.org/wiki/Gift_tax_in_the_United_States#Gift_tax_exemptions
http://www.irs.gov/Businesses/Small-Businesses-&-Self-Employed/What%27s-New---Estate-and-Gift-Tax
AMT: http://en.wikipedia.org/wiki/Alternative_minimum_tax
<u>Estate</u> planning fun. http://tonyp4idea.blogspot.com/2014/08/estate-planning-101-for-me.html
Taxes on stocks: https://www.youtube.com/watch?v=EKYMbsjUUtE
Tax <u>avoidance</u>: https://www.youtube.com/watch?v=tXou5pM7zh0
Capital <u>gain</u>: https://www.youtube.com/watch?v=ezPs4ibFsNU&t=2678s
Trading course: https://www.youtube.com/watch?v=8sbfrusR5Eo
How <u>safe</u> our brokers. https://www.youtube.com/watch?v=wz64z1YuL0A

Fidelity funds: https://www.youtube.com/watch?v=xdEunmLrhb4
Fidelity core money market fund:
https://www.youtube.com/watch?v=KU6HYRHj3jg

Government bond <u>default</u>? https://www.youtube.com/watch?v=wMxj6iB92ZA
<u>Broker</u> CDs (Recommended): https://www.youtube.com/watch?v=zhEiyW2N7KE
<u>Money market</u> fund: https://www.youtube.com/watch?v=N53wZ_80abU

Economy
YouTube <u>video</u> (highly recommended): https://www.youtube.com/watch?v=Q6NIDJZdQH4

What will the world be in 5 years (<u>2027</u>).
https://www.youtube.com/watch?v=LzipwDQBUyc

Inflation and interest rate: https://www.youtube.com/watch?v=q8KJSNyAHLE
Wealth gap widens with low interest rate:
https://www.youtube.com/watch?v=t6m49vNjEGs

Investing helps the economy: https://www.youtube.com/watch?v=W6ICRTqsxk8

Filler: Max. drawdown

'Max. drawdown' should be understood for short-term investors. It is the maximum money you can lose. If your tested strategy tells you that you can lose 40% in this strategy, then you should place the stops accordingly. To illustrate, you bought MSFT for $100, and it dipped to $50, your max. drawdown is $50 or 50%. If you use margin, your broker would issue a margin call on its way to the $50 drop. Eventually the stock would recover and hit the $200 mark, and the long-term holders are glad that they did not close the position.

Appendix 4 - Our window to the investing world

- **General**
  Wikipedia / Investopedia /Yahoo!Finance / MarketWatch / Cnnfn / Morningstar /CNBC / Bloomberg / WSJ / Barron's / Motley Fool / TheStreet
- **Evaluate stocks**
  Finviz / SeekingAlpha / MSN Money / Zacks / Daily Finance / ADR / Fidelity / Earnings Impact / OpenInsider / NYSE / NASDAQ / SEC / SEC for 10K and 10Q (quarterly) reports required to file for listed stocks in major exchanges.
- **Charts**
  BigCharts / FreeStockCharts / StockCharts /
- **Screens**
  Yahoo!Finance / Finviz / CNBC / Morningstar /
- **Besides stocks**
  123Jump / Hoover's Online / FINRA Bond Market Data / REIT / Commodity Futures / Option Industry
- **Vendors**
  AAII / Zacks / IBD / GuruFocus / VectorVest / Fidelity / Interactive Brokers / Merrill Lynch /
- **Economy.**
  Econday / EcoconStats / Federal Reserve / Economist /
- **Misc.**
  Dow Jones Indices / Russell / Wilshire / IRS / Wikinvest / ETF Database / ETF Trends / Nolo (estate planning) / AARP /

Appendix 5 - ETFs / Mutual Funds

What is an ETF
ETFs have basic differences from mutual funds: 1. Lower management expenses, 2. Trade ETFs same as stocks, and 3. Usually more diversified but not more selective than the related mutual funds such as NOBL vs FRDPX.

The major classifications of ETFs are 1. Simulating an index such as SPY, QQQ and DIA, 2. Simulating a sector such as XLE and SOXX, 3. Simulating an asset class such as GLD and SLV, 4. Simulating a country or a group of countries such as EWC and FXI, 5. Managed by a manager(s) such as ARKK, 6. Betting a market or sector to go down such as SH and PSQ, and 7. Leveraged (not recommended for beginners).
Fidelity: Index ETFs (https://www.fidelity.com/etfs/overview).
Wikipedia on ETF (http://en.wikipedia.org/wiki/Exchange-traded_fund).

List of ETFs
ETF database (Recommended): http://etfdb.com/
ETF Bloomberg: http://www.bloomberg.com/markets/etfs/
ETF Trends: http://www.etftrends.com/
A list of ETFs. Seeking Alpha.
http://etf.stock-encyclopedia.com/category/)
A list of contra ETFs (or bear ETFs)
http://www.tradermike.net/inverse-short-etfs-bearish-etf-funds/
Misc.: ETFGuide, ETFReplay
Fidelity low-cost index funds:
https://www.youtube.com/watch?v=zpKi4_IJvlY
Fidelity Annuity funds with performance data.
http://fundresearch.fidelity.com/annuities/category-performance-annual-total-returns-quarterly/FPRAI?refann=005
ETFs vs mutual funds; https://www.youtube.com/watch?v=Vmz0CzlQvHk
Three ETFs: https://www.youtube.com/watch?v=MVi2RhpffuU

Other resources
Most subscription services offer research on ETFs. IBD has a strategy dedicated to ETFs and so does AAII to name a couple. Seeking Alpha has extensive resources for ETF including an ETF screener and investing ideas. So is ETFdb.

Not all ETFs are created equal
Check their performances and their expenses.

When to use or not to use ETFs

I prefer sector mutual funds in some industries, as they have many bad stocks such as drug industry, banks, miners and insurers. Most mutual funds cannot time the market.

When you believe a sector is heading up (or contra ETF for heading down), but you do not have time to do research on specific stocks, buy an ETF for the sector; it is same for the market.

Half ETF

Taking out half of the stocks that score below the average in an index ETF could beat the same full ETF itself. I call it HETF (half the ETF). You heard it here first.

To illustrate, sort the expected P/E (not including stocks with negative earnings) in ascending order and only include the stocks on the first half. Add more fundamental metrics. It will take a few minutes.

Disadvantages of ETFs

- When you have two stocks in a sector ETF one good one and one bad one, the ETF treats them the same. Stock pickers would buy the one that has a better appreciation potential.
- Sometimes the return could be misleading due to stock rotation. To illustrate this, on August 29, 2012, SHLD was replaced by LYB in a sector fund. SHLD was down by 4% and LYB was up by 4% primarily due to the switch. Unless you sell and buy at the right time (which is impossible), your return would not match the ETF's returns due to the replacement.
- Ensure the performance matches the corresponding index; it is hard due to excluding dividends.

Advantages of ETFs

- We have demonstrated that you can beat the market by using market timing. Between 2000 and Nov., 2013, you only exit and reenter the market 3 times and the result is astonishing.
- It is easy to rotate a sector vs. buying/selling all of the stocks in this sector. Rotating a sector is the same as trading a stock.
- The risk is spread out, and your portfolio is diversified especially for a market ETF or buying three or more ETFs in different sectors.
- Periodically the bad stocks in most funds are replaced by better stocks.
- Eliminate the time in researching stocks.

Leveraged ETFs
I do not recommend them. Some are 2x, 3x and even higher. They're too risky for beginners. However, when you are very sure or your tested strategy has very low drawdown, you may want to use them to improve performance. Most leveraged ETFs and contra ETFs have higher fees.

My basic ETF tables
I include some contra ETFs, mutual funds and Fidelity's annuity. Some of these may be interesting to you. Most Vanguard's ETFs have lower fees.

ETFs and funds come and go. Some ideas and classifications are my own interpretation. Refer to ETFdb for updated information. Not responsible for any error. Check out the ETF or fund before you take any action.

I prefer VFINX over SPY for the lower fees; both simulate the S&P 500 index. The stocks in the ETF can be either equally weighted or weighted by market caps. The latter is more like using momentum strategy, as the rising stocks usually have larger market caps. The index usually kicks out some poor-performing stocks and replaced them with better stocks. These ETFs are suited for long-term investing without constant reviews.

Table by market cap:

Category	ETF	Mutual Funds	Fidelity's Annuity	Contra ETF	Alternate
Size:					
Large Cap	DIA			DOG	
	SPY			SH	VOO VFINX RSP FXAIX
	QQQ			PSQ	FNCMX
	RYH				
Blend	IWD	BEQGX			
Growth	SPYG	FBGRX			FSPGX
Value	SPYV	DOGGX			FLCOX
Dividend	NOBL	FRDPX			
	VYM				
Mid Cap			FNBSC	MYY	
Blend	MDY	VSEQX			
Growth		STDIX			
		BPTRX			
Value		FSMVX			
Small Cap			FPRGC	SBB	FSSNX
Blend	IWM	HDPSX			
Growth		PRDSX			FECGX

Value		SKSEX			FISVX	
Micro	IWC					
Multi						
Blend		VDEOX				
Growth		VHCOX				
Value		TCLCX				
Total					FSKAX VTI	
Bond						
Long Term (20)	VLV	BTTTX		TBF		
Mid Term (7 – 10)	VCIT	FSTGX				
Short Term (1 – 3 yrs.)	VCSH	THOPX				
Total	BOND	PONDX				
Corp Invest Grade	VCIT	NTHEX				
High Yield (junk)	PHB	SPHIX				
Muni	MUB	Check state				
Special situation						
Buy back	PKW					

Table by sectors:

Sector	ETF	Mutual Funds	Fidelity's Annuity
Banking[1]		FSRBK	
Regional	IAT		
Biotech	IBB	FBIOX	
	XBI	Large	
Consumer Dis.	XLY	FSCPX	FVHAC
Consumer Staple	XLP	FDFAX	FCSAC
Defense + Aero	PPA		
Finance	KIE	FIDSX	FONNC
	IYF		
Energy	XLE	FSENX	FJLLC
Energy Service		FSESX	
Farm	DBA		
Gold	GLD	FSAGX	BAR
Gold Miner	GDX	VGPMX	
Health Care	IYH	FSPHX	FPDRC

	VHT	VGHCX	
House Builder	ITB	FSHOX	
Industrial	IYJ	FCYIX	FBALC
Material	VAW	FSDPX	GSG
	IYM		
Natural Gas	UNG		
Oil	USO		
Oil Service	OIH	FSESX	
Oil Exploration	XOP		
Real Estate	VNQ	FRIFX	FFWLC
REIT	VNQ		
Retail	RTH	FSRPX	
	XRT		
Regional bank	KRE	FSRBX	
Semi Conduct	SMH		
Software	XSW	FSCSX	
	IGV		
Technology	XLK	FSPTX	FYENC
	FDN	FBSOX	
		ROGSX	
Telecomm.	VOX	FSTCX	FVTAC
Transport	XTN		
	IYT		
Utilities	XLU	FSUTX	FKMSC
Wireless		FWRLX	

Footnote. [1] Also check Finance.

Table by countries outside the USA:

Country	ETF	Mutual Funds	Fidelity's Annuity	Alternate
Australia	EWA			
Brazil	EWZ			
Canada	EWC	FICDX		
China	FXI	FHKCX		
EAFE	EFA			
Emerging	VWO	FEMEX	FEMAC	FPADX
Europe	VGK	FIEUX		
Global	KXI	PGVFX		
Greece	GREK			
India	INDY	MINDX		
Indonesia	EIDO			
Latin America	ILF	FLATX		
Nordic		FNORX		

Hong Kong	EWH			
Japan	EWJ	FJPNX		
S. Africa	EZA			
S. Korea	EWY	MAKOX		
Singapore	EWS			
Taiwan	EWT			
Turkey	TUR			
United Kingdom	EWU			
Foreign:				
Combination				
Intern. Div.	IDV			FTIHX
Small Cap	SCZ			
Value	EFV			
Europe	VGK			

#Filler: Miss Mia

In my first job and just after the Vietnam War, everyone (yes, guys and ladies) tried to date my beautiful officemate Mia except me. If we married, then her name would be Mia Pow ('missing-in-action' and 'prisoner-of-war'). She would be very popular or very unpopular without showing her beautiful face. In any case, when she becomes a mother, she will be Mamma Mia.

#Filler: Honey, my book can play music.
https://www.youtube.com/watch?v=HxGT5z6d-GA&list=PLMZa6mP7jZ2b1otqG4tfbgZpLEdh6YiNF

www.ingramcontent.com/pod-product-compliance
Lightning Source LLC
Chambersburg PA
CBHW021809170526

45157CB00007B/2520